A STORY FOR ALL AMERICANS

A STORY FOR ALL AMERICANS

Vietnam, Victims, and Veterans

Compiled and Edited by
Frank L. Grzyb

Introduction by Senator John F. Kerry

Purdue University Press
West Lafayette, Indiana

04   03   02   01   00   5   4   3   2   1

The paper used in this book meets the minimum requirements of American National Standard for Information Sciences—Permanence of Paper for Printed Library Materials, ANSI Z39.48-1992.

Printed in the United States of America

Illustrations by Matthew Garthee

Library of Congress Cataloging-in-Publication Data

A story for all Americans : Vietnam, Victims, and Veterans / compiled and edited by Frank L. Grzyb.
    p. cm.
    Previously published under the title: Touched by the dragon.
    Includes bibliographical references.
    ISBN 1-55753-199-4 (pbk : alk. paper)
    1. Vietnamese Conflict, 1961–1975—Veterans—United States—Interviews.
2. Vietnamese Conflict, 1961–1975—Rhode Island—Newport—Interviews.
I. Grzyb, Frank L., 1946– . II. Grzyb, Frank L., 1946– Touched by the dragon.

DS559.73.U6T68 2000
959.704'3373—dc21   00-023316

To the memory of

William J. Cyr

Because of his unselfish dedication to duty,
total disregard for his own personal safety,
and his heroic deeds, he was awarded the
Silver Star and Purple Heart (posthumously).

Not only was Billy a close personal friend
and companion, he was, above all,
a wonderful human being;

and to the memory of all those who served in Vietnam
and paid the ultimate sacrifice,
especially those from Newport County,
Rhode Island.

May God keep them all in his loving arms.

CONTENTS

PREFACE

F OR those of us who served, Vietnam was more than just a war. It was an experience, albeit a difficult one. It awakened our senses. It grabbed us and held on relentlessly. For some, it never let go. Our innocence and our youth were swept away. The lasting impression it left upon our souls was like none other ever to be experienced again in our lifetimes.

Although we veterans may not realize it, we wear an invisible yet indelible mark that Vietnam stamped on us. It is resident in the unconscious of our minds. The memories associated with this strange and turbulent yet exciting period of time (the mid-to-late 1960s and early '70s), combined with the trauma of war, took a physical as well as a psychological toll upon many of us.

Of the nearly 3 million Americans who served in Vietnam, 47,253 were classified as killed in action (KIA) or missing in action (MIA), while another 10,449 died from non-hostile causes. Approximately 303,000 troops were listed as wounded; nearly half of those were categorized as seriously wounded.

Although no accurate count can be ascertained, it is estimated that close to 30,000 Rhode Island men and women, of which approximately 2,500 were from Newport County, served in Vietnam; a seemingly insignificant number. Yet the experiences of these local veterans were no less meaningful than the majority that served from our entire country. Rhode Island lost 207 of its young men in the war (171 hostile and 36 non-hostile). From the one city and five towns which make up Newport County, Rhode Island (Newport, Middletown, Portsmouth, Jamestown, Tiverton, and Little Compton), 18 citizens died and an undetermined number were wounded as a consequence of the war. Many who survived the ordeal were decorated for valor.

Several books list the average age of Americans who fought in the war at nineteen, although some sources placed the age as high as twenty-two. Most likely, it was somewhere in between. Regardless, they were still considerably younger than their counterparts who served in World War II. There is no reason to believe that those who served from Newport County were any older. In truth, our men who went off to war were, in fact, boys.

I can attribute no single factor as the primary reason why I decided to write this book. Perhaps it was the culmination of many years of listening to fellow Vietnam veterans recount their experiences. I heard them on golf courses, at cocktail parties, at sporting events, in restaurants and other places where people socialize. Some stories were sad, others were entertaining, and some downright funny. Occasionally, I even heard tales which seemed almost inconceivable, and maybe they were.

In 1996, it had been twenty-five years since my departure from Vietnam. Veterans' Day was approaching, and it seemed like an appropriate time to write about my experiences while there. I drafted a brief memoir over a period of a few months, and the finished article appeared in two separate editions of the *Newport Daily News* during the 1996 Veterans' Day period. The articles were generally well received by veterans and non-veterans alike.

While writing my Vietnam memoirs, I realized it would have been unfortunate not to capture other Newport County veterans' stories for posterity. With this in mind, I set out on nearly a year's journey of reading unpublished personal memoirs and personally interviewing a number of local Vietnam veterans with the ultimate objective of writing a book about their experiences.

While doing the research, I had the privilege of interviewing former draftees, enlisted men, and officers who served in South Vietnam. Some were assigned as support personnel and saw little or no combat action, while others were marines, army infantry soldiers, or in one case a naval flight officer, who all experienced their fair share of combat. From another perspective, a nurse was interviewed and relates what she experienced as the aftereffects of war and what it did to the men, women, and children who were placed under her care. Regardless of which group they belonged to, all the veterans had an interesting tale to relate; some were incredibly moving.

Unfortunately, a few of the veterans who took part in this endeavor are partially disabled. Some have been diagnosed with post-traumatic stress disorder (PTSD), an aftereffect of combat, and were still under medical care at the time of my interviews. Yet these veterans chose to be a part of this effort. It was no easy task for them to convey their experiences. Their remarkable fortitude is to be admired and commended.

Since the end of American combat involvement in 1973, hundreds of books have been written about Vietnam; several became literary successes, although some of the authors never stepped foot in Southeast Asia, or Vietnam in particular. In my opinion, that's a natural prerequisite for writing any book about the war. Although they wrote about Vietnam, I find it difficult to believe they actually felt and embraced it, making their writings more of a history lesson in tactical warfare than a recounting of empirical knowledge from those who fought. I feel that actual experience is a necessary ingredient in understanding the war's complexities and, more importantly, what it did to those who served.

In fairness, Vietnam wasn't easy to characterize, even by those who did serve. Personally, I found it to be a peculiar and puzzling place—you could get anything that you wanted—liquor, drugs, and prostitutes. Indeed, all vices were in general abundance. Despite the potential for so-called enjoyment, you could also get killed. Let us not forget, there was a war going on. It was a quagmire that became confusing to understand, not just for the troops that served, but for the people on the home front as well. History has confirmed it to be a mismanaged effort from the standpoint of tactics and lack of a clear vision on how it was to be fought and hopefully won.

Although the word "Vietnam" conjures up images of war, that wasn't exactly the scenario we all lived through. Perhaps I'm doing a disservice to some by oversimplifying it; certainly, one is not intended. However, if I had to classify Vietnam veterans into only two general and distinct categories, there were those who experienced combat (infantry soldiers) and the horrors of war (doctors, nurses, medics and corpsmen who took care of battlefield wounded) and those who were support troops who encountered little enemy activity. Normally, for the latter, the only action they witnessed was in the form of late night mortar and rocket attacks.

Although it seems improbable, an even smaller percentage of support personnel found Vietnam to be an adult playground. It was a chance to evade authority, let loose, party, drink alcohol, do drugs, and, if possible, consort with the local women. Indeed, the famous in-country adage, "In the rear with the beer," certainly must have been devised with this sentiment in mind.

It should be remembered that even for those who were in so-called secure locations, Vietnam was still a war zone, and no one was totally insulated from enemy attacks. This reality was brought home in a jarring way during the Communist Tet Offensive of 1968, when nearly the entire country was overrun by the enemy.

Vietnam was a land of startling contrasts. It was an incredibly beautiful place, picturesque and pleasing to the eye, with an air of mystique surrounding it. Conversely, the general population could be brutally uncivilized, with some but not all of the primitive conditions attributable to the effects of the war. Over a number of generations, poverty was a condition that many Vietnamese had become accustomed to, and it was almost always evident to an American soldier on a daily basis.

During the interview process, I attempted to talk to a cross section of local veterans to afford the reader an opportunity to understand the unique differences between combat and support personnel in Vietnam. The differences weren't just combat experiences, or the lack thereof, but included distinct lifestyles, living standards, and unique ways of looking at life and survival. The stories are interspersed in such a way that they offer an interesting perspective of what it was like for each type of veteran before, during, and after his or her military experience.

The reader is advised that the majority of participants were drafted or enlisted from the community, while a few either received military training here or moved to the community during the war years. Those individuals have since setup a permanent residence in the county. One participant was born and brought up in Newport but moved to another state after the war. Some of his relatives still live in the county.

This book is presented in a narrative format; that is to say, it uses the veterans' first person accounts. Due consideration must be extended to each veteran in that some 25 to 30 years have transpired since their individual Vietnam experience. It is as factual as they can remember.

The veterans' stories begin with discussions about their lives as a civilian and continue with descriptions of the adjustments made as new military recruits. Subsequent chapters describe the training required to become reasonably proficient at one's military occupation, receiving orders to go to Vietnam, the actual Vietnam experiences, and the return to America. Finally, the veterans recount their sentiments and feelings about the overall experience from the perspective that 25 to 30 years has brought.

One of the closing chapters pays tribute to those fallen heroes of battle who did not survive the ordeal. I had the distinct honor and privilege of interviewing surviving relatives from three families, who provided me with some wonderful insights into the deceased veterans' personalities. I have tried my best to describe the families' feelings in this chapter. The families were also thoughtful enough to allow me access to some very personal documents and photographs, which are respectfully reproduced and published here for the first time.

Although the passage of years has contributed to many of us finally being able to share our inner feelings about the war, there are still those who are either reluctant or emotionally unprepared to recount them. This is their right, and this decision is to be respected. However, their silence, for whatever reason, makes them no less a part of this endeavor.

The reader is advised that the words Vietnam and South Vietnam were used interchangeably by the veterans. Vietnam always meant the Republic of South Vietnam. North Vietnam (the communist enemy of South Vietnam and the United States during the war) was so stated. After the loss of the war by the South Vietnamese in 1975, both North Vietnam and South Vietnam were reunited as one nation. Now the country is simply referred to as Vietnam, although the official title is the Socialist Republic of Vietnam.

Some editing of the veterans' stories was necessary for the purpose of brevity and also to ensure that this book could be read by a diverse age group. During the Vietnam War, as in World War II and the Korean War, the "f-word" was used liberally by the military contingent. It was spoken as an adjective, adverb, verb, a noun, and what have you. In specific places in the text, it has been eliminated where the editors felt it did not add to the veteran's narrative. In other places, where it better served to emphasize a point, it was kept and printed as *f—*. Hopefully, this minute amount of censorship will not diminish the readability and impact of these stories.

Some vulgarities were stricken from the text, although those relating to bodily functions remained. In select stories, they were used quite profusely, and some readers may be offended by this. To answer why they were not censored, I simply state the following: This was a war, and I used the soldiers' exact dialog and expressions to realistically describe their experiences.

Although the stories in this book are about veterans who resided or currently live in Newport County, Rhode Island, they could as well have been the experiences taken from veterans from any small city or town in this country.

To the adventurous reader, I hope you find this book enjoyable, enlightening, yet in some ways, just a trifle unsettling. I trust you will come away with a sincere appreciation of what these veterans lived through and sacrificed during their individual tours of duty.

To my fellow Vietnam veterans, I salute you. My desire has always been that this book will serve as a cathartic experience for you, just as it has for me. I am proud that we can call each other friends. We have earned that right through the fraternal association we gained while serving during a very difficult time in our country's history. Regardless of location, period of service or branch of service while in Vietnam, we really have, to the best of our ability, survived our private ordeals, both before and after the war.

ACKNOWLEDGMENTS

I T would have been impossible to write this book without the support and sacrifices of the fifteen veterans who provided narratives of their wartime experiences. I owe each of them a sincere debt of gratitude for taking the time away from their families and busy work schedules. For several participants, it was the first time that their Vietnam experiences would be revealed to family and friends in such intense, emotional, and graphic detail. I respect and praise their candor, as several veterans had withheld so much for far too long.

My heartfelt appreciation is extended to those I interviewed who lost their sons or brothers in the war. I can only imagine how difficult it was for them to talk about their deceased loved ones. Undoubtedly this book would have suffered an emotional void had they not contributed their innermost thoughts and feelings. I am truly humbled that they allowed me the privilege of reproducing and publishing some of their most cherished photographs and private family documents. Hopefully this book will help preserve the memories of these fine young men.

I am deeply indebted to Captain Robert Barney Rubel, USN—a successful author in his own right—for his initial words of encouragement. The letter I received from him, written while he was serving on an overseas duty assignment, offered his personal and expert insight and gave me the will as well as the drive to persevere. Quite simply, he helped me believe in myself.

Additional notes of appreciation go to Marguerite Beal, John Blomstedt, Russell DeSimone, Philip Jackman, Peter St. Jacques, and my brother Dick Grzyb for reading one of several versions of the manuscript and providing many beneficial comments, critiques, and suggestions in return.

Jim Dion secured the rubbings at the Vietnam Veterans Memorial (the Wall) in Washington, D.C. For this, I extend my sincere appreciation for going above and beyond the call of duty.

Without Bob Pimentel's assistance, I may not have found the funding to help finance the initial stages of this project. His research skills, honed at the Portsmouth Free Public Library, were also invaluable.

Gary Ruff, of the *Newport Daily News,* offered constructive criticisms to make this book considerably better. I deeply appreciate all of his professional assistance and advice and am greatly indebted to him for his friendship and support throughout the entire project.

Many thanks go to Pauline Peter for laboriously reviewing manuscript after manuscript, usually on short notice. Her expert and invaluable assistance was proven time and again.

A special debt of gratitude is extended to Chris Duckworth for her expert proofing and outstanding professional editorial assistance. Her fine talents significantly contributed to making this book so much more cohesive and meaningful.

Chris Burns and I spent significant time working together scanning illustrations, documents, and photographs, as well as designing the preliminary text layout. Quickly I came to know and greatly respect his unique ideas, skills, and professional capabilities.

Matthew Garthee's lifelike drawings add an essential touch to better illustrate several of the veterans' stories. Although still a young man, his talents are already self-evident.

To David Douglas Duncan, a sincere thank-you for granting me the privilege of reproducing, as illustrations, several of his critically acclaimed photographs from the Vietnam War. Many of his photographs were published in *Life* magazine during the war years, and in my opinion, are some of the most moving and realistic portraits of what the Vietnam War was like for the typical combat soldier.

The final illustration in chapter 11, symbolic of a soldier killed in battle, was inspired by a photograph currently in the possession of Jack E. Clarkin, Jr. It was taken at a memorial service in Phu Bai, Vietnam, by an unidentified member of the 1st Battalion, 501st Infantry, 101st Airborne Division (Airmobile).

Tom Bacher, director of Purdue University Press, has my deepest appreciation for accepting my work for publication and recognizing its value.

I am also grateful to Margaret Hunt, managing editor of Purdue University Press. The finishing touches she applied to the book shaped a "diamond in the rough" into a reasonable piece of military historical work. After several rewrites of the manuscript, I quickly realized that without her professional guidance and direction, this book would have had little chance of any literary merit.

Dr. Heath Twichell's assistance in crucial publishing and funding matters was a godsend. I wish we had worked together earlier in the project, as his encouragement and advice proved to be invaluable. His award-winning book, *Northwest Epic,* truly inspired me. Not only did it serve as a fine example of an author's outstanding research and writing skills, but in a greater sense signified an untiring effort, through sheer perseverance and extreme dedication, to honor the legacy and memory of his father. Hopefully some of his intellect and sensitivity has brushed off on me.

My greatest debt is to my wife, Ginny, who provided not only additional help with the proofreading but, more importantly, the love and emotional support I needed to bring this project to completion.

INTRODUCTION

FRANK Grzyb has performed a great service for all of us by collecting the memories of so many Vietnam veterans from Newport County. To extract our recollections of the war in which we fought is an arduous and delicate task. Some memories flow easily with smiles and hearty laughter; some can be barely articulated by throats choked with emotion, eyes clouded over with tears. There are memories still that remain locked inside, wounds every bit as fresh as they were the day we sustained them in a distant land.

Vietnam remains an experience of unresolved feelings. But each time veterans come together and speak out, we help each other repair the breach in our lives.

We struggle to heal ourselves, to put words to our experience, even though nothing about Vietnam lends itself to encapsulation. It was a whirlwind—a place and period of our history which profoundly changed the way we thought of ourselves and acted. I remember how young we were, ready to win, ready to continue the unfinished business of World War II and Korea, how enthusiastically and idealistically we committed ourselves to assume President Kennedy's challenge to "bear any burden and pay any price." Then I remember the clash of ideal and reality—the politics which played havoc with the truth, the terrible struggle between fathers and sons, brothers and sisters—whole families denied the traditional growing pains of life in normal America—people going to prison, to Canada—anywhere but Vietnam.

I remember how extraordinarily beautiful Vietnam was and how strange it seemed to be engaged in a life and death struggle in such surroundings. I remember the rivers of the Mekong Delta, stunningly beautiful, eerily quiet and romantic, suddenly erupting in firefight; rolling thunder B-52 strikes so near that boat, river, and rice paddy shook with the force of explosions; nighttime ambushes, search and destroy missions, water snakes, the piercing cry on the radio set for a medevac which always left one more grateful to be alive and haunted for what had happened. I remember at times being incredibly tired, at times incredibly

1

scared and always incredibly proud of the people I served with and the honesty of our effort to do decent things in a situation that invited indecency.

I remember the evening smell of wood fires burning in markets, of *nuoc-mam* fish sauce cooking, of water buffalo dragging plows through lush green rice paddies and always, everywhere, children massing around us, hands outstretched, looking for American largesse. Despite all that was happening, the smiles and laughter of children were overwhelming.

I particularly remember the remarkable camaraderie of all who manned our boats, the quiet moments before a mission, the raucous moments of letting off steam—the shared struggle to do more than survive—to do honor for our service and to our friends who were lost.

I remember the moment I realized that, although I was lucky to leave Vietnam alive, I could never leave my experiences behind—and the country to which I was returning was not ready to welcome home anyone who couldn't escape the grip of the Vietnam experience. On my return flight from Vietnam, still in my uniform, exhausted, I fell asleep. Not much later I awoke from a nightmare—still in Vietnam in my mind—to find myself in unfamiliar territory. People in the plane had moved away from my seat. There were whispers throughout the remainder of the flight. No one dared make conversation let alone eye contact with an American veteran who reminded them too starkly of the war. With one shout during a restless dream, even in uniform I had become an object of curiosity and misunderstanding. Vietnam changed who I was and transformed who we are in a way I could never have predicted.

It is hard for us still to put the conflicting memories of Vietnam behind us—experiences of great brotherhood and great betrayal—but A *Story for All Americans* reminds us of those things we have in common, and in that shared experience there is healing. The words of veterans from Newport County, Rhode Island, belong to all of us who served in Vietnam—the stories are more than just familiar, they are intimate and personal. It is our story, our past retold in frank and honest language by those who shared it. But now, through the publication of this important book, it is—finally—becoming a story for all Americans.

—Senator John F. Kerry

ONE

THE TRANSITION

There never was a just one, never an honorable one—on the part of the instigator of the war. I can see a million years ahead, and this rule will never change in so many as half a dozen instances. The loud little handful—as usual—will shout for the war. The pulpit will object at first, the great dull bulk of the nation will rub its sleepy eyes and try to make out why there should be a war and will say earnestly and indignantly, "It is unjust and dishonorable and there is no necessity for it." Then the handful will shout louder. A few fair men on the other side will argue and reason against the war with speech and pen, and at first will have a hearing and be applauded; but it will not last long; those others will out shout them, and presently the anti-war audiences will thin out and lose popularity.—Mark Twain

WHILE STILL A CIVILIAN

FOR an unencumbered, happy-go-lucky teenager in the 1960s, Newport County was a fun place to live, especially after all the cold weather and snow disappeared from the previous winter. The warmer weather of late spring and early summer was heralded with much fanfare, and its arrival seemed to rejuvenate the City-by-the-Sea as well as its youthful inhabitants.

There was the usual abundance of activities for the average teenager living in the Newport area, but perhaps nothing was more important or more enjoyable than the pursuit of the opposite sex. There were strategic

3

locations throughout the city where teenagers gathered regularly, but the busy downtown commercial district seemed to be the best place to congregate. And having an automobile, regardless of its condition, was a distinct advantage for the pursuer.

Three of the more popular nightclubs in the county were situated in downtown Newport. Dorian's and Bambi's were known exclusively for live rock 'n' roll music, while Hurley's distinguished itself for its fine jazz ensembles with an occasional rock 'n' roll band thrown in for good measure.* At the time, racial harmony was far from a reality; however, Hurley's had to be considered unique, as blacks and whites seemed to coexist there with relatively few problems.

Sports was a favorite pastime in the area. For a number of years, baseball and softball leagues were an institution on the island. Many teenagers were Boston Red Sox fans, but there always seemed to be an occasional New York Yankee fan thrown in for good measure. As to be expected, arguments would occasionally ensue between the two as to which team or what player was more talented.

Tennis, basketball, and golf were some of the other recreational activities engaged in. Tennis, the so-called sport of the rich and famous, was not only played on the island by the affluent of society, but also by the middle-class as well. In the community, the sport owed its popularity to the influence of professional tennis tournaments scheduled each year at the Newport Casino on fashionable Bellevue Avenue. Amateur and professional tennis matches had been held there since 1881. For a number of years, the Casino was also home to the National Lawn Tennis Hall of Fame, later to be known as the International Tennis Hall of Fame.

Basketball was enjoyed throughout the county, but some of the more spirited games were held at a place called The Hut, where recreational leagues had played for a number of years. It was located within a quarter mile of the Newport Casino and right next to municipal tennis courts.

As Newport and the surrounding towns were situated along the Atlantic Ocean, many took advantage of the sandy beaches for sunning and bathing. Surfing was a sport still in its infancy in Newport County, but it gained in popularity as several adventurous souls joined in the fun and challenge.

Sailing enthusiasts took to the coastal waters for racing or just for the sheer enjoyment of the sport. For a landlubber watching from the shoreline, it was a beautiful and picturesque sight to observe the sailors tack-

---

* All these nightclubs have long since disappeared.

ing their boats in order to catch New England's mighty winds and hoisting their colorful spinnaker sails to realize the ride of their lives.

Admittedly, there were a few whose extracurricular activities as juvenile delinquents resulted in some close encounters with the law. Those who were truants, underage drinkers, or marijuana smokers were fortunate, for the most part, in avoiding any legal ramifications.

In order to cover expenses for summer enjoyment (food, entertainment, and gas for the car), many teenagers were employed at various odd jobs on the Island, ranging from supermarket checkout clerks to delivery men. Holding a job was a small price to pay when considering the potential advantages of having extra cash in the wallet.

Rarely did these youthful individuals realize the benefits of being a civilian until that status was abruptly taken away after they were drafted into the armed services. For the majority, living as a civilian meant enjoying the comforts of home, family, and friends. It meant being able to come and go as one pleased, sleeping late, eating what, when, and where one wanted, and, except for occasional parental guidance, living the life of a free spirit. Indeed, most of the comforts of life were taken care of. Conversely, being in the military meant relinquishing all of the above.

Thomas Finn, *Specialist Four, U.S. Army, Company A, 519th Military Intelligence Battalion, 525th Military Intelligence Group, MACV-J2, Saigon, 1966–67*

It was summertime, 1965, and my friends and I usually spent considerable time at the beach. I was employed part time at my father's variety store here on the corner. The store had been in the family for about thirty years. I worked there a little bit before and all during high school.

I didn't really know much about Vietnam at the time. All I knew was that it was a faraway place, and I probably had to look it up on the map to find it. I knew there was a little bit of a war going on, and we Americans were not too involved.

I said to myself, "It's not going to affect me, it's something someone else does, not me."

Rob Roche, *Sergeant, U.S. Army, 101st Airborne Division, Da Nang, 1967–69*

I was raised in the Fifth Ward [predominantly an Irish section of Newport], in the Morton Park area, to be more specific. Newport wasn't the same tourist town it is today. The group I hung out with was kind of a wild bunch. We used to roll sailors and stuff like that. You could say we got into a little bit of trouble. Growing up, we were delinquents. You had to picture Newport at the time. Along Thames Street, you had Skipper's Dock* and all those other bars. We used to go down to the cliffs, along First Beach, and drink. We made a habit of skipping school as frequently as possible.

Mike Pinksaw, Specialist Four, U.S. Army, 60th Land Clearing Company, 62nd Engineering Battalion, 20th Engineering Brigade, Long Binh, Bien Hoa, Lai Khe, 1968–69

I lived in the Fifth Ward of Newport. It was the old Newport, not like it is today. It was great. I lived near the downtown area, and our neighborhood was strictly blue-collar workers.

I went to high school at Rogers. One of the things that prepared me for the military was my experience at Rogers with the ROTC program. I have no real idea why I joined; I guess it just looked interesting to me at the time. One of my high-school classmates was John Braga. He would later lose his life in Vietnam.

David Rossi, Specialist Four, U.S. Army, 1st Infantry Division and 25th Infantry Division, Di An, Tay Ninh, and Cu Chi, 1969–70

I was working in my father's ice business prior to going into the service. My job was an easy one. I simply bagged ice.

Stephen Butler, Lance Corporal, U.S. Marine Corps, 7th Marine Combat Engineers, Da Nang, 1966–67

I was from Portsmouth. I did about the same things other teenagers did at the time, except I spent a lot more time working than most, because my father had passed on when I was only twelve years old. My mother had four kids to take care of, so we all had to work to pretty much pay our bills.

I worked for a guy who was a full-time produce farmer, and he kind of took me under his wing and treated me almost like his adopted son. I worked for him every day of the school week and every single day of the summer from the time I was twelve until the time I went away to Connecticut.

Portsmouth at the time was somewhat similar to the way it is today,

---

* Skipper's Dock was located in an area once referred to as Blood Alley. Most of the bars there were patronized by a number of sailors, and for good reason. For instance, Skipper's Dock, like some of the other bars in Newport, conducted striptease shows. Fights were frequent, and the Navy Shore Police had many a busy weekend.

but much more agrarian and laid-back. I hate to say it, but I think it was a little bit more close-knit than it is today.

Salvatore T. Raffa, *Airman Second Class, U.S. Air Force, 377th Security Police Squadron, Tan Son Nhut Air Base, Saigon, 1967–68*

I was in college—Rhode Island Junior College, matter of fact. I remember hanging out on Bellevue Avenue, sitting on the wall in front of the Newport Creamery with not a care in the world, doing absolutely nothing. We just watched the cars go by and, of course, looked at the girls. I just loved Newport, especially the summers.

Michael Toner Farrell, *Specialist Five, U.S. Army, 544th Replacement Company, Cam Ranh Bay, 1969–70*

I was a sickly child. I had had congenital heart disease, which required open-heart surgery while I was still young. Because of my condition, I was sort of a protected child; my mother had me tied to her apron strings. I guess you could've called me an eighteen-year-old child—a baby, for that matter.

I lived in Newport, and drugs weren't visible yet. Newport was very, very navy, laid-back; and tourism was low, not like it is today. Occasionally I'd go out to a rundown deserted mansion along Ocean Drive. You could go to Purgatory Rock and hardly see anyone the entire time you were there. Try that today! I was working as a truck driver delivering beer, cigarettes, and things like that.

Ironically, I was also a rebel. I left home when I was seventeen years old. Although it seems strange to talk about being protected, I really was. Unfortunately for me, I had been given everything; I was from a family that could afford anything. We had a Cadillac and sports cars, and I had everything I wanted. It was the typical poor-little-rich-boy story. But one day I started to let my hair grow long, and that bothered the family.

I was told, "Cut your hair or we'll take the car away from you." I gave them the keys.

Then it came down to, "Cut your hair or don't come home," so I moved out.

Ken Garthee, *Private First Class, U.S. Marine Corps, 3rd Battalion, 3rd Marines, 3rd Marine Division, Da Nang, Rock Pile, 1966–67*

I wasn't from this area originally, although I spent a better portion of my life here. In fact, I was brought up in Milwaukee.

Looking back, I guess you could say I was as much an islander as a midwesterner. Indeed, I loved both places.

My best friend and I used to work on cars together, and for fun we tooled around the streets in an old 1949 Willys sedan. We had known each other since the eighth grade. We used to talk about everything, but neither one of us knew what we were going to do after graduating from high school.

Doug Johnson, *Specialist Four, U.S. Army, 25th Infantry Division, 2nd Battalion, 12th Infantry, 1968*

Before entering the army in 1968, I attended Fairfield University for four years and graduated in June 1968 with a bachelor of arts in English. I was only home in Newport over the summer months from 1965 to 1968, and because I had to earn enough money to pay for my own education, it was usually a very busy time. I would get up early on the weekdays and work all day delivering everything from wallboard to shingles to the major contractors in the Newport County area.

After a school year of stress and study, and probably too much partying, it was great to be outdoors getting great physical exercise and not having to think. It was also a great lesson in what I did not want to do with the rest of my life.

I also worked at a local supermarket. Since I had worked there throughout high school, I knew a lot of the regular customers and could catch up on what had been happening during the year while I was at school. My favorite activities were trying to brighten up the day for the elderly people and terrorizing the young female population.

When I wasn't working, I was usually sunning and swimming at Gooseberry Beach, a wonderful family beach that my family had enjoyed for as long as I can remember. It may just be my imagination, but I tell people today that my recollection of the water temperature in Newport in early June was about 55 degrees. As you walked into the water, your legs would hurt, and your body would swear it would do unspeakable things to you if you went any further. After you dove into the water, the greatest mystery was how long it would take for your heart to start pumping again.

One of my favorite summer activities in Newport was sailing. A good friend of mine was a great sailor and had access to two large sailboats, and we made many a sunset cruise throughout Newport Harbor. It was great excitement to become engrossed in our dates and look up to see a large tanker or freighter bearing down on a crash course with our boat— but we always seemed to survive.

I also have fond recollections of the Newport Jazz and Folk Festivals and all the fantastic groups that came to Newport every summer to participate. Once again, I mixed business with pleasure, and by working as an usher at the festivals, I was able to make money while seeing the greatest artists in folk and jazz night after night.

THAT DREADED DRAFT NOTICE

With the exception of contracting a life-threatening illness or losing one's manhood, there was perhaps no greater fear for a young man than opening the mailbox and finding his induction notice. The correct government term for this process of manpower mobilization for the military was called *conscription*, but everyone knew it as *the draft*. Indeed, receiving one's draft notice from the Selective Service was thought to be the worst luck imaginable.

There were those who looked for ways to avoid induction into the armed services, and because of this, new professions sprang up to serve this need, especially in larger cities. They were called draft lawyers and draft counselors. Some agencies operated with the profit motive in mind, while others were nonprofit organizations that offered assistance because of their creed and convictions of moral necessity. Whatever the motive, the main objective for either group was to assist potential draftees with their legal rights and, more importantly, to beat the draft system.

Legal advice would include any of the following actions:

- Enlisting (obviously the least desirable option)
- Serving as a reservist (the next-least desirable option)
- Refusing to register for the draft and facing the consequences
- Escaping to Canada or any other country
- Disappearing from planet earth (not as difficult as one can imagine)
- Refusing induction
- Claiming conscientious objector status
- Requesting immediate discharge
- Obtaining a dependency deferment for financial, emotional, or physical reasons
- Claiming sole surviving son status
- Claiming ministry or theology student deferments
- Securing a medical disqualification
- Working in a civilian profession designated as a critical position to the defense of the country

- Claiming to be gay (not something readily admitted during the Vietnam era)

For those who came from smaller cities and towns like in the Newport County area, especially from lower- or middle-class families, the chances of finding alternatives, such as serving in the National Guard, Reserves, or Peace Corps, were nearly impossible. It was extremely difficult to find influential people who had the right connections to find an open billet in any of these units.

Several of the other deferment options were never even thought of, let alone seriously considered. Why not? Seemingly, the legal consequences of failure could have been embarrassing not only to the young men but also to their immediate families. Therefore, most resigned themselves to the inevitable.

For many local residents, the draft was a rude awakening. There weren't too many individuals who were eager to perform military service, never mind fighting in Vietnam—those few made up a very small minority indeed.

Thomas Finn, *Specialist Four, U.S. Army, Company A, 519th Military Intelligence Battalion, 525th Military Intelligence Group, MACV-J2, Saigon, 1966–67*

I actually received two previous notices to report to Field's Point in Providence for examinations. I reported there because I was trying to get into a reserve unit. After the first two times, I was just sent home. This time, I thought, would be like the previous ones, so I simply packed my bag and told my mother and father that I'd be home for dinner that evening. But this time, they kept me.

It was September 9, 1965. We were not up in Providence too long when we realized this could be a slightly different day for us. But I still didn't know. Maybe it was after lunch when we were doing the *I do*'s, then I knew: This was it, and I wasn't going home for dinner that night.

Prior to boarding the bus, we were told that they were drafting into the army, navy, and marines. Fortunately, I was told that I was going into the army, but I kind of still thought that I was going home. I probably didn't believe it, or didn't want to, because the other two times I had gone home.

The next thing I can remember is being on the bus and going down Route 95 through Connecticut. We tried to bribe the bus driver to stop anywhere in New York to get a few brews [the drinking age in New York

SELECTIVE SERVICE SYSTEM

Approval Not Required.

ORDER TO RÉPORT FOR INDUCTION

The President of the United States,

To

Thomas Michael Finn
21 Dresser St.
Newport, R.I.

(LOCAL BOARD STAMP)

(Date of mailing)

SELECTIVE SERVICE NO.			
37	3	45	378

GREETING:

You are hereby ordered for induction into the Armed Forces of the United States, and to report

at ___Short Line Bus Terminal, Court House Square, Newport, Rhode Island___
(Place of reporting)

on ___SEP 9 1965___ at ___6:50 A.M.___
    (Date)   (Hour)

for forwarding to an Armed Forces Induction Station.

J.E. Ibbotson
(Member or clerk of Local Board)

IMPORTANT NOTICE

IF YOU HAVE HAD PREVIOUS MILITARY SERVICE, OR ARE NOW A MEMBER OF THE NATIONAL GUARD OR A RESERVE COMPONENT OF THE ARMED FORCES, BRING EVIDENCE WITH YOU. IF YOU WEAR GLASSES, BRING THEM. IF MARRIED, BRING PROOF OF YOUR MARRIAGE. IF YOU HAVE ANY PHYSICAL OR MENTAL CONDITION WHICH, IN YOUR OPINION, MAY DISQUALIFY YOU FOR SERVICE IN THE ARMED FORCES, BRING A PHYSICIAN'S CERTIFICATE DESCRIBING THAT CONDITION, IF NOT ALREADY FURNISHED TO YOUR LOCAL BOARD.

Valid documents are required to substantiate dependency claims in order to receive basic allowance for quarters. Be sure to take the following with you when reporting to the induction station. The documents will be returned to you. (a) FOR LAWFUL WIFE OR LEGITIMATE CHILD UNDER 21 YEARS OF AGE—original, certified copy or photostat of a certified copy of marriage certificate, child's birth certificate, or a public or church record of marriage issued over the signature and seal of the custodian of the church or public records; (b) FOR LEGALLY ADOPTED CHILD—certified court order of adoption; (c) FOR CHILD OF DIVORCED SERVICE MEMBER (Child in custody of person other than claimant)—(1) Certified or photostatic copies of receipts from custodian of child evidencing serviceman's contributions for support, and (2) Divorce decree, court support order or separation order; (d) FOR DEPENDENT PARENT—affidavits establishing that dependency.

Bring your Social Security Account Number Card. If you do not have one, apply at nearest Social Security Administration Office. If you have life insurance, bring a record of the insurance company's address and your policy number. Bring enough clean clothes for 3 days. Bring enough money to last 1 month for personal purchases.

This Local Board will furnish transportation, and meals and lodging when necessary, from the place of reporting to the induction station where you will be examined. If found qualified, you will be inducted into the Armed Forces. If found not qualified, return transportation and meals and lodging when necessary, will be furnished to the place of reporting.

You may be found not qualified for induction. Keep this in mind in arranging your affairs, to prevent any undue hardship if you are not inducted. If employed, inform your employer of this possibility. Your employer can then be prepared to continue your employment if you are not inducted. To protect your right to return to your job if you are not inducted, you must report for work as soon as possible after the completion of your induction examination. You may jeopardize your reemployment rights if you do not report for work at the beginning of your next regularly scheduled working period after you have returned to your place of employment.

Willful failure to report at the place and hour of the day named in this Order subjects the violator to fine and imprisonment. Bring this Order with you when you report.

If you are so far from your own local board that reporting in compliance with this Order will be a serious hardship, go immediately to any local board and make written request for transfer of your delivery for induction, taking this Order with you.

An induction (draft) notice. (Courtesy of Tom Finn)

at the time was eighteen years old] and we'd pay him all kinds of money, but he didn't buy that one.

It was dinnertime, and I think we stopped in New York for a box lunch. We had our lunch, and the next thing I remember is we're in New Jersey and approaching Fort Dix. Then the hush came over the bus. "This is it, boys," I said to myself. You could've dropped a pin in the bus, and you would have heard it!

David Rossi, Specialist Four, U.S. Army, 1st Infantry Division and 25th Infantry Division, Di An, Tay Ninh, and Cu Chi, 1969–70

I wasn't college material, so I was just sitting back waiting for it to happen, which of course it did.

Doug Johnson, Specialist Four, U.S. Army, 25th Infantry Division, 2nd Battalion, 12th Infantry, 1968

In my senior year of college I began to realize that the world was a much larger place than my college campus and its environs. As graduation approached, it seemed that I was watching with increasing curiosity the events unfolding on TV and in the papers in a faraway place called Vietnam. Although I didn't exactly know why we were in Vietnam, I believed that we were trying to help another country in a struggle against communism and oppression, and they had asked for our help. Being a realist, I recognized that with no student deferment and living in a small town like Newport, it was only a matter of time before I would be drafted. I decided that I did not want to get a job or launch out on a new career with a draft notice hanging over my head. As soon as I graduated from college in June 1968, I visited my local draft board with mixed feelings of pride, confusion, curiosity, and uncertainty, and volunteered. It was a decision that was to teach me much about survival, forever alter my philosophy of life, challenge many long-held beliefs, and lead me to stare death in the face, but it is a decision that I have never regretted.

Michael Toner Farrell, Specialist Five, U.S. Army, 544th Replacement Company, Cam Ranh Bay, 1969–70

After my draft notice arrived, I reported for my physical examination. Because I had had open-heart surgery, they gave me a 4-F, which meant "not fit for military service." All my friends and even people I didn't know who were being processed at the induction center were saying, "God, you're so lucky," because at the time just about everyone was doing whatever they could to stay out of the service and especially Vietnam. Some were even claiming they were homosexuals, just to get a 4-F.

I felt invalidated, cheated, that there was something wrong with me, and I didn't like it. Previously, I had been told by the doctors that I was perfectly healthy, but behind my back my parents were told by one doctor that I probably would be lucky if I made it past 1969. Thank God he was just a little wrong with his estimate, 'cause here I am today.

As soon as I left the induction center, I went right to Boston to see my doctor. I really wanted to serve my country, and I knew that there was no future for me in Newport. I said to the doctor, "You told me that there was nothing wrong with me, and I had absolutely no restrictions. Now the military tells me that I'm not medically qualified." The doctor gave me a note giving me a clean bill of health. I took the note, along with one from a lawyer saying that they needed to accept me, and brought it back to the draft board. I was sent to the induction center, and this time I was accepted.

Being drafted and finally accepted had its good points. It renewed my relationship with my parents. The day before I was supposed to leave for the service, I went to my parents' house, rang the front doorbell, and my mother answered. I told her I was going into the army and had come to say good-bye. When I told her I was leaving for the army in the morning, of course she said, "Why don't you come in." I know they never, ever expected me to join the service.

ENLISTING

Enlisting in the armed services meant that a person had the luxury of predetermining his training assignments and ultimately his military occupation. However, enlisting always meant a commitment of an additional year or more over the two years obligated by the draft. If the training that a recruit received was unsuccessful, he was reassigned to a new military occupation, usually infantry. Unfortunately, the recruit was still required to serve out his entire term of enlistment.

Some individuals were college graduates and enlisted to become officers, which they became only after successful completion of officer candidate school. Each branch of the service had its own school. These individuals became known as "Ninety Day Wonders," which referred to the minimum number of training days required before the candidate received his officer's commission. It was a derogatory phrase, one most definitely undeserved by the vast majority of those completing the course.

Enlisting, whether to become a soldier or to be commissioned as an officer, did not insulate a person from going to South Vietnam. Whether drafted or enlisted, the recruit was just as susceptible to being sent off to war.

Rob Roche, *Sergeant, U.S. Army, 101st Airborne Division, Da Nang, 1967–69*

I and two others quit school because we had such low draft numbers. We had heard about Vietnam and were patriotic and figured it was our turn to do our duty like our fathers and grandfathers had done, not knowing that our attitudes would quickly change once we experienced Vietnam and the realities of war. At the time, however, we figured we were doing the right thing. My decision to join the army was made even easier, as my parents couldn't afford to send me to college. It was evident that as soon as I finished high school, the military was going to get us anyway, so two of my friends and I enlisted in the army just to get it over with.

Dick Turner, *Boatswain's Mate Third Class, U.S. Navy, River Assault Squadron 15, River Division 152, Task Force 117, Dong Tam and My Tho, 1968–69*

I enlisted, although I did receive a draft notice to report for a draft board physical. It was February 1964. The navy appealed to me the most because they traveled around the world, and I figured it would give me a chance to see it. My maternal grandfather was a captain in the British Royal Navy, and so in a way, it was sort of a family tradition to serve in the navy.

Mike Pinksaw, *Specialist Four, U.S. Army, 60th Land Clearing Company, 62nd Engineering Battalion, 20th Engineering Brigade, Long Binh, Bien Hoa, Lai Khe 1968–69*

I enlisted in the service on February 11, 1968, because, quite frankly, I wanted to pick my military occupational series in advance of the army drafting me. I didn't want to be stuck in a grunt* unit like the infantry. I wanted to have a good occupation.

---

* Grunt was the sound an infantry soldier made when he leaned over to pick up his ruck-sack. Hence the name stuck.

Bill McCollum, *Sergeant, U.S. Army, 173rd Airborne Brigade, Charlie Company, 4th Battalion, 503rd Infantry, LZ-English, 1969–71*

When I enlisted, I selected the light infantry program. Looking back, I guess what motivated me to join the service was the comments of my older brother, who told me I'd never make it in the military, especially as a paratrooper. Time proved him wrong, 'cause I did it.

Salvatore T. Raffa, *Airman Second Class, U.S. Air Force, 377th Security Police Squadron, Tan Son Nhut Air Base, Saigon, 1967–68*

I flunked out of college, and shortly thereafter I got a letter from Uncle Sam telling me I lost my student deferment. I immediately became 1-A, which meant I went to the top of the list for the draft. I knew they were going to get me, so I started looking into things like the National Guard, which didn't work out. On my way down to the armory, I said to myself, "I think I'll go in for a second." I met the air force recruiter, and I started talking to him with another friend of mine about opportunities in the air force. Next thing I knew, don't ask me how it happened, I'm signing up.

Well, actually, the air force seemed the best choice, because I was petrified about going to Vietnam.

People were telling me, "Go into the air force; it's the closest thing to civilian life, and you'll never go to Vietnam." I'm as patriotic as the rest of them, but I'm no hero. I didn't want to go to Vietnam, so I enlisted in the air force for four years.

Ken Garthee, *Private First Class, U.S. Marine Corps, 3rd Battalion, 3rd Marines, 3rd Marine Division, Da Nang, Rock Pile, 1966–67*

A group of the guys met during the Easter break in April 1965. None of us were sure what we were going to do after graduation. One of the guys said, "Let's all go down to the marine corps recruiter and enlist." All of us thought it was a great idea. After all, we were all over eighteen years old and didn't require our parents' permission to do anything anymore.

So off we went, down to see the marine recruiter, and we all enlisted in what was called the delayed entry program. What this meant was, we could all enlist as *buddies* but didn't have to go to boot camp until August 1965. In this same program, we were allowed to pick the boot camp we wanted to go to. Parris Island, South Carolina, had a reputation for being tough, so we selected the warmth of San Diego. We thought we were going to become Hollywood marines.

All kidding aside, coming from the Midwest, we were patriotic and loved America. Remember President Kennedy's "Ask not . . ." speech? We thought, "Why not join the marines?" We did it, and that was that, but in fact, there was much more to it than that. All the men in my family had served in the armed forces—my father in the navy as a cook in World War II in the Mediterranean off the coast of Africa, and my Uncle Bill was a marine in 1942 with the 2nd Marine Division when they landed on Guadalcanal. Both survived and came back home. My Uncle Jack was a paratrooper with the 82nd Airborne Division. He was all set to go to Korea in 1952 but was never called upon to go. My Uncle Keith, who was an aerial photographer with the air force, did go to Korea in 1953. As you can tell, the military tradition was embedded in my family.

When I came home and told my parents that I had joined the marines, my dad never said a word; however, my mother was in shock. I never did get any outright rejection from either one of my parents, though.

I remember it like it was yesterday—the day Mom and I visited my Uncle Bill to let him know that I was going to become a marine like he was. When we walked into his home, he was asleep on the sofa. I looked down on him and touched him, oh so gently. He jumped up with a start, almost touching the ceiling. In fact, he reacted like he was being assaulted. After a few seconds, he regained his composure and apologized for his unpredictable behavior. It had to have been his time during the war that made him react that way.

When Uncle Bill was fully awake, I told him I had enlisted to become a marine. For the longest time, no one said a word. Uncle Bill broke the silence and said, "Why did you go and do a stupid thing like that? You should have gone into the navy or air force, where they have good schools."

I never said a word. What could I say? On my way back home with my mother, neither of us said a word.

In order to get prepared for the marine experience, every day my friend and I went to a park across the street from my house and ran with full backpacks loaded with rocks or whatever heavy objects we could find. We figured this would get us in shape so we wouldn't have to work so hard in boot camp.

A few weeks later, I went to work on a relative's farm for the remainder of the summer. It was here that I realized how satisfying being a farmer could be. What impressed me the most was that, although spending long hours and having to work awfully hard doing typical farm hand chores, you could measure your results. It was a really positive experience. Yes, it was on this farm that I learned to do my best, how to work as a team, and also how to have fun.

Peggy R. Zarek, *Lieutenant Commander, U.S. Navy, U.S.S. Sanctuary (AH-17), Coastal Waters off South Vietnam, Military Region 1, 1969–70*

In the early '60s, I was already in the service as a registered nurse. I was stationed at the navy hospital in Philadelphia, and I was taking care of the amputees who had come back from Vietnam.

My mother was a nurse and my father was a doctor, although that wasn't the real reason why I became a nurse. I used to work in a hospital in high school, and I always wanted to take care of people, so I guess that's why I went into nursing.

Betsy Wylie, *Lieutenant, U.S. Navy, Management Information Center, Headquarters, Naval Forces Vietnam (NAVFORV), Saigon, 1967–68*

As I was getting ready to graduate from college, the most important thing for me was finding a job. I looked at several civilian jobs, and nothing was in the offing, so I decided to go to women officers' school. The obligation at that time for women joining the navy, was only two years, so I figured I'd work in the navy for two years and then go back and find a civilian job.

Howard North, *Lieutenant j.g., US Coast Guard Coast Guard Squadron One, USCGC Point Clear (WPB 82315), An Thoi and Cat Lo, 1967–68*

I had just graduated from college with a degree in mathematics and education, and I really didn't know what I wanted to do. When I was younger, I had read a number of books about the Arctic and Antarctic, and I always wanted to know what it would be like to serve on an icebreaker. I had a couple of uncles who were in the coast guard, and I had listened intently to their stories. With this in mind, I decided to pick up a recruitment brochure. I liked what I read. Not long after, I took the written aptitude test and passed it. Then I went up to Boston for my physical and interviews. I was accepted in July 1965, and in less than two months I was off to officer candidate school in the coast guard.

TWO

YOUR ASS IS MINE!

The more you sweat in peace, the less you bleed in war.
—Chinese Proverb

BASIC AND ADVANCED TRAINING

A RMY basic training (boot camp to a marine) didn't exactly prepare a person for the rigors of war, nor was it designed to. Seventeen-plus years of living as a civilian were difficult to wash away in just eight weeks of military indoctrination. A draftee's metamorphosis from civilian to military life wasn't exactly a smooth transition. Although nearly everyone successfully completed the physical aspects of the training process, some never made the mental adjustment. They may have been trained for military service, been dressed appropriately, and received the short haircuts to look the part; but in their minds and through their silent resistance, they were still civilians at heart.

Basic training was, quite simply, an introduction into the military way of life. It included daily physical training, discipline, marching, and starting in the fourth week, marksmanship qualification at the rifle range. Bayonet training was also introduced during the fourth week.

"What is the spirit of the bayonet?" the drill sergeant would yell.

The recruits would scream back, "To kill!"

Then the drill sergeant would ask, "What types of bayonet fighters are there?"

The recruits would yell, "The quick and the dead!"

In actuality, not too many of the enemy were ever really injured or killed by a bayonet in Vietnam. Why bayonet training then? Most likely it was nothing more than a dexterity and discipline drill.

Everyone got to throw at least one armed hand grenade during week six. A live-fire exercise was brought into play during the trainees' seventh week. At night, the recruits had to crawl approximately seventy-five yards from one end of an obstacle course to another, with live machine gun bullets whizzing over their heads while self-contained explosive charges were set off at unpredictable intervals at locations throughout the course. It sounded worse than it actually was. As long as the trainee didn't jump up, he had no fear of being hit. Everyone knew that. Still it was somewhat unsettling.

One of the most memorable yet most unpleasant experiences was the inhalation of tear gas. A group of fifteen to twenty recruits wearing gas masks was led into a concrete bunker. The instructor dropped a tear gas pellet into a container and ordered each recruit, one at a time, to remove his mask and inhale until he gagged on the gas for several seconds. Only then was he allowed to put his mask back on. Everyone's eyes burned for an hour or so afterward, even after splashing them with cold water.

Support troops destined for South Vietnam received additional training before their departure. It included such lessons as understanding the Vietnamese culture, the Geneva Convention, first-aid and lifesaving techniques, additional marksmanship training (requalification with the M14 or M16 rifle) and the standard get-down-and-dirty training of jumping out of moving trucks in full combat gear. This exercise simulated an attack by the enemy, who were played rather poorly by Vietnam veterans wearing appropriate costume.

Advanced training—especially for those chosen to become infantry soldiers and a smaller contingent of troops selected to attend jump school to become paratroopers—was a whole different scenario. This training was intense, physically demanding, and mentally stressful. As good as it was, however, there was no training in the world that could satisfactorily prepare a new recruit for the magnitude of what he was about to experience.

Thomas Finn, *Specialist Four, U.S. Army, Company A, 519th Military Intelligence Battalion, 525th Military Intelligence Group, MACV-J2, Saigon, 1966–67*

As we approached the gate at Fort Dix, I could see out the window that the military police were waiting for us. It was around midnight now. I wasn't sure of the time, but it was very late. I was wondering to myself, "Why are these MPs waiting for us?"

We stopped at the gate. The next thing I remember, this drill sergeant came on the bus, you know, the big honcho thing, hup-two and whatever, and what the hell was that all about? We got off the bus and they took us into the barracks. We were issued clean linens, but nobody really slept that night.

Early the next morning, we went to the reception station, located high on a hill. We were issued a duffel bag, which you had to drag everywhere, all your gear, you know; it was like dragging fourteen tons of bad news. We spent a week at the reception station.*

I remember the sergeant boarded the bus before our departure for basic training and said, "Your ass is mine," you know, the usual rhetoric. I still remember his name, and I think he was from Clearwater, Florida. He was a tall, black sergeant and was actually a pretty nice guy. At least, no one wanted to kill him.

In 1965, there was only one drill sergeant per platoon because it was at the very beginning of the big call-up. So you had this one poor sergeant, this dude, who had this platoon of fifty guys. He had to be there morning, noon, and night. He must have had no life for himself whatsoever. This one guy had to do it all.

Basic training was a different story. At the time, I thought the training was extremely difficult. It was hard for me, as I had come from a very soft life here in Newport. But as I reflect on it, the training was not as hard as it should have been, considering the fact that in nine more months I would be in Vietnam—a combat zone. Of course, I would never tell the sergeant that I got shortchanged, but I probably was. Fortunately, it turned out okay.

We graduated at the time of the great Northeast Blackout in November 1965. They called us out one night. We were days from graduation from basic, and they were telling us that the greater Northeast had lost all electricity. Fort Dix was not in trouble because it had its own power. We all thought we were going to be called up the next morning to quell the riots. Fortunately, nothing ever materialized, although we were put on alert.

From basic training, I was sent to Fort Holabird in Baltimore, Maryland, for military intelligence training. That was a really nice time in my life. It was party time. It was like college, that's what it was! We were in the downtown area of Baltimore and had a great time.

Michael Toner Farrell, *Specialist Five, U.S. Army, 544th Replacement Company, Cam Ranh Bay, 1969–70*

I left with my friend from a bus station in Newport and went to the

---

* This week was called zero week, as it counted toward the recruits' time but not toward the eight-week basic training period.

induction center in Providence to be sworn into the army. From there, we took a train down to Augusta, Georgia, with other recruits from Rhode Island whom we did not know. What a horror show! We were all packed in like sardines. It was hot, the food was bad, and we were on the train for twenty-six hours. Trust me when I say it wasn't a luxury trip.

I arrived at Fort Gordon, Georgia, on June 6, 1968.

As I reflect back, I remember I had been in basic training for only two weeks when I said to myself, "This is not what I want to do. I've got to get the hell out of here." Looking back, all I really had to do at the time was fall on the ground, and I'd probably be collecting military disability today.

It was difficult, because I was very frail, but I kept up. It took me forever to run the mile. I did everything except the gas chamber, which I was exempted from. They knew I had had open-heart surgery and were kind to me when it came to the gas. Other than that, I did it all. Basic training turned me into a man.

For advanced training, I was sent to Fort Lee, Virginia, to become a cook, but I didn't get this assignment at first. When I completed basic training, I was told I was going into the infantry. And I said to myself, "No way!" I knew who I was, the limits of my own physical and mental capabilities, and that I would be dead in no time flat. So I asked how I could change my military occupational series. I was told I could reenlist for another year and choose any MOS I wanted. Reflecting back, I wish I had chosen helicopter repairman, but I took what I knew best: being a cook. I had considerable cooking experience at my mother's diner back home, and I figured I couldn't go wrong.

When I got to Fort Lee, I was taught how to cook all over again, and I learned. They had this recipe book that was incredible, with all these recipes for a minimum of five hundred people up to a maximum of three thousand.

Mike Pinksaw, *Specialist Four, U.S. Army, 60th Land Clearing Company, 62nd Engineering Battalion, 20th Engineering Brigade, Long Binh, Bien Hoa, Lai Khe 1968–69*

By bus, we traveled from Newport to Providence. There, the recruiter met us and took us to the induction center. We were all sworn in as a group, and after the brief ceremony we were all put back on the bus for transportation to the main train terminal in Providence. We took this train all the way down to Washington, D.C., where we switched trains on our way to Fort Jackson, South Carolina. The ride down was long and boring, and it took us two days to get there. We arrived around two o'clock in the afternoon.

Ugh, the first thing I remember upon arrival at Fort Jackson was everyone yelling at us like, "Get off the f—in' train, move it, get the f— off!" They lined us all up outside. I thought it was going to be warm in South Carolina, but it wasn't. It was freezing cold.

We were marched up to the induction center and spent a week there. This is where we all were issued our uniforms. I remember that first week we were all forced to live in a barracks that was heated with a potbellied stove.

The day came when we were to be transported to our basic training company. I stayed right at Fort Jackson, while others went to Fort Gordon, Georgia. We were put on trucks, and the next thing I can remember is arriving at the barracks and the drill sergeant yelling, "Get off that f—in' truck!" Someone behind me was so scared that he threw his duffel bag on top of me in his haste to get off the truck.

All kidding aside, I was scared shitless. I said to myself, "What the f— am I doing here?"

My basic training was a typical one. I had more experience with tear gas than I would ever want to encounter again in a lifetime. Even later, when I was in Vietnam, I had some experiences with it.

We trained with the M14 rifle, not the newer version, the M16.* I really never understood why. Finally, when I got into advanced training, I did get the M16.

Tom Finn in a Jeep holding an M14 rifle. (Courtesy of Tom Finn)

---

* Production of the M14, a 7.62mm rifle, ceased in 1964; however, it was still used in Vietnam for a number of years thereafter. The M16 (officially designated the M16A1) was a 5.56mm rifle and quickly proved to be an excellent weapon in jungle warfare due to its lightness and versatility.

After advanced training, I went to Fort Leonard Wood, Missouri, for training as a heavy equipment operator. The course I was assigned to was to teach you how to operate bulldozers. I learned to be a D-7 operator. We trained on Caterpillar D-7s and Allis-Chalmers HD-16s. The training consisted of learning how to grade land and how to maintain the heavy machinery we were operating, such as changing blades and performing preventive maintenance—stuff like that. Only later in Vietnam would I find out why I needed to know how to change blades.

Doug Johnson, *Specialist Four, U.S. Army, 25th Infantry Division, 2nd Battalion, 12th Infantry, 1968*

I recall that when I arrived at the recruit center, we were given a battery of tests, one of which was an attempt to identify those individuals who qualified for officer training. These tests could have been passed by a monkey having a good day. When I was informed by the exuberant administrator that I had passed the test, I was forced to give them their first example of Johnson's basic mathematics. I inquired how long I would have to remain in the army if I took officer training and was informed that it would be three years. As a draftee, I only had a two-year obligation, so I most humbly turned down the invitation to become an officer. So on my very first day in the military, I was able to piss off a superior, something I became quite good at during my short but distinguished military career.

My first day in the mess hall I remember a cook who yelled at us the entire time we were eating, "Hurry up and eat and get out of my mess hall, you bunch of pigs." In retrospect, I realize that this poor excuse for a human being with the intelligence of an amoeba was probably a private E-1 just like me. But being in the army at least one day longer than me, he outranked me, and I had to put up with his cretin ravings.

Mornings we were greeted with the music of trash cans being thrown onto the floor, various objects being clanged on our bedposts, and all sorts of new and soothing words to remind us that we were no longer civilians: it was time to face another day in hell. The cast of characters in my basic training company was not necessarily a group of guys I would have hung out with under different circumstances. They ranged from college graduates to guys who were given the choice to join the army or go to jail.

Although I can't remember a lot of names, I know that I shared a closeness and a bond—one that I was later to feel in Vietnam—from experiencing tough times and challenges together. The first few weeks of basic seemed to be full of terror and fatigue, as we were physically and mentally challenged in ways I have not previously experienced. I remember many days when I thought I couldn't run another step and would collapse into my bunk in a state of exhaustion. In the process, I learned a lot about the benefits of being challenged, the durability of the human body, and the toughness of the human mind and spirit.

About halfway through basic, I discovered that I was now in shape, didn't fear the tyrants known as drill instructors, and began to see this experience as a game. I realized that I could no longer be intimidated by the physical demands, and as long as I kept my opinions about what was going on to myself, that I could cope just fine. The drill instructor that was assigned to my squad was a seasoned veteran, and he was tough but fair. As a veteran of multiple tours in Vietnam, I really believe that he wanted to train us to face the rigors that he knew awaited us in that far-off jungle. I respected him as a man, because although he never really exhibited it in outward displays, I believe that he cared for us and wanted to train us to survive an experience that he could not convey in words but that we would all have to experience on our own. I learned a lot about myself and grew up a lot in those three long months of basic training.

My military occupational series for the army was as a radio/telephone operator (RTO), which, I believe, was an 05B20. I don't remember much of my advanced infantry training, but it took place at Fort Dix, New Jersey. From what I remember, we spent a lot of time in class and learned something valuable that I have been called upon to use many times since AIT—Morse code. At some time not far into our advanced training, we all were struck with the revelation that being a radio/telephone operator was not exactly the most glamorous position to occupy in an infantry unit. Somehow, either through word of mouth, or maybe from some sadistic army instructors, we learned that the life expectancy of a radio/telephone operator was probably a matter of seconds. It seems that the radio you carried on your back, along with the prominent antenna and the enemy's knowledge that you were the main means of communication in the unit, placed the radio operator high on the enemy hit list. Coupled with these unsettling thoughts was the knowledge that most, if not all, of the graduates from our class would be heading straight to Vietnam. Two interesting developments resulted from this knowledge. Many of the students in class did not want to go to Vietnam, and they intentionally altered their academic performance to wash out of the RTO school, hoping to avoid the jungle tour. They were to go on to distinguish themselves in cook school, mechanic school, and other esoteric duties offered by the army.

For those of us who stayed with the program—the few, the proud, and probably, in the view of many, the stupid—we were soon offered the opportunity to attend radio teletype school. Since this involved another three months of training in Fort Huachuca, Arizona, I decided that I would do well enough to graduate from RTO training but not qualify for additional training. I was sick of being a trainee and wanted to move on to whatever fate awaited me.

Perhaps the most ludicrous portion of my advanced infantry training was the actual infantry portion of the training at Fort Dix. We were training during the depth of the winter months, and there was often snow on the ground as we performed our various maneuvers. I vividly remember our first attempts at practicing ambush techniques on the snow-covered ground. While I had not yet been to Vietnam, I knew it was a jungle and that there was not likely to be any accumulation of snow on the ground. I also wondered how successfully we were hiding ourselves from our prospective ambushers as we lay on the white snow-covered fields in our olive drab army uniforms. The most frightening moments in AIT were when we participated in night-ambush training. I'll never forget the panic and terror of being ambushed at night and the realization that had this been real life instead of training that I would probably be returning in a body bag. Nothing could have adequately prepared us for the nightmare that was Vietnam, but this training left a lot to be desired.

Ken Garthee, *Private First Class, U.S. Marine Corps, 3rd Battalion, 3rd Marines, 3rd Marine Division, Da Nang, Rock Pile, 1966–67*

In the early morning hours of August 15, 1965, I woke up to get ready to leave for boot camp. It was about four A.M. when I got up. I packed the rest of my personal items in a bag and was about to leave to catch the bus. Standing in the living room, waiting to say good-bye, were my mom and dad. We had already said good-bye the night before. My dad didn't say much; he just looked me in the eye, shook my hand and said, "Take care of yourself." My mom gave me a big hug.

I didn't think about too much on the bus. I just looked at the streets going by and thought about how my life was going to change in the not-so-distant future. In a short time, I met up with some of my friends, and we all went to the airport together to catch the flight to San Diego.

The flight to San Diego was my first flight. I had a window seat, and when the plane took off, I saw white vapor trails streaming from the wings. Being new at this game, I thought the plane was going to crash, and I swear, I nearly fainted. When I finally realized we were not in danger, I felt really stupid. So much for the big bad marine.

We were greeted at the San Diego Airport by a USMC drill instructor (DI), who herded us into a military bus along with other recruits. When we arrived at the marine corps recruit depot, that's when all the fun started. We didn't even get a chance to get up from our seats when the DI started to scream and yell instructions to all of us. Quickly getting off the bus, we were told to stand on a pair of yellow footprints that were painted on the pavement. Some guys didn't move fast enough, but they quickly found their way with the help of the DI, by being pushed and shoved and pulled and tossed. It didn't take me long to find a pair of footprints. We were told when to speak and how to speak and to begin and end each response with "Sir." Our eyes always had to look forward, and we learned never, ever to refer to our drill instructor as "you." We were told what to do and when and how to do it.

It would be a while before we earned the right to be called a marine; we were called a lot of things, but marine wasn't one of them.

Just when we thought we were beginning to square things away, the drill instructor would always find fault with something or someone. If the problem was caused by an individual, we had what was called a late-night blanket party. We'd put a blanket over the guy's head, and by knocking some sense into him, made him realize that his poor performance or conduct had an effect on all of us. Having an occasional party like this quickly brought these individuals around. I was lucky. I never had a blanket party.

I can remember doing a lot of running and double-time marches in boot camp, as well as an overabundance of push-ups and/or squat-thrusts. Every push-up had to be counted, using the word "sir" after each one was completed. Of course, there was always someone who never seemed to do them right, and the DI would make us start all over again.

The most important skill a marine recruit had to learn was how to shoot a rifle. The practice of shooting a rifle was called snapping-in. We would lie in the hot sand for hours sighting the rifle and shooting at targets. Some guys actually fell asleep doing this, and that was not good in the eyes of the DI. Our penalty, as a unit, was squat-thrusts. I qualified as a sharpshooter, only a few points from being an expert.* All the friends I enlisted with also qualified.

---

* In the marines, as it was in the army, there were three qualification badges granted to a rifleman. Those least proficient on the rifle range were awarded a marksmanship badge. Those more proficient were awarded a sharpshooter badge, while the most proficient received the expert badge.

Eventually we graduated from boot camp and finally earned the right to be called a marine by the drill instructor. When I think back to my self-training with rocks in my backpack, I realize the futility of that effort. Boot camp was really hard, and the marines were getting us prepared for something much more difficult.

Next came ITR (infantry training reserve). There we learned how to shoot every weapon the marine corps had in its arsenal—bazookas, automatic weapons, rocket launchers, and more. We were taught combat tactics, escape and evasion strategy, and jungle maneuvers. Jungle maneuvers were difficult to conduct in such open areas at Camp Pendleton, but we did them anyway. In wooded areas of the camp, we learned how to detect booby traps and how to prepare for or prevent ambushes.

ITR was considerably easier than boot camp. The instructors were not yelling at us all the time, nor were we required to do push-ups for punishment. We did, however, maintain our physical conditioning by doing daily calisthenics. Eventually we finished all of our infantry training.

Bill McCollum, *Sergeant, U.S. Army, 173rd Airborne Brigade, Charlie Company, 4th Battalion, 503rd Infantry, LZ-English, 1969–71*

I left town with four other guys. I guess I thought at the time that it was going to be pretty great. We flew out of Providence and landed in Washington, D.C., where we had a several-hour delay. So here we are: a lengthy delay, a little bit of money, and no place to go. We saw this military guy in the airport and asked him if there was any place we could go to eat. We told him we had just been inducted into the army. He said he was just getting off duty and to come with him. He not only took us for something to eat, but gave us a brief tour of the area. We saw Fort Myers and President Kennedy's grave site and the Tomb of the Unknown Soldier, with the changing of the guard at Arlington National Cemetery. It was a tour of the metropolitan Washington area like you wouldn't believe. It was great.

When we eventually got to South Carolina, it was kind of scary. We were picked up at the airport by a limousine; that's right, a limousine. There was another soldier and an officer already inside the vehicle.

As we were riding to Fort Jackson, the guy with the officer said to us, "You're not going to like this." He continued, "This is the third time they caught me." I started laughing to myself, figuring he's pulling our leg.

Again he said, "Hey, you're not going to like it there."

One of the guys finally said, "Why not?"

His response was, "Because they treat you like shit!"

The officer turned to the guy and said, "Be quiet!"

Finally, we realized that he was in handcuffs and was being transported back to the stockade for being AWOL. Our first stop was to drop this boy off at the stockade.

Now we were there in the middle of the night and they took us to the mess hall to feed us. The next thing I knew a guy walked by and whacked me with a fly swatter. I said to myself, "This isn't what they said it was going to be."

The next morning, we were in a tent city; there were so many guys coming in, we had to live under canvas until a barracks opened up. I happened to look over to a tent near me and I see the son-of-a-bitch who hit me with the fly swatter the night before. He had gotten there only a few days before me. All the while, I thought he was part of the permanent cadre at Fort Jackson.

Basic training was a process of determining who could cut it and who couldn't. I guess that's what eventually made me become a drill sergeant. I wanted to be tough and prove I could survive the ordeal.

My basic training was difficult but quite good because I had an excellent drill sergeant. This guy was tough. He was wounded in the arm in Vietnam, and when he came back, he used to carry this ball in his hand all the time and squeezed it constantly for therapy. He always used to tell us stories about being there.

Basic was rough, not like it is today. I can remember them whacking me around a bit. I had short legs, so the running killed me, but still I was able to maintain a good outlook. Being a practical joker helped a great deal.

I had the attitude that no matter what they did to me, they just couldn't hurt me. I guess I followed this approach because I heard stories from others who went through basic and said, "Once you get through it, and you will, you'll have it made."

My father told me basically the same thing: "Don't let the bastards get you down!"

In the end I made it.

I took my advanced infantry training (AIT) at Fort Gordon—more specifically Camp Crockett, which was out in the wilderness far away from the PXs and stuff, and they had to truck everything out to us. In fact, we went everywhere in cattle car trucks. The training was good; however, the area really stank of raw sewage. I think we were near a sewage plant.

I had the attitude, "Teach me something; I'm not going to be ignorant, I'm going to learn." When I reflect on what happened to me in Vietnam, if it hadn't been for my basic and AIT training, I'd probably not be standing here today. I paid attention, and I was a good learner.

After AIT, I went directly to Fort Benning, Georgia, for airborne training, or jump school, as it was called. It lasted three weeks. If you weren't in shape, you were dead. My running was bad because I had short legs, and we had to run everywhere. I managed to make it through—I was not going to fail.

Stephen Butler, *Lance Corporal, U.S. Marine Corps, 7th Marine Combat Engineers, Da Nang, 1966–67*

Frankly, I enjoyed basic training. Remember, I went to work when I was twelve years old working for a guy who treated me as his equal. He taught me how to work, and he taught me some things as fundamental as how to shovel dirt—believe me, there's a right way to shovel dirt and a wrong way to shovel dirt. He was a workhorse. It was not unusual for me to have to load an entire truck of cabbage by myself. At the end of the day I'd go back home, have supper, and drive with him to the produce market at night, unload the stuff, and come back home, only to get up the next morning and do the same thing all over again.

So when I got to Parris Island, most of the guys were complaining; and I thought it was a Vegas holiday or something. My mother didn't have much money, and I thought the food was just absolutely . . . well, I mean, I'd never been in a place that had such a selection: chocolate milk, and regular milk, and ice cream with meals.

Yeah! I didn't have a problem there at all. I was never an outstanding athletic type because I never got a chance to play sports, but in terms of the work and drill and all, it wasn't a problem.

I didn't really get a lot of advance training. I went from Parris Island, where I received the typical training for a marine, up to infantry training reserve in North Carolina, and then I went to NBC school, which was training in nuclear, chemical, and biological warfare. Then I was stationed for a while in South Carolina.

Rob Roche, *Sergeant, U.S. Army, 101st Airborne Division, Da Nang, 1967–69*

After enlisting, two of my friends and I received orders to report to Fort Gordon, Georgia, for basic training. We left Providence by train on August 27, 1967, and boy, was it hot! As we traveled down the coast, we made stops in major cities like New York and Washington and picked up others who had enlisted. When we got to Fort Jackson, South Carolina, we all got off the train for initial processing. I remember it like it was yesterday.

They had a wooden barrel set out in front of this building. A sergeant stepped forward and said, "Anyone who has zip guns, knives, or any other type of weapon should put them in the barrel."

We're all standing there thinking to ourselves, "This is nothing more than a big joke." Well, I want you to know, they nearly filled that barrel! There were a good number of Hispanics from inner-city gangs who were present in the formation. After that, I said to myself, "Oh no, we're in trouble now."

Not long after, we boarded the train again, and of course we partied like hell all the way to Georgia. In fact, because we had partied so hard at home a few days earlier, by the time we arrived in Augusta, we were exhausted and really sick. Two of us had high fevers due to the extreme heat. Of course, all the booze we had consumed on the way down didn't help, either. We spent the next eight weeks doing physical training, marching, running, and learning to shoot the M14 rifle.

I signed up to be supply clerk. I think the army classification numbers for this series was 76Y3B. As I remember it today, I was relieved that I did not have to go to advanced infantry training. After completing our basic training, we were to report to Fort Lee, Virginia, for training in lightweight armor. We also trained as supply clerks. Unfortunately for my other friend, he got an 11B10 MOS—infantryman.

For whatever reason, I decided to go airborne. There was another fellow I met, Russell, who became a very close friend, and we both volunteered for jump school. Mike, another friend of mine, didn't want to go either. Wouldn't you know it, he immediately received orders for Vietnam. Russell and I received orders for jump school, which was a three-week parachuting and infantry course to be given at Fort Benning, Georgia. Today, I remember it as one tough course. I'd much prefer basic training than jump school any day. It was all physical training. You had to run everywhere, even in place. The only time you stopped running was in the mess hall or in the barracks.

In the final week, we took a number of jumps from the tower and then later from a plane. Eventually, we qualified as airborne infantry soldiers.

David Rossi, *Specialist Four, U.S. Army, 1st Infantry Division and 25th Infantry Division, Di An, Tay Ninh, and Cu Chi, 1969–70*

I took my indoctrination at Fort Jackson, South Carolina, and my basic training at Fort Gordon, Georgia. After a few weeks of leave back home, I was assigned to Fort Sam Houston in Texas for training as a medic. I didn't ask for this training. This was the occupation that the army selected for me.

Salvatore T. Raffa, *Airman Second Class, U.S. Air Force, 377th Security Police Squadron, Tan Son Nhut Air Base, Saigon, 1967–68*

Basic training was horrible. The heat, you know—I was at Lackland Air Force Base in Texas. Sometimes it got so hot there they'd run up a red flag, and training was canceled for the day. You didn't dare venture outside.

I was homesick, and I had a girlfriend back home, who, by the way, is now my wife. I mean it was mentally tough on me.

Matter of fact, the training instructor happened to retire near the end of my basic training, and he came over to me and shook my hand saying, "Raffa, I didn't think you were going to make it."

I said, "I didn't either, Sarge!"

I just couldn't adapt. I was always hiding in the lockers having a cigarette or getting lost somewhere else to avoid duty. The physical part of the training was really no problem for me. I just didn't like the military.

I went on to advanced training, but it was not an extensive course. Matter of fact, just before going to Vietnam, they gave us all one week, *one week* of combat training. That was it. I didn't have a lot of training.

Dick Turner, *Boatswain's Mate Third Class, U.S. Navy, River Assault Squadron 15, River Division 152, Task Force 117, Dong Tam and My Tho, 1968–69*

In the navy, we called it recruit training or boot camp. I was sworn in on February 25, 1964, and we were all loaded on a bus and taken to Logan International Airport in Boston, where we boarded a commercial plane and flew to Chicago. There we boarded navy buses and were driven to Waukegan, Illinois, where the navy recruit training command was situated. We arrived around 3:30 A.M. and were immediately herded into a building. We had to fill out a lot of paperwork, and then they let us sleep a couple of hours. Reveille sounded at 5 A.M. and consisted of someone kicking a trash can down a passageway, followed by a lot of yelling and screaming. I said to myself, "Wow, what have I got myself into?"

Later on that same day, we had to fill out more paperwork. We were asked what we wanted to do after we graduated from recruit training, and I picked the rate of boatswain's mate. We were formed into individual companies and were greeted by our company commander. Then it was eight weeks of training. After completion of recruit training, I received my orders to report to a tug boat in the Philadelphia naval shipyard. On the tug, I worked as a deck hand.

In the navy they have these things called dream sheets, and that's exactly what they were—nothing but a dream. I wrote on a dream sheet that I wanted to go to small-boat school and learn how to operate small boats. I submitted it and reenlisted for six years. I never really got exactly what I wanted.

OFFICER TRAINING

During the war years, an individual with a college degree and a 1-A draft status had three choices—to be drafted, to enlist, or if qualified, to enter officer candidate school (OCS). Those who chose OCS obtained a minimum of ninety days of concentrated training, both academic as well as physical. Depending on the service branch, the type of training varied considerably. One subject that was universally taught was leadership skills. Regardless of service branch, without the ability to lead men effectively, a candidate had little chance of receiving his commission as an officer.

It was a well-known fact during the Vietnam era that the army OCS program was much less difficult to qualify for than the navy or the air force programs. The army was desperate for infantry officers due to personnel losses in Vietnam; and because of this need, the army's standards were less stringent than those of other services. This lowering of standards would be a subject of debate for a number of years after the war had officially ended. In later years even General William Westmoreland admitted that some officers who served in Vietnam were not officer material.

For the record, approximately one out of every ten military personnel serving in Vietnam was an officer. An even smaller percentage served as infantry officers, pilots, and aviators.

Howard North and William Sullivan were both involved in some pretty intensive programs. Here is what they had to say about their training programs.

Howard North, *Lieutenant j.g., U.S. Coast Guard, Coast Guard Squadron One, USCGC* Point Clear *(WPB 82315), An Thoi and Cat Lo, 1967–68*

I went to officer candidate school in Yorktown, Virginia, where I was placed in a class of approximately two hundred people. There was a good cross section of candidates in the class—twenty-five had enlisted earlier, while the balance were college graduates. It was really good training. They taught us how to navigate, how to work in a combat information center, and all the other military stuff. Naturally, we also did physical training; however, it was more demanding academically than it was physically. When I graduated, I was commissioned as an ensign in the Coast Guard and shipped off to the cutter *Vigilant* out of New Bedford, Massachusetts. The *Vigilant* was a 210-foot medium-endurance cutter, and its function was to do fishery patrols and search-and-rescue missions along George's Bank off the coast of Massachusetts. I did this for about fourteen to fifteen months.

In between assignments, I was sent to communications officer's school, to classified publications school, and a few others. It took up about two months of my time in the service.

William Sullivan, *Lieutenant Commander, U.S. Navy, Fighter Squadron 213, U.S.S.* Intrepid, *Air Wing, U.S.S.* Kitty Hawk *(CVA-63), U.S.S.* Intrepid *(CVA-11), U.S.S.* Paul Revere, *and U.S.S.* Blue Ridge, *1965–68 and 1971–72*

I went to officer candidate school in Newport in 1955, graduating and commissioned as an ensign in 1956. I didn't get a chance to see much of the city, because I had all I could do concentrating on my studies. I found it extremely difficult.

After I graduated from OCS in Newport, the navy, in its infinite wisdom, cut the group in half alphabetically. Everybody from *a* through *n* was going to carrier air, and *o* through *z* to land-based air in Hawaii. I was in the latter half, but I really wanted to go into the carrier air, so I found a guy who was willing to trade assignments. The navy allowed that to happen.

I trained on naval aviation observers in order to become a naval flight officer. At the time, it was really on-the-job training. In order to get my wings, I was assigned to a squadron, and I trained for six months with this unit.

My first tour of duty was with the Carrier Airborne Early Warning Squadron-11 (VAW-11), in North Island, San Diego. This is where I first trained and learned how to operate from an aircraft carrier. Initially, you do what's called field carrier landing practices, and after you become reasonably proficient at this, you then train takeoffs and landings from carriers off the coast of California. I was in this squadron for four years, from November 1956 to September 1960, and was deployed three times to the Western Pacific aboard the U.S.S. *Ticonderoga* (CVA-14).

Betsy Wylie, *Lieutenant, U.S. Navy, Management Information Center, Headquarters, Naval Forces Vietnam (NAVFORV), Saigon, 1967–68*

I really rather enjoyed women officers' school. I had no major problems with it. I know some of my classmates had problems with the discipline, but I didn't think it was that bad. It was certainly not the emphasis on physical education and physical training that there is today. It was being in good health, maintaining the correct weight, being able to climb up and down the stairs, and that was about it.

I thought the academic program was pretty good. We had homework every night, yes, but not insurmountable.

Peggy R. Zarek, *Lieutenant Commander, U.S. Navy, U.S.S. Sanctuary (AH-17), Coastal Waters off South Vietnam, Military Region 1, 1969–70*

We didn't get any kind of special training to serve on a hospital ship. I did go to Philadelphia to take a six-month orthopedic course because of all the amputees returning from Vietnam. That's the extent of the training I got—the orthopedic course and taking care of the amputees.

VIETNAM, HERE I COME!

Depending upon where one was stationed, the type of unit he or she was assigned to, and military occupation and training, the way an individual received his or her orders for assignment after advanced training varied considerably. For a majority of the troops in the mid- to late '60s and early '70s, there was one inescapable conclusion: no matter what military occupation you held, whether it be infantry, cook, clerk typist, or supply clerk, it all too frequently led to an assignment to Vietnam.

Surprisingly, a significant percentage of troops levied for Vietnam were volunteers. Some volunteered out of sheer patriotism, while others were looking for adventure. There were others who simply wanted to avoid what was called "the chickenshit duty," associated with stateside assignments. Spit and polish inspections were all too frequent in the States. In a war zone, however, there was relatively little time for such military tradition.

Armed and Ready—an F-4 Phantom Jet

Bill McCollum, *Sergeant, U.S. Army, 73rd Airborne Brigade, Charlie Company, 4th Battalion, 503rd Infantry, LZ-English, 1969–71*

I asked to go to Vietnam.

When I came out of airborne training, I got orders for the 82nd Airborne at Fort Bragg; however, at the last minute the black-hatted instructor came out and said, "There's been a change."

Well, we're all looking at each other thinking, "We're going right over."

He walked in front of us and said, "This is the deal. You guys are now part of the 24th Mechanized Unit out of Fort Riley, Kansas. For one month you're gonna go to Germany to take part in war games. When you come back, you'll be put back into an airborne unit."

So off we went Germany to play games for a month. When we came back to Fort Riley, the 24th Mechanized Unit soldiers hated us because we were all gung-ho about airborne and always talking about it.

We asked the powers to be, "What's going to happen to us?"

The answer was a simple one: "We haven't decided what we're going to do with you guys yet."

We were then told we would be doing prison detail and riot control training, and it seemed like it was never going to end.

We'd go out to the training field, and guys would be throwing garbage at us, pretending that a riot was in progress; and they'd bring a unit out to face us; and we'd learn to do wedge formations, this formation and that formation. Next week I'd be at the stockade taking prisoners out to cut grass and cleanup in graveyards and dig graves. I'd just supervise.

Finally, I thought to myself, "This is not for me." I said to one of the guys in charge, "How do I get out of this duty, and what do I have to do to get out of this place?"

He said, "Where do you want to go?"

"Christ sakes," I said, "I think Vietnam is better than this."

He said, "That's easy, just put in a 1049 form and volunteer for Vietnam."

Next thing I know, he gave me a pass, I went down to the personnel office and did just that. About five days later, my name was on the list for Vietnam. I said to myself, "I'm out of here."

That was it.

Thomas Finn, *Specialist Four, U.S. Army, Company A, 519th Military Intelligence Battalion, 525th Military Intelligence Group, MACV-J2, Saigon, 1966–67*

After taking advanced training in military intelligence for three to four months in Baltimore, Maryland, we received orders for Fort Bragg, North Carolina. This was in March 1966. When we got to Fort Bragg, we knew we were destined to go to Vietnam. While there, we were assigned into units; the military called them packets. We were identified as Packet A-1. We left Bragg in May '66, over five hundred of us, to go to Vietnam. For all intents and purposes, it was a battalion.

From Fort Holabird through Fort Bragg, all those I had met and made friends with were to travel with me, pretty much as a group, to Vietnam.

Ken Garthee, *Private First Class, U.S. Marine Corps, 3rd Battalion, 3rd Marines, 3rd Marine Division, Da Nang, Rock Pile, 1966–67*

After completing ITR in mid-November 1965, we were all called together in a group; some were given orders for Da Nang, South Vietnam. We had no idea where Vietnam was located and had to look at a map to find it. When we found it, we realized it was a long way from home.

Stephen Butler, *Lance Corporal, U.S. Marine Corps, 7th Marine Combat Engineers, Da Nang, 1966–67*

When I was stationed in South Carolina, I basically had two jobs. I was working over at Parris Island as an adjunct from time to time, and I was working at Beaufort, which was a navy base of marine fighter pilots, and I did some support work there. The first shirt [first sergeant] came and said they had cut a bunch of orders for critical military occupational series they needed in Vietnam. My MOS had rolled down, and I was one of those selected. But the first shirt said that I didn't have to go there because my brother was stationed in Vietnam, and also because I was on a 2-2-2 enlistment—two years of active duty, two years of active reserve, and two years of inactive reserve. He said there was no way they could combine the active into the reserve and send me over, as it was outside the enlistment time. But I didn't want to spend all my remaining time in South Carolina, so I ended up telling them that I would go to Vietnam.

Dick Turner, *Boatswain's Mate Third Class, U.S. Navy, River Assault Squadron 15, River Division 152, Task Force 117, Dong Tam and My Tho, 1968–69*

The officer in charge called me up to his office. He said, "I've got a set of orders for you." He closed the door behind us and read the orders: "You are hereby ordered to report to the Republic of South Vietnam." But first, I had to report to survival, escape, evasion, and resistance school for twelve weeks of intensive training at Mare Island, California. So I reported there.

At the school they had a mock POW camp that made a real believer out of me. If I had ever been captured in Vietnam, I would have been prepared for it. We were made to undress and stand in a fifty-five-gallon drum filled to the brim with cold water, and we got slapped around a lot.

One day we were driven out into the wilderness and dropped off in the middle of nowhere. All we were given was a parachute, a compass, a toothbrush, and a tube of toothpaste. Our mission was to make it back without being captured. In the meantime, we had to live off the land. We were given checkpoints that we had to find along the way. Not too long after, we were captured and sent to the POW camp.

Well, some of us managed to escape, a rare occurrence in a camp such as this. We were eventually found walking on a paved road not far from the camp. Because we were successful in our escape, we were taken to the mess hall and treated to a steak dinner. That was our prize.

Betsy Wylie, *Lieutenant, U.S. Navy, Management Information Center, Headquarters, Naval Forces Vietnam (NAVFORV), Saigon, 1967–68*

I volunteered for Vietnam. I thought it was the appropriate thing to do. I had originally volunteered, probably in 1966, when I was stationed in

Germany; and I got a letter back from the Bureau of Personnel saying, "Thanks, but no thanks." I volunteered again and never heard from them. I assumed they had forgotten about me.

When I was stationed at a training school in Maryland, I got a call from the assistant chief of naval personnel for women, who said, "We're going to order you into Vietnam, but you can't tell anybody."

And I said, "All right. But I will tell my parents." And her concern, at that time, was that I was going to be the first woman line officer sent to Vietnam from the navy, and she didn't want any publicity until they were ready to release it in Washington and all of this sort of hoopla. So I told my commanding officer (as I thought that was appropriate), and I called my parents (I thought that was appropriate), and I called my brother. But I must have sat on it for a month to six weeks before the high mucky-mucks in Washington decided they could make the press release saying that they were going to send a woman who was not a nurse corps officer to Vietnam.

I was at the Schools Command in Bainbridge, Maryland, when the news release was finally made about my going to Vietnam as the first female line officer. After that, I got some very weird phone calls and also some really weird letters. I just turned them over to the Office of Naval Intelligence. I called them and told them, "Hey look! I'm getting these weird telephone calls and letters." They were strange, not particularly vindictive. Nobody threatened my life or anything, but they were weird letters. And as I said, I just turned them all over, and eventually it all went away.

Rob Roche, *Sergeant, U.S. Army, 101st Airborne Division, Da Nang, 1967–69*

It's difficult for me to remember, but I'm pretty certain I received orders for Vietnam immediately after graduating from jump school. We had just graduated that morning and were still in formation when the orders were handed out. As I remember it, not all of us received orders for Vietnam. I did, of course. I also received a thirty-day leave. Immediately, I packed my bags, caught a commercial flight, and went home to visit my family and friends.

Doug Johnson, *Specialist Four, U.S. Army, 25th Infantry Division, 2nd Battalion, 12th Infantry, 1968*

Upon completion of my advanced infantry training, I received the confirmation of what until then had only been an expectation: that I would be ordered to Vietnam. I don't remember feeling any particular emotion when I received the orders. I can't say that I was afraid or exuberant—maybe curious or resolved best summed up my state of mind. From what I recall, the entire class from the radio/telephone program was summoned together, and a list was read of each person and his new duty assignment. There was a sense of finality as name after name was matched with a distant land known to us only by name and reputation. In retrospect, it was a recitation for some of what would prove to be a sentence of death.

David Rossi, *Specialist Four, U.S. Army, 1st Infantry Division and 25th Infantry Division, Di An, Tay Ninh, and Cu Chi, 1969–70*

We were originally told at Fort Sam Houston that we were going to Vietnam, but in San Francisco, for whatever reason, we were delayed for a while. Some were reassigned to Hawaii, a couple went to South Korea, and so it went. Naturally, I would have wanted Hawaii, but I was finally told I was going to Vietnam. I'd guess that 95 percent of us [those trained as medics] ended up there.

When I finally found out I was going to Nam, it really didn't bother me. I actually preferred going there than ending up in cold places like Germany or South Korea and having to pull meaningless duty.

Salvatore T. Raffa, *Airman Second Class, U.S. Air Force, 77th Security Police Squadron, Tan Son Nhut Air Base, Saigon, 1967–68*

I was stationed in Wilmington, North Carolina, and one day I just got orders issued to me, reassigning me to Vietnam. I went home and told my wife, whom I had just married, and we both cried.

Howard North, *Lieutenant j.g., U.S. Coast Guard, Coast Guard Squadron One, USCGC* Point Clear *(WPB 82315), An Thoi and Cat Lo, 1967–68*

I found out I was going to Vietnam about three months before I went. One day I got called up to the executive officer's (XO) stateroom. I rapped on the door, and I was told to come in. The XO said, "I don't want to lose you, but I've got a set of orders for you." He handed them to me. I slowly read them. They were all typed out. The first thing I saw was, "Transferred to Coast Guard Station, Alameda, California." I said to myself, "California! That sounds good." Then the next line down said, "For further assignment to Coast Guard District 11 or 13"—I don't remember the number, but it was to San Francisco. I said to myself, "That doesn't sound bad." The next line down said, "For further assignment to Squadron One, Saigon, Vietnam." Now I said to myself, "That doesn't look too good!"

That's the way I found out. I was in a state of shock for the next two or three days.

William Sullivan, *Lieutenant Commander, U.S. Navy, Fighter Squadron 213, U.S.S.* Intrepid, *Air Wing, U.S.S.* Kitty Hawk *(CVA-63), U.S.S.* Intrepid *(CVA-11), U.S.S.* Paul Revere, *and U.S.S.* Blue Ridge, *1965– 68 and 1971–72*

I pretty much asked to go to Vietnam. At the time, I was stationed at the Naval Missile Test Center in Port Mugu, California. There I volunteered to fly the navy's newest jet fighter aircraft, the F-4 Phantom. I accumulated enough time there to qualify as an air intercept officer, and on the basis of that experience, I was assigned to sea duty as a crew member in Fighter Squadron 213 on the carrier U.S.S. *Kitty Hawk,* which was deployed to the Western Pacific.

Sullivan as a lieutenant in a picture taken at Headquarters, Pacific Missile Range, Port Mugu, California. (Courtesy of William Sullivan)

Michael Toner Farrell, *Specialist Five, U.S. Army, 544th Replacement Company, Cam Ranh Bay, 1969–70*

When I graduated from advanced training, I was reassigned to Fort Bragg, North Carolina. In the meantime, I was granted a two-week leave to go home. While still at Fort Lee, I took all my uniforms and recklessly stuffed them into my duffel bag. I was just happy to be going home after seventeen weeks in the army.

After my leave expired, I made my way down to Fort Bragg. Arriving around 2 A.M., I checked into my new company. The guy on duty told me to go to the barracks and find myself a bunk and get ready to fall out in the morning. I asked him whether I should fall out in my civvies or in my fatigues. He said, "In your uniform."

So I made it back to the barracks around 3 A.M., fell asleep, and was awakened at 6 A.M. I went into my duffel bag and found my shoes caked with mud and my fatigues badly wrinkled, and the brass buckle on my belt was black with tarnish. I had no choice, so I dressed and ran outside for formation. There must have been five hundred GIs outside, as far as you could see in either direction.

I was in the third row of a four-row formation. Of all the mornings I had to arrive, it was the morning of the uniform inspection by the commanding officer (CO). Standing next to me on one side was this guy whose shoes were so clean I could see my face reflected in them. His brass was blinding me. Clearly, I was in an airborne unit.

So the CO went through the line and made a quick turn and inspected each soldier individually. Each trooper saluted and the CO looked him over, spun around on his heel, and continued on to the next guy. By the time he reached me, he was about halfway through. He took one look at me and said, "What in the hell are you?" He just walked directly out of the formation without continuing on. Getting to the podium, he yells out, "Gentlemen. I had planned on a nice ten-mile hike for you today, but because of that"—he's looking directly at me when he said it—"you now have the weekend off." "You"—pointing to me—"are on garbage detail for the rest of the weekend." I did that for two hours on, two hours off, for the entire weekend. It was November, and I was cold. During the few hours I had to myself that weekend, I took my fatigues to the dry cleaners.

When Monday morning came, I was dressed to kill, at least in army terms. My fatigues were starched like cardboard, and I polished my shoes and brass. I walked to the CO's headquarters and asked to see him. When I was finally granted permission by the first sergeant, I walked in and saluted.

He said to me, "What can I do for you?"

I said, "Off the record, sir, how can I get the heck out of this company? What you did to me on Friday was disgusting. I just want out!"

He said, "You want to get out of here?"

"Yeah," I said.

He handed me a paper he pulled from his desk drawer and said, "Sign this paper, and you'll be in Vietnam in three months."

I signed it.

THREE

FINAL PREPARATIONS AND DEPARTURE

These are the times that try men's souls. The summer soldier and the sunshine patriot will, in this crisis, shrink from the service of their country; but he that stands it now, deserves the love and thanks of man and woman.—Thomas Paine

SAYING GOOD-BYE

PATRIOTISM was highly regarded by many post–World War II and Korean War families, especially those who had fathers, brothers, sisters, or other relatives who had served. Fathers and mothers were not only patriotic, but many of them lived by old-fashioned values and ideals—love of God and country and the simpler things in life. Initially, it was not a question of whether the Vietnam War was right or wrong; a son or daughter was simply expected to do his duty because of family tradition. This is not to say that parents wanted to give up their offspring to the military; they simply felt it was their duty and an honor to do so. This honorable attitude would eventually dissipate as the battle victories became meaningless and the bodies came home at an alarming rate.

Indeed, there were others who immediately saw the fruitlessness and the evils of the whole endeavor. Although they felt that the war was wrong, they were unable to prevent the sacrificing of one of their own. For these parents, it was a terrible predicament.

Some families decided to spend the remaining time with their sons or daughters as quietly and leisurely as possible, while others organized a going-away party with relatives and friends. These festivities were looked upon as an individual's last chance to celebrate while still at home. Some found that being the guest of honor was somewhat embarrassing. They may have felt they didn't deserve it, but their parents knew better. These departing GIs—marines, air force, navy, and coast guard personnel, both men and women—were young and extremely naive about what they were about to experience.

Ken Garthee, *Private First Class, U.S. Marine Corps, 3rd Battalion, 3rd Marines, 3rd Marine Division, Da Nang, Rock Pile, 1966–67*

After receiving my orders for Vietnam, I was sent home on a thirty-day leave before I had to report back to Camp Pendleton. When I got home, I looked great! I had my dress blues on with a stripe stitched on the arm of my coat and my National Defense Service Medal pinned on the front.

Being home was a proud time for me. All my family and uncles were there, and just by the way they looked at me, I could tell they were proud, too. I felt like the best marine on my block.

When things settled down a little, I had to show my parents where Vietnam was located on a map. They had no idea, just as I hadn't a few weeks before. But my Uncle Jack, who worked in the legal system as a court reporter, was considerably more attuned to the situation. He not only knew where and what Vietnam was all about, but he was able to talk to me about what was going on in Vietnam, how political the war was, and how he felt that nothing good was going to come by our involvement. All I did was listen to him. What more could I do?

While home, I paid a visit to my high school, wearing my dress blues. I went to a basketball game and sat at the top of the bleachers. Only a few students and teachers said anything to me that night. For some reason, the high school seemed smaller that night, while only a few months earlier it seemed so much larger.

I relaxed and visited friends and relatives as much as I could. On occasion, I also cruised in a car with my friend John.

For my last dinner at home, my mom said she would prepare my favorite meal—deep-fried shrimp with homemade French fries and lemon meringue pie. Everyone in my family was there, and we had a great time. It reminded me of our typical family reunions, only our reunions usually happened during the summer in our backyard or a large park, not inside the house during the cold month of December.

While the shrimp was cooking, the fryer overheated and burned a large spot on the new kitchen countertop. Surprisingly, my mom never got upset. She said that she would always remember that burned spot, and how and when it got there.

Stephen Butler, *Lance Corporal, U.S. Marine Corps, 7th Marine Combat Engineers, Da Nang, 1966–67*

I married my wife a week before I went to Vietnam. My mind-set was, we had been dating since we were fifteen, and although I had dated other girls when I was first in the marine corps at nineteen, I figured that if I went to Nam, she probably wouldn't be there when I got back. I thought she was a dynamite woman, and somebody else would take her. So I got married.

Then I went to the West Coast for training. My mother had previously moved to Arizona, so on my way over, I stopped in Arizona to see her. She had moved there because of her health. She had respiratory problems with the humidity in Rhode Island, so she and my aunt went out there.

Now, my mother was a very, very strong person because she had raised the kids all by herself. But when I got on the bus to leave, for the first time ever that I can remember, she was crying as she waved good-bye. That was the only point that I really said to myself, "I may be in some serious trouble here."

Bill McCollum, *Sergeant, U.S. Army, 173rd Airborne Brigade, Charlie Company, 4th Battalion, 503rd Infantry, LZ-English, 1969–71*

Of course, when I came back home, I partied with all my friends.

Mike Pinksaw, *Specialist Four, U.S. Army, 60th Land Clearing Company, 62nd Engineering Battalion, 20th Engineering Brigade, Long Binh, Bien Hoa, Lai Khe 1968–69*

It was very emotional—very emotional—mostly for my mother, my father, and me. My father was just recovering from a heart attack at the time. He had been stricken when I was training at Fort Leonard Wood, Missouri.

My friends and I went out and had a little drinking party before I left. It was nothing special, mostly just hanging around and drinking beer.

Rob Roche, *Sergeant, U.S. Army, 101st Airborne Division, Da Nang, 1967–69*

During leave, I was home in Newport and raised all kinds of hell. My parents were breaking up then, so I didn't have a formal party from them.

Doug Johnson, Specialist Four, U.S. Army, 25th Infantry Division, 2nd Battalion, 12th Infantry, 1968

After receiving the orders that I was to leave for Vietnam in early February 1969, I was given leave to straighten out my affairs and say my last farewells. I got engaged over Christmas 1968 to my sweetheart from Washington, D.C., and we had a party with family and friends to celebrate. The mood at this party was festive, and as typical young, starry-eyed lovers, we were hopeful for our future together. I don't remember much talk about Vietnam because I frankly don't think anyone knew much about it. We had dated throughout much of college and were ready to settle down and get married—if Vietnam were not looming so close in our future. I was enough of a realist to know that there was a distinct possibility that I would never return, and I informed her that I was not an advocate of young widows.

After my good-byes in Washington, my fiancée and I traveled to visit my family in Newport. We had a great visit, but there was a sense of urgency that I felt in visiting friends and relatives. I grew up in a really close family; I was the second-oldest of eight children—six boys and two girls. I really don't recall that I ever sat down with my mom and dad and my younger siblings and discussed the reality that I was going to Vietnam. In many ways it was too painful a subject, and we were all probably trying to protect ourselves and each other from the twin scourges of separation and uncertainty.

I'll never forget the last glances I exchanged with Mom and Dad at the Newport Air Park before my fiancée and I boarded the twin-engine plane on a flight to an uncertain future. An expression of helplessness and pain could not be veiled by the courageous face they attempted to put on, and my heart was heavy as I watched them and Newport fade into the distance of memory, to be summoned up at some later time in a moment of reverie.

David Rossi, Specialist Four, U.S. Army, 1st Infantry Division and 25th Infantry Division, Di An, Tay Ninh, and Cu Chi, 1969–70

I left for Vietnam a couple of days after the astronauts first landed on the moon. Prior to my departure, I had a party given in my honor at my mother and father's house. My relatives were there. In attendance was a veteran from World War I, and his advice to me was, "If anybody gives you any shit or whatever, take him down to the latrine and. . . ." Of course, being from the World War I era, he was talking about horses and other things, which would not be of very much use where I was going.

Salvatore T. Raffa, *Airman Second Class, U.S. Air Force, 377th Security Police Squadron, Tan Son Nhut Air Base, Saigon, 1967–68*

You have to understand, when I came home, I was in shock. This was all horrible to me.

Howard North, *Lieutenant j.g., U.S. Coast Guard, Coast Guard Squadron One, USCGC* Point Clear *(WPB 82315), An Thoi and Cat Lo, 1967–68*

My mother was in the hospital at the time I received my orders for Vietnam, and I didn't know how to tell her. Finally I said to myself, "I've got to tell her." Considering her condition, she took it as well as could be expected.

Michael Toner Farrell, *Specialist Five, U.S. Army, 544th Replacement Company, Cam Ranh Bay, 1969–70*

When I got home from Fort Bragg, I spent two weeks in Newport. I visited my folks and said my good-byes. My brother, at the time, was already in Vietnam as an officer in the air force.

THE GIRL I LEFT BEHIND

Some soldiers were married and had small children, but the vast majority of men going off to war were single. Many did have girlfriends.

Undeniably, one of the most difficult duties a soldier had to perform was to say good-bye to his wife or girlfriend. It was difficult enough for both partners to accept that they were not going to see each other for a year. The fact that one of the partners was going to a war zone made the good-byes all the more unbearable. Many tears were shed during these partings.

William Sullivan, *Lieutenant Commander, U.S. Navy, Fighter Squadron 213, U.S.S.* Intrepid, *Air Wing, U.S.S.* Kitty Hawk *(CVA-63), U.S.S.* Intrepid *(CVA-11), U.S.S.* Paul Revere, *and U.S.S.* Blue Ridge, *1965–68 and 1971–72*

Well, my wife has always been very supportive of my career. I'm sure she had some qualms about me going into combat for the first time, but she never expressed them, at least not to me. I could tell sometimes that she was concerned. I've been very fortunate to have the best wife in the world.

Thomas Finn, *Specialist Four, U.S. Army, Company A, 519th Military Intelligence Battalion, 525th Military Intelligence Group, MACV-J2, Saigon, 1966–67*

I was dating a girl in Newport. She was a very nice person. I was fond of her, but only at that time.

Rob Roche, *Sergeant, U.S. Army, 101st Airborne Division, Da Nang, 1967–69*

I hung out with my girl, Barbara, and we got kind of serious. We also went to a number of different parties together.

Stephen Butler, *Lance Corporal, U.S. Marine Corps, 7th Marine Combat Engineers, Da Nang, 1966–67*

We were kids, and we acted as typically as you'd expect. This is what I cannot believe today as an adult with a son of my own: I had absolutely no idea at all that this was going to be anything other than a typical drill that they had taught me at Parris Island. I can honest-to-God say that at that point in time, I felt like I was gonna do my job and I was going to come back. And that's the way I left.

My wife was crying, of course. She was always much more intelligent than me and much more mature. She was devastated by it. Me, well, I was a lot more sexist than I am today, and at the time I said that my wife's reaction was a female kind of thing.

Doug Johnson, *Specialist Four, U.S. Army, 25th Infantry Division, 2nd Battalion, 12th Infantry, 1968*

The most painful farewell took place at Newark Airport when I had to say a final good-bye to my beloved. By this time, the reality of our situation was crashing down upon us as she had to board a plane to return to Washington and I had to report to Maguire Air Force Base for my flight to Vietnam. There were no words left to comfort one another, and I recall both of us holding hands and crying unashamedly as our only remaining form of communication. I have never again in my lifetime experienced such a sense of hopelessness and despair as I did when I realized that we might never again hold and kiss each other and have the opportunity to settle down and raise a family together. I was one of the lucky ones who returned—but there is an empty place in my heart for all those who were not so lucky to return and realize their dreams. In a sense, that day marked the beginning of our relationship; we would never take life or our relationship for granted again.

THE FRIENDLY SENDOFFS

Perhaps no one conveyed it better and more simply than William Shakespeare when he wrote, "Parting is such sweet sorrow." Leaving loved ones makes an individual more appreciative of what he or she possessed yet was about to lose. For no one has Shakespeare's sentiment been more suitable than for those families whose sons and daughters would soon be heading off to war.

Nearly everyone destined for a Vietnam tour of duty was granted some type of official military leave. The duration of such a leave varied from one service component to the next and ranged from two weeks to thirty days. It afforded these young men and women an opportunity to relax, have fun, raise hell, and, above all, to spend some quality time with their loved ones.

It only seemed natural and right for family and friends to gather and say their final good-byes. Many of those who came from caring families knew they could count on their parents for words of encouragement and advice, but, even more importantly, for their unconditional love. Whether willing to admit it or not, these individuals really wouldn't have wanted it any other way.

For the families and their military sons and daughters, having to say good-bye became an extremely emotional and gut-wrenching affair. Knowing full well this occasion would be their last encounter together for a year or so made the departure even more difficult. No one wanted to succumb to a sense of finality, but it was not possible to suppress fears and tears.

Now those who went to war and the families who remained at home had to face the reality of departure and absence.

Rob Roche, *Sergeant, U.S. Army, 101st Airborne Division, Da Nang, 1967–69*

My mother gave me and my friend Cliff, who also had orders for Vietnam, a ride to Logan Airport in Boston. Within hours of our arrival, we left Logan airport on a commercial flight to Vietnam.

Dick Turner, *Boatswain's Mate Third Class, U.S. Navy, River Assault Squadron 15, River Division 152, Task Force 117, Dong Tam and My Tho, 1968–69*

When I first came home, I didn't tell my parents that I was going. My father and mother couldn't understand why I was on leave. So I let it lie for a few days, and when the whole family was together, I said to them, "The reason I'm home on leave is I'm on my way to Vietnam." The next day, my father and I went to a travel agency to get a military discount one-way ticket to San Francisco.

The neighbors all got together and threw a big party for me. They gave me gifts and everything. It was a really great sendoff. One of the neighbors had known me when I was just a kid. She said to me, "You're too smart to get killed." And, you know, she prayed for me every night while I was over there.

The day I had to leave, my mother and father drove me to Boston. We all ate at a restaurant together before I caught the plane to San Francisco.

Bill McCollum, *Sergeant, U.S. Army, 173rd Airborne Brigade, Charlie Company, 4th Battalion, 503rd Infantry, LZ-English, 1969–71*

My father gave me a ride to the airport. His final words to me were, "Come home!" My father cried, and I cried, of course.

My mother had been sick all this time. She had had this run-in with cancer for the longest time and had just completed chemotherapy. I tried to tell her that I was going to Vietnam. She said, "Why do you have to go?" I didn't know how to answer her. Of course, I couldn't tell her that I volunteered to go. Anyway, she took it hard.

I even saw some of my friends cry before I left for Vietnam.

Salvatore T. Raffa, *Airman Second Class, U.S. Air Force, 377th Security Police Squadron, Tan Son Nhut Air Base, Saigon, 1967–68*

I can remember being at the airport, and everybody was crying. Crying is what I remember most. My family, my in-laws, my wife, and my relatives—everyone was crying.

Before I left for Vietnam, I tried to live a normal life. It wasn't easy, but I did the best I could to keep things on an even keel.

William Sullivan, *Lieutenant Commander, U.S. Navy, Fighter Squadron 213, U.S.S.* Intrepid, *Air Wing, U.S.S.* Kitty Hawk *(CVA-63), U.S.S.* Intrepid *(CVA-11), U.S.S.* Paul Revere, *and U.S.S.* Blue Ridge, *1965–68 and 1971–72*

I had heard of people having unpleasant experiences prior to their departure to Vietnam or upon their return, but I myself never had one adverse encounter. I can't remember anyone who was not supportive of me at the time. Matter of fact, people were just the opposite. They were buying me drinks and treating me very well.

THE UNFRIENDLY SENDOFF

As the war escalated in South Vietnam and as our country's strategies and objectives became more uncertain, the treatment of American soldiers being sent off to war worsened. This would continue until the American troop pullout many years later.

Being spat at, insulted, given dirty looks, or ignored happened to only a small minority of those leaving for war. Though only a few were subjected to such a sendoff, it was no less painful for them.

Those who insulted soldiers may have acted out of a sense of mob sentiment. Their anger or contempt, most likely, was directed against the entire military establishment through the person wearing the uniform. Unfortunately, this was of little comfort to those who happened to be wearing it at the time.

It is a tribute to the citizens of Newport County that during the war, not one veteran interviewed experienced a single incident of harassment before leaving Newport County for their tour in Vietnam. Perhaps most of the antiwar sentiment and negative behavior was confined to and exhibited in the bigger cities and at the larger airports.

Stephen Butler, *Lance Corporal, U.S. Marine Corps, 7th Marine Combat Engineers, Da Nang, 1966–67*

When we were in California, we went on liberty, or leave, a couple of times, and there were some situations. In those days, you had to go on liberty in uniform. We were in temporary barracks prior to our departure for Nam. We went out one time, and it was ugly, so I didn't go anymore.

After that, when I had the chance, I visited my mother in Arizona. I took a short puddle-jumper flight to where she lived. She was living in this nice little spot on the Colorado River. There was no trouble there.

LEAVING ON A JET PLANE—OR SHIP

In the early stages of the war, troops departed for South Vietnam by transport ships or military aircraft. As the war escalated and a larger number of troops was rotating in and out of the country, commercial airlines were chartered by the government. Civilian pilots flew 707 jets with a full contingent of female stewardesses on board.

The passengers were unique, however. They were all dressed in jungle fatigues. Sometimes they carried their rifles and gear on board, but most of the time they were unarmed.

The airlines flew a number of different routes, all with the same final destination: South Vietnam. The majority of flights landed in Bien Hoa or Cam Ranh Bay, in the south. Some went to Da Nang, in the north.

Thomas Finn, *Specialist Four, U.S. Army, Company A, 519th Military Intelligence Battalion, 525th Military Intelligence Group, MACV-J2, Saigon, 1966–67*

They gathered us at Pope Air Force Base, which is adjacent to Fort Bragg, at around seven in the evening. It seemed like we were there for hours. At about midnight, we were ordered to board the plane. It was a commercial prop job. As I remember it today, it was a really small airline—a wing and a prayer, literally. I suspect they had only a few planes in their fleet.

Someone had a bright idea, the colonel's wife perhaps, that she should gather all the officers' wives and bid us adieu. Visualize a plane loaded with GIs and you've got some of these young lieutenants' wives coming on board to wish us well. Indeed, it was kind of humorous. Let me tell you, it was not one of the colonel's wife's best ideas. It was one of those funny scenes right out of the movies. You just had to be there to appreciate it. Here you've got some of these women, with good intentions, prancing through the aisle trying to shake our hands or whatever, and all of a sudden the groping, slapping, and pinching start, along with the hoots and whistles. Needless to say, they didn't stay too long. Fortunately, before anyone could get in any real trouble, we departed.

AIRLINE PASSENGER TICKET, BAGGAGE CHECK
AND
MAC BOARDING PASS

MISSION NUMBER	BOARDING TIME DATE	BOARDING NUMBER	ORIGIN/DESTINATION VIA	BAGGAGE PIECES POUNDS
↑ G2B3	TIME 1315			No. 2
	DAY MO YEAR			Lb. 41

The Following Constitutes A Statement By the Carrier Which Is Hereby Delivered To the Passenger At the Carrier's Request

CONDITIONS OF CARRIAGE AND ADVICE TO INTERNATIONAL PASSENGER ON LIMITATION OF LIABILITY

Passengers on a journey involving an ultimate destination or a stop in a country other than the country of origin are advised that the provisions of a treaty known as the Warsaw Convention may be applicable to the entire journey, including any portion entirely within the country of origin or destination, that in most cases limits the liability of the carrier for death or personal injury and in respect of loss of or damage to baggage. For such passengers, the convention and special contracts of carriage embodied in applicable tariffs provide that the limit of liability for each passenger for death, wounding, or other bodily injury shall be the sum of U.S. $75,000 inclusive of legal fees and costs, except that, in case of a claim brought in a state where provision is made for separate award of legal fees and costs, the limit shall be the sum of U.S. $58,000 exclusive of legal fees and costs. The carrier shall not, with respect to any claim arising out of the death, wounding, or other bodily injury of a passenger, avail itself of any defense under Article 20(1) of said Convention as amended by the Hague Protocol signed September 28, 1955. The names of carriers parties to such special contracts are available at all ticket offices of such carriers and may be examined on request. Additional protection can usually be obtained by purchasing insurance from a private company. Such insurance is not affected by any limitation of the carrier's liability under the Warsaw Convention or such special contracts of carriage. For further information please consult your airline or insurance company representative.

FOR THE PURPOSES OF ARTICLE 3 AND 4 OF THE WARSAW CONVENTION, THE FOLLOWING CONSTITUTES PARTICULARS GIVEN BY THE CARRIER TO THE PASSENGER

A. The place of issue of the passenger ticket and the baggage check is that place designated as "origin" in the "Origin/Destination" block on the front page of this document; the date of said issue is set forth in the "Boarding Time and Date" block on the front page of this document.

B. The place of departure is the place of "origin" as set forth in the "Origin/Destination" block on the front page of this document; the place of destination is in the same block. The agreed stopping places are also in the same block.

C. The letter symbol which is the prefix of the mission number shown in the "Mission Number" block on the front page of this document is the symbol of the carrier for this flight. The name and address of this carrier is shown opposite the same letters symbol set forth below under the heading "Mission Number Prefix Code".

D. The number of the passenger ticket is set forth in the "Boarding Number" block on the front page of this document. Your name is on the flight manifest for this flight opposite this same number on said manifest.

E. The number and weight of the packages or baggage are shown in the "Baggage/Pounds" block on the front page of this document.

F. Delivery of said baggage will be made to the bearer of the baggage check.

G. This transportation of the passenger and the baggage is subject to the rules relating to liability established by the Convention, but the higher limits of liability as set forth elsewhere on this document apply.

MAC (Military Assistance Command) Airline Boarding Pass required for final boarding and flight to Vietnam. (Property of the editor)

The flight across the country pretty much tired us out, and we slept quite a bit. When we pulled into Oakland Army Air Terminal, it was still early in the morning. We took a short bus ride from this small airfield to Oakland Army Terminal, which is the pier. Arriving there, we were ordered to board a troop ship, the *General Gordon*. There were also several other troop ships being loaded at the time. I mean, they were coming by the busloads. I'm guessing that there were as many as three thousand to four thousand troops loaded on each ship, and there were at least four of them.

Some time later, I saw something I've never seen before or since. Coming over the horizon was a troop train. I know they used these quite extensively in World War II, but who would have guessed that they would still be using them in this era? Lo and behold, the train pulls down to the pier and hundreds more got off this train. Later we found out it had traveled all day and all the previous night from Texas.

As God is my witness, there were donut dollies, these women from the Red Cross, handing out coffee and doughnuts at the pier. I tried to make one last call home from one of the phone booths on the pier, but the lines were just incredible.

We stayed on the ship for one or two more nights while the ship was being provisioned, then early on a Monday morning, we pulled out.

From our departure in Oakland to our arrival in Vietnam, it took twenty-two days.

I remember going under the Golden Gate Bridge. Initially we were doing all right on the trip across. Then we hit a few swells a couple of miles out from San Francisco, and everybody got sick. The entire ship smelled bad because nearly everyone was throwing up.

The best time on the ship was when I got KP (kitchen police) for five days running. You could eat constantly, and the consumption of food kept your stomach at an even keel—no pun intended. So I volunteered for fifteen more days of KP.

Our first stop was Guam, where we dropped off some troops and picked up some others. It wasn't long before we were approaching the coast of South Vietnam.

Salvatore T. Raffa, *Airman Second Class, U.S. Air Force, 377th Security Police Squadron, Tan Son Nhut Air Base, Saigon, 1967–68*

They were sending me to Seattle, and from there I was supposed to be sent to Tuy Hoa, Vietnam, which I never got to. I arrived at McCord Air Force Base in Seattle, and for one week they delayed my departure. They lost my orders or something.

So I was calling my wife up every night. Every night I was calling her, and we'd both be crying. Toward the end of the week, she was just sick of hearing from me. I mean she couldn't cry anymore, and she just said, "Tore, you know, it's sad, but you've got to go now." It was just too long for us to say our good-byes.

My wife ended up writing a letter to one of our state senators, asking, "Why was my husband delayed so long?" I think they wrote back that it was an unusual situation.

I was supposed to go to Tuy Hoa. I ended up being reassigned to Tan Son Nhut.

On the plane ride over, I was a scared little boy. I was petrified, and because of it, I got sick to my stomach. You've got to remember, I'd never left home before, and now I was going halfway around the world to fight in a war.

Doug Johnson, *Specialist Four, U.S. Army, 25th Infantry Division, 2nd Battalion, 12th Infantry, 1968*

My most lasting memory about the trip to Vietnam was the drastic shift of mood from the time we boarded the plane at Maguire Air Force Base in New Jersey until we arrived at Bien Hoa Airport in Vietnam. First of all, the Capitol Airlines jet was perhaps the largest plane I had ever set eyes upon. I wondered how it could ever get off the ground with all the passengers we were carrying. The mood of the troops was almost buoyant as we took off and began our journey. There was lots of excited chatter as we all began introducing ourselves to those seated around us and learning a little about each other's history, both military and personal. I remember specifically two guys that I spoke with at length on the flight. One guy, who appeared to be in his early twenties, was returning to Vietnam on a second tour of duty. He had met and fallen in love with a Vietnamese girl during his first tour and had attempted to marry her and bring her back to the States. As he described it, there was so much red tape involved that he was unable to get it all together before his tour of duty was over, so he was back to give it another shot. After all the horror stories I had heard about Vietnam, I couldn't believe that anyone in their right mind would go back for seconds.

The other guy I met was so nervous about going to Vietnam that he couldn't sit still. He kept lamenting that he had a wife—or maybe it was a girlfriend—back in the States and worried about whether he would ever see her again. As fate would have it, his worrying was all for naught, as he was eventually assigned to some photography unit in Saigon and I am relatively certain that he made it back.

The first leg of our journey took us for a fuel stop in Anchorage. We had not even been issued field jackets, so we practically froze our butts off just walking into the airport. After approximately a one-hour stop, we were off to Japan for another fuel stop. I don't remember anything about the trip from Alaska to Japan, but I am certain that the mood on the plane was becoming more subdued and pensive the closer we progressed toward Vietnam.

The final leg of the journey took us to Bien Hoa Airport. The flight to Vietnam, as I recall, lasted about twenty-four hours, and by the time we approached Vietnam, I'm sure we were all exhausted. I don't remember sleeping, but I'm sure I did a lot of thinking, and if I was smart, I should have done a lot of praying.

When the pilot or stewardess announced that we were landing at Ben Hoa Airport in Vietnam, you could have heard a pin drop. It was as if suddenly the impact of where we were and what we were about to do hit everyone at the same time, and we sat in stunned silence contemplating the unknown fate that awaited each of us.

Dick Turner, *Boatswain's Mate Third Class, U.S. Navy, River Assault Squadron 15, River Division 152, Task Force 117, Dong Tam and My Tho, 1968–69*

The flight over was uneventful with the exception that many of us got drunk on the plane while going over. I mean, we were potted.

It was a long flight. I think it took us something like twenty-five hours to fly there.

Betsy Wylie, *Lieutenant, U.S. Navy, Management Information Center, Headquarters, Naval Forces Vietnam (NAVFORV), Saigon, 1967–68*

I had dinner at Travis Air Force Base, at the Officers' Club, with a friend of mine before I left for Vietnam. It was a night flight. Because it was going to be a long flight and because I was as nervous as anybody else, I took a Valium after I got on the plane; and it had an absolute magical effect. However, nobody told me that the first leg was only going to Seattle.

In order to refuel the plane, they had to unload all of us. Now here I was, ready for a long winter's nap, and I had to get off the plane and go into the terminal. I recollect walking about fifteen feet each way from the entry port, right back on to the airplane, because I thought if I sat down, I was going to miss the plane. The rest of the flight was very uneventful.

We stopped for probably two hours in Yokota, Japan; I presume for refueling, and about that time, I was wide awake.

There were several nurses and a civilian woman on the plane who ended up in the same headquarters where I worked. She volunteered to go to Vietnam, but she was scared to death of flying. I mean, so frightened that she was almost unable to control herself. And yet she wanted to volunteer so badly that she took medication so she could make that long flight, a flight that took about twenty-two hours. I remember her medication was starting to wear off when we were getting off the plane in Yokota. So several of us women stuck very close to her to make sure she'd be all right.

Peggy R. Zarek, *Lieutenant Commander, U.S. Navy, U.S.S. Sanctuary (AH-17), Coastal Waters off South Vietnam, Military Region 1, 1969–70*

I flew out of Norton Air Force Base in California. Another girl, one who had been to Vietnam, told me before I left that there would be plenty of girls on the plane. That wasn't the case. I was the only girl on board.

On the way over, I was apprehensive about what I was going to encounter when I got there. I remember it as a long trip.

William Sullivan, *Lieutenant Commander, U.S. Navy, Fighter Squadron 213, U.S.S.* Intrepid, *Air Wing, U.S.S.* Kitty Hawk *(CVA-63), U.S.S.* Intrepid *(CVA-11), U.S.S.* Paul Revere, *and U.S.S.* Blue Ridge, *1965–68 and 1971–72*

I was very anxious going to Vietnam. You think about how you're going to react in combat the first time and whether you're going to survive the ordeal. But you were distracted from some of this type of thinking by the duties you had to perform to keep your unit functioning on a daily basis.

Ken Garthee, *Private First Class, U.S. Marine Corps, 3rd Battalion, 3rd Marines, 3rd Marine Division, Da Nang, Rock Pile, 1966–67*

After saying good-bye to everyone at home, I was driven to the airport and flew military standby back to Camp Pendleton, California. It was just before Christmas when I reported in. Everyone in my company was assigned guard duty for the next few evenings. My assignment was to guard an empty warehouse in the middle of nowhere on Christmas night. The warehouse wasn't the only thing empty; so was my rifle. We weren't allowed bullets. And to make matters worse, it rained all night.

We still hadn't a clue what to expect when we got to Vietnam. Marines who had been there were telling us what to expect, but we were pretty naive and just a little bit too stupid to comprehend the full meaning of what they were trying to convey. They told us it was hot, it rained a great deal, and not to trust anyone except another marine.

Prior to our departure for Vietnam, we were given more training. We learned about the changing climates, the culture of the South Vietnamese people, booby traps, a review of escape and evasion tactics, and we even got to camp outside, pitching our tents, eating C-rations,* and learning to shoot our rifles at night. We also played war games like "capture the flag." Those who got caught learned the lesson the hard way. They were interrogated until they were so tired that they would tell the "enemy" (played by other marines) anything. We learned not to get caught.

While we were at Camp Pendleton, we were issued plenty of combat gear—jungle boots, several pairs of utility pants, long-sleeved shirts, a steel helmet, an entrenching tool, a shelter half (half of a tent, that is), and a bayonet. Whether we were prepared for Vietnam or for combat I'm not sure, but we certainly were well-equipped.

We took off from Travis Air Force Base in January 1966, aboard a C-130, strapped in our mesh seats. Along with replacement marines like me were Jeeps and skids stacked high with sundry military gear. The flight itself was uncomfortable, noisy, and cold. In midflight they gave us box lunches. We landed only once, at Hickham Air Force Base in Hawaii, for refueling, and there they let us get off the plane.

We were allowed to go the air force dining hall for dinner, and I just couldn't believe what I saw. They had linen table cloths on the tables and china plates and silverware for place settings. We proceeded to eat like gentlemen and enjoyed everything they put in front of us. I don't think we were there for much more than six hours when we were called back to the plane to reboard and head to Da Nang, South Vietnam.

Mike Pinksaw, *Specialist Four, U.S. Army, 60th Land Clearing Company, 62nd Engineering Battalion, 20th Engineering Brigade, Long Binh, Bien Hoa, Lai Khe 1968–69*

I had to report to Oakland Army Base. Incredibly, when I arrived, I met most of the guys who'd done advanced infantry training with me.

One thing that stands out in my mind is that, the night before my departure for Vietnam, they let us go into San Francisco. We went to a topless nightclub. It was the first time that I had ever experienced a woman

---

* C-rations were canned meals consisting of breakfast or dinner and intended for consumption by the military troops in the field. Also called "C." The cans were all painted drab green and tightly packaged in a small box.

topless, you know. Naturally, we spent most of the night in this bar. Then we went back to the barracks at the base.

The next morning, they moved us to this huge building that looked like a converted warehouse. From there, we were processed for final departure. When finished with all the usual military formality, we were taken to Travis Air Force Base, boarded a plane, and took off for Vietnam. It was a long, long ride. We landed in Alaska and Japan, and then it was on to Bien Hoa, Vietnam.

Rob Roche, *Sergeant, U.S. Army, 101st Airborne Division, Da Nang, 1967–69*

I flew from Logan Airport to Seattle. I was to report to Fort Lewis. When I arrived in Seattle, I decided to go into the city. Mind you now, I was by myself. Somehow or other, I got into a poker game with a bunch of old-timers in the back of a bar. They proceeded to take every nickel I had. They were sharp. I won the first few hands, and that was it.

I finally arrived at Fort Lewis. We were all issued our gear there. After only a few days, I was manifested for a flight on a C-130 troop transport to Vietnam. It was a four-prop job. There were no seats on it. You lay on your duffel bag.

We had to refuel first in Hawaii, where they let us off the plane. Naturally, we went to an airport bar for about an hour. We were just sitting there thinking how nice it was with the palm trees and all. One of the guys I was with said, "Do we have to get back on that plane?" Of course, we all knew the consequences of not reboarding. We certainly thought about it, but we quickly brushed it aside as a wild idea.

It was a long, tough flight. I was kind of looking forward to seeing what in the hell we were in for.

Bill McCollum, *Sergeant, U.S. Army, 173rd Airborne Brigade, Charlie Company, 4th Battalion, 503rd Infantry, LZ-English, 1969–71*

We flew from Logan Airport in Boston, to Fort Lewis, Washington, then through Japan and on to Vietnam. Going over, it was very quiet on the plane. When we finally approached the airport in Cam Ranh Bay, we had to circle because the pilot was advised that the runway was being shelled. Eventually, we were diverted to Tan Son Nhut in the Saigon area.

David Rossi, Specialist Four, U.S. Army, 1st Infantry Division and 25th Infantry Division, Di An, Tay Ninh, and Cu Chi, 1969–70

I flew out of Travis Air Force Base on a commercial jet, Northwest Orient, to Seattle, up to Alaska, down to Okinawa, and on to South Vietnam. I remember when we landed some of the stewardesses had tears in their eyes.

Stephen Butler, Lance Corporal, U.S. Marine Corps, 7th Marine Combat Engineers, Da Nang, 1966–67

It was really interesting. We left in the middle of the night and went up to El Toro Air Base, a marine air base, but they had civilian airlines flying out of there, which I thought was really weird. We took a Continental goldentail across to Vietnam.

The most interesting thing was—and I guess this is a typical dumb marine story—there was this colonel loading up a full company of guys on a couple of planes. And his boarding instructions to us were, "This isn't much of a war, Marines, but it's the only thing we have to do right now." The idea being, try to keep it going until you find something better. So then we all got on the plane; it was an endless ride. We flew to Hawaii, refueled, had maintenance done on the plane, stopped in Okinawa. I mean, it seemed like we were on this plane . . . Well, I don't remember how long it actually took, but it seemed like we were on this plane forever. It was terrible.

Howard North, Lieutenant j.g., U.S. Coast Guard, Coast Guard Squadron One, USCGC Point Clear *(WPB 82315), An Thoi and Cat Lo, 1967–68*

I left on a 707 commercial jet, Pan Am to be exact, and I flew from Logan Airport in Boston to San Francisco, where I took additional training for the next five weeks. In fact, I continued to train all the way to Vietnam. I attended damage control school in Alameda, where we played the ship is sinking, plugged up holes, and all that kind of stuff. Then I was sent to Camp Pendleton for a week of weapons familiarization. From there, I went to San Diego to attend survival school with all the navy pilots. At the school they gave us all parachutes and sent us out in the woods near the Mount Palomar observatory. We spent a week in the woods playing the game of attempting to avoid capture by the enemy and being thrown in a makeshift prison camp. The enemy in this case were trained American soldiers, dressed in the uniform of the North Vietnamese Army, who spoke with phony accents. It was a really tremendous experience. But the thing I remember most about it was the snow and freezing cold. It was the wrong time of the year to be there.

During the first four or five days in the hills, it was strictly survival. We were given the skimpiest of rations for the entire week—a cubic inch of corned beef and a half-a-cup of rice. For the rest of our food, we were expected to eat off the land.

It was a little scary at night. On the final day, they captured us. After being caught, we got the crap beat out of us. No one ever made it to the final objective without being caught. There were about twenty of us in the group, all Coast Guard guys, and about a hundred total in the entire school. They put us in the stockade, in black boxes, the kind of greeting you would receive if you were captured by the real enemy. When they got done beating us up and everything, I think in our group, we had one guy with a broken rib and another with two black eyes, all inflicted by the camp prison guard. It wasn't really done intentionally, but the training tended to get rough, due to the intimidation factor. As strange as it sounds, we all liked it, even the guys who got hurt.

The camp was originally conceived and started by guys who were captured by the North Koreans during the Korean War, and they still served as advisors on how the camp was to operate. There were only a few of them left when I went through the school. I don't know how many other permanent training personnel were stationed there, but they seemed like they were everywhere, especially when you were trying to evade them.

Upon conclusion of survival school, I flew from Travis Air Force Base to Vietnam via the northern route through Alaska and Tokyo. It seemed like the sun was always rising. It was a nice flight, and they fed us really well. We all got filet mignon. The airline was Pan Am, and ever since, I've always had a soft spot in my heart for that airline because of how well we were treated. We landed in Vietnam at noon.

Michael Toner Farrell, Specialist Five, U.S. Army, 544th Replacement Company, Cam Ranh Bay, 1969–70

I flew out of Providence to Seattle. From Seattle, I flew Flying Tiger Airlines to Vietnam. I don't remember much about the trip, but I do remember when the plane touched down and I saw the countryside from the window. I immediately became terrified. Until that moment, it hadn't hit me. I never thought about what I had done—that is, to volunteer for a tour of duty in Vietnam just to get away from the bullshit handed out in the States. I mean, I had no fear whatsoever. I said to myself, "I'm going to Vietnam, I'm going to be a cook, that's cool." Reality had not yet set in.

FOUR

IN-COUNTRY

*There is many a boy here today who looks on war all
glory, but boys, it is all hell. You can bear this warning
voice to generations yet to come. I look upon war with
horror.*—William Tecumseh Sherman

POPULATION, TOPOGRAPHY,
AND CLIMATE

DURING the late sixties and early seventies, Vietnam had a population of approximately 33 million people, almost equally distributed between North Vietnam and South Vietnam. The exact population during that period may never be known due to war casualties and refugee movements.*

The people of Vietnam were—and still are—highly dependent upon agriculture. Competition for fertile farmland was and will continue to be a political problem—there are just too many people and not enough productive land to adequately support the entire population.

Vietnam consists of mountains, coastal plains, and river deltas. It has a coastline of approximately 1,200 miles along the South China Sea. The country itself is long, narrow, and S-shaped. The central and southeast areas of Vietnam have a tropical rain forest climate, with high temperatures, humidity, and considerable precipitation. The average yearly rainfall for both Ho Chi Minh City—Saigon, as it was called during the war—and Hanoi in the north is six feet, although eight feet is not uncommon. In

---

* *Collier's Encyclopedia* (New York: P. F. Collier, 1995), vol. 23, p. 130.

the southwest, there are both wet and dry periods, with temperatures generally higher than in the north.*

For the troops in base camp, the heat could be unbearable, but it became even worse in the jungle. Add to that the high humidity, and conditions could best be described as stifling. It became a daily problem for those in the field and jungle to maintain a safe body temperature and to keep the sweat from constantly blurring one's vision. Infantry soldiers usually wrapped a towel around their necks and poured water from canteens over their heads to stay as comfortable as possible. Only the cooler nights brought any comfort or relief.

Just when the troops thought it couldn't get much worse, the monsoons blew in. This unique weather condition prevailed mainly in the Indian Ocean and signaled the change of seasons. Depending upon where one was stationed in South Vietnam, the north or the south, the monsoons started at different times, usually a few months apart. When the heavy winds arrived, they were always accompanied by a deluge of rain. When the inclement weather briefly subsided, the clouds would cover the sun for extended periods. The monsoon season lasted for approximately five to six months. Needless to say, for those experiencing combat and for others in the field, the monsoons made life not only uncomfortable but downright depressing.

Mike Pinksaw, *Specialist Four, U.S. Army, 60th Land Clearing Company, 62nd Engineering Battalion, 20th Engineering Brigade, Long Binh, Bien Hoa, Lai Khe 1968–69*

The heat was incredibly worse than what we could ever envision in New England during the summer. It was unbearable.

Like many others, I was there during the monsoons. I've never seen rain like that before. It rained every which way: horizontal, vertical, upside down, as far as I was concerned.

Dick Turner, *Boatswain's Mate Third Class, U.S. Navy, River Assault Squadron 15, River Division 152, Task Force 117, Dong Tam and My Tho, 1968–69*

It rained so hard, you couldn't even see. We'd be in an operation in a column of boats and you couldn't see the boat in front of you. We were wet all the time.

---

* *Encyclopedia Americana International Edition* (New York: Encyclopedia Americana Corp., 1970), vol. 28, pp. 107–8.

Bill McCollum, *Sergeant, U.S. Army, 173rd Airborne Brigade, Charlie Company, 4th Battalion, 503rd Infantry, LZ-English, 1969–71*

When you got off the plane it felt like you were standing behind a back blast of heat—it was that hot. My skin blistered badly within a few days. Being a fair-haired Irishman didn't help matters much. I virtually burned up. My face, my arms, were all blistered; I was in tough shape.

I remember the rain. It would rain, and I mean rain! When I was on an outpost, you could see it coming toward you as you looked down the valley. "Here it comes," you'd say to yourself, and come it did! Within minutes, the place would be flooded, and you'd be soaked to the skin. Maybe an hour later the sun would come out, and you'd change clothes, only to see it coming again a few minutes later. I mean, you'd begin to wonder if you needed Noah's Ark to protect yourself. There were times I wondered whether it was ever going to stop.

Betsy Wylie, *Lieutenant, U.S. Navy, Management Information Center, Headquarters, Naval Forces Vietnam (NAVFORV), Saigon, 1967–68*

Hot and muggy was what it was like. I divided my year in Vietnam into two weather patterns: the hot and wet, and the hot and dry. For somebody who really doesn't like hot weather, it was a very long year.

Michael Toner Farrell, *Specialist Five, U.S. Army, 544th Replacement Company, Cam Ranh Bay, 1969–70*

It was brutally hot; plus I was just terrified when I walked off the airplane. That gives you an idea of how much I really didn't want to be there.

After a few months, I kind of got acclimated to the temperature, which was normally over one hundred degrees during the day. But at night during the monsoon season I had to wear a winter fatigue coat; it was still seventy to eighty degrees outside, but I was freezing. Think about it. In Newport, when it's ninety degrees in the summer and the next day it gets down into the sixties, you feel that change. It was no different in Vietnam. A twenty- to twenty-five-degree temperature drop could make it feel like a cold spell. Remember, we had very little body fat, so we got cold quickly.

Dick Turner, *Boatswain's Mate Third Class, U.S. Navy, River Assault Squadron 15, River Division 152, Task Force 117, Dong Tam and My Tho, 1968–69*

The pilot came on the intercom and said, "We have to circle the field, because the airfield is under attack."

We were stacked up over Tan Son Nhut, and finally we landed and were escorted into the building, real quick. We were then put on buses.

When I got on the bus, I said to the guy sitting next to me, "Wow, we're actually in a war zone." I saw screens on the bus windows and I asked the driver, "Where are we going, to a prison or something?"

He said, "The screens are there to keep the hand grenades out."

We were taken downtown to Saigon, to a hotel that was run by some kind of a naval support activity. I was processed there and received some of my equipment, including a weapon. I think I stayed there for approximately three weeks. I took some more vaccinations at the hotel. We were told about the malaria pills we had to take every day, you know, the big horse pills. Of course, we were also advised not to get involved with the civilians, and that if you were to go out at night, you were to go in twos.

While there we had to stand watches on the roof of the building. We had a machine-gun nest up there.

Rob Roche, *Sergeant, U.S. Army, 101st Airborne Division, Da Nang, 1967–69*

I remember when we landed and the door to the plane was opened. It was hot! Looking across to the land area from the top of the plane steps, you could see the heat moving up off the ground, so that the ground appeared out of focus. And I mean, it was really hot!

Ken Garthee, *Private First Class, U.S. Marine Corps, 3rd Battalion, 3rd Marines, 3rd Marine Division, Da Nang, Rock Pile, 1966–67*

The C-130 landed, and no one said a word. The door of the airplane was opened, and you could immediately feel the heat; it took your breath away. The funny thing was that was supposed to be the cool time of the year; the rainy season was just about to end. I just couldn't imagine what the summer would be like.

When we got our gear and got off the plane, we were escorted to a huge hangar to await processing and reassignment to a combat unit. The heat was still intense, and I can only describe it like opening the door to an oven which was set at five hundred degrees.

Howard North, *Lieutenant j.g., U.S. Coast Guard, Coast Guard Squadron One, USCGC* Point Clear *(WPB 82315), An Thoi and Cat Lo, 1967–68*

The monsoons were one of the worst things I had to deal with, especially being out in the water and all. The first month I was there, the southwest monsoon hadn't started yet, and that's why we were patrolling in the Gulf of Thailand. Once the monsoons started, the winds blew in one direction for two to three months at a time. And the rain—oh, man!

I think it was either my first or second patrol, and we were going back to our home port when the radar went dead. We really didn't have any good way to navigate. Inside the boat it was pitch black, and it started to rain. I mean, I had never seen it rain so hard. I turned the searchlight on in the boat and I couldn't see the bow, yet it was only about thirty feet away. We decided to drop anchor until it stopped raining, 'cause we didn't know where the hell we were.

Doug Johnson, *Specialist Four, U.S. Army, 25th Infantry Division, 2nd Battalion, 12th Infantry, 1968*

The weather in Vietnam, especially when I first arrived and before I became more acclimated, could be described in one word—oppressive. I remember that it was very easy to become dehydrated because we were constantly sweating, and the sweat would immediately evaporate. If you didn't consume lots of water, you were in for big trouble. The temperature during the day seemed to be over one hundred degrees and you really had to pace your activities to keep from succumbing to heat exhaustion.

I remember that the first time I had guard duty on the perimeter at Cu Chi, I didn't bring a field jacket with me. The temperature that night probably dipped into the seventies, and I spent a miserable night shivering and believing I was going to freeze to death before anyone found me in the morning.

Another lasting memory about the weather was the difference between the rainy and dry seasons. When I first arrived in-country, I believe it was the dry season. Day after day, the sun would beat down mercilessly and not a drop of rain was to be found. The dust on the ground seemed to reach up to our ankles. Convoys could be seen for miles by the huge dust trails that followed closely in their tracks. Then, rather unceremoniously, the rainy season would come. Every day it would rain heavily, and then the sun would come out, and it would be over for another day. I truly learned the meaning of monsoon in Vietnam and almost began to enjoy the cleansing that seemed to come with the heavy deluge. I didn't bitch much about the rainy season because I think that these sudden deluges not only kept the Viet Cong out of their holes, but also slowed them down.

Salvatore T. Raffa, Airman Second Class, U.S. Air Force, 377th Security Police Squadron, Tan Son Nhut Air Base, Saigon, 1967–68

I landed in Cam Ranh Bay, and I think it was still daytime. Getting off that plane, the heat hit you like a hot stove. It was unbelievable. I didn't stay that long in Cam Ranh Bay because I was being reassigned to Tan Son Nhut on a C-130.

I never was in a C-130 before, and I can remember the pilot saying, "If the red light flashes, that means we're in danger."

All the while I'm saying to myself, "I can't believe this is happening to me." So the whole time I'm flying, I'm just staring at that red light.

Stephen Butler, Lance Corporal, U.S. Marine Corps, 7th Marine Combat Engineers, Da Nang, 1966–67

Compared to California, it wasn't bad at all. In California, where I had training, it was the worst drought—in fact, that was the time, I guess, about four hundred marines were killed. The local firefighters decided to use the marines as firefighters, but the wind shifted and they didn't know what the hell they were doing and got burned up.

California had been real hot, so it wasn't a big transition for me.

THE SIGHTS

In the movie *The Wizard of Oz*, Dorothy is swept away from her home by a cyclone and deposited in a strange land. Looking around at her new surroundings, she turns to her dog and says, "Toto, I have a feeling we're not in Kansas anymore!" Well, the feeling wasn't much different for those from Newport County who witnessed a tropical area for the first time. After traveling for many hours by plane or days by boat and being somewhat exhausted upon their arrival, many must have said to themselves, "Guys, I have a feeling we're not in Rhode Island anymore!" The contrasts were startling.

Regardless of where one arrived in-country, the sights were certainly nothing like home. As the war dragged on, vast troop and supply areas became more prevalent. These military compounds had wooden buildings for the troops and fairly elaborate roads to get them where they needed to go. Indeed, it was possible to serve an entire tour of duty at one of these major installations (Cam Ranh Bay or Long Bien, for example) without ever experiencing any of the war. The area was that large and secure.

Villages with shanty huts, "hooches," as they were called by the Americans, were everywhere. Except for Saigon and in some of the other major cities, all the Vietnamese houses were small and inexpensively constructed. Most resembled shacks. The signs of poverty and the lack of sanitation that went along with it were easy to see. Garbage was strewn everywhere, and lavatories were simply open areas located just outside the homes.

It was a beautiful country, despite its dichotomies. In a single glance it was possible to see a Vietnamese native squatting to do his or her business, while also viewing a beautiful white sandy beach, flowery tropical vegetation, lush green jungle, or majestic mountains.

Peggy R. Zarek, *Lieutenant Commander, U.S. Navy, U.S.S.* Sanctuary *(AH-17), Coastal Waters off South Vietnam, Military Region 1, 1969–70*

When I landed in Da Nang, that was a shock. That's when it really hit me, 'cause I saw the sandbags, fellows walking around in fatigues, carrying guns and whatever. It was like another world to me. I just couldn't believe I was there.

When we first got to Vietnam, we had to stay in the navy hospital in Da Nang because our ship was out to sea, up north. We were picked up at the airport by an army guy who gave us a ride to the hospital. The first night we were there we were told about incoming fire. They also told us that under our bunks were flak jackets. This other young nurse and I got so scared, we didn't get to bed until I don't know when.

The next morning, someone asked us, "How'd you do?"

I said, "What do you mean?" Apparently, during the night, some area took incoming rounds, but we never heard it.

So we stayed there for two days and two nights. For some reason, instead of the ship coming into Da Nang harbor, we had to go to the ship. That was another experience. We took a helicopter to get there. Inside the helicopter were fellows at the open doors and guns mounted to the deck.

Thomas Finn, *Specialist Four, U.S. Army, Company A, 519th Military Intelligence Battalion, 525th Military Intelligence Group, MACV-J2, Saigon, 1966–67*

It was early morning hours when they woke everyone on the ship and told us to go topside. On the horizon we could see the coastline of Vietnam. We pulled into Vung Tau, a port city not far from Saigon. It was formerly called Cape St. Jacques by the French. When the French troops occupied the area in the early 1950s, it was transformed into a resort. I still remember the beautiful beaches and white sand.

First the landing ships were let down. Later in the afternoon we boarded them. We knew we weren't going into a combat beach like in Normandy during World War II, although looking at us, you'd never know the difference. We were dressed in full combat gear with steel pot helmets, weapons, the whole shebang. Man, we were ready for anything. By then it was five or six o'clock at night.

So we storm the beach. The door slams down into shallow water and we charge out. It was one of those weird scenes. You had to be there to appreciate the hilarity of the entire scene. There were support troops already stationed there, and apparently they had just gotten off work, as they were sitting on the beach enjoying a beer. So, if you can, visualize us charging off the ships and these support troops are looking at us like we had three heads. They must have said, "Oh no, more FNGs!" It was weird.

Within a reasonable time we boarded a plane for a short flight to Tan Son Nhut Air Base in Saigon. There we boarded buses and were taken to our new compound. It was late, maybe nine or ten at night, and we were wide-eyed but fatigued from all the travel. After traveling through the streets of Saigon, the bus finally arrived.

As we were disembarking, someone was shouting instructions: "The mess hall is this way, the bar is that way. . . ." You can only imagine which way everyone turned. I tied one on that night like you wouldn't believe. There it was, my first night in Vietnam, and I was passed out under a Ping-Pong table.

David Rossi, Specialist Four, U.S. Army, 1st Infantry Division and 25th Infantry Division, Di An, Tay Ninh, and Cu Chi, 1969–70

We landed in Bien Hoa. We didn't know if we were going to be shot getting off the plane or what. None of us had any clue that Bien Hoa was a pretty secure place. For the next few hours all we did was fill out paperwork and wait for a unit assignment.

---

* FNG, short for "a f—in' new guy," was one of the most common names used to describe a new person in-country.

Doug Johnson, *Specialist Four, U.S. Army, 25th Infantry Division, 2nd Battalion, 12th Infantry, 1968*

My first lasting impression is that Vietnam was a land of simplicity and pastoral beauty. There was a certain simplicity and dignity in the people that I believe came from their closeness to the soil and their simple values of live and let live. I am certain that the villagers would have been perfectly content to allow life to go on in their villages as it had for centuries between wars. Their simple hooches or huts and unpretentious dress did not reflect their resourceful and hard-working nature. They didn't have much, but they did a lot with the little they had. America could have learned a lot about recycling from the Vietnamese.

The most unsettling sight for me was the begging children in the villages as our convoys would pass by. We would toss C-rations to them, and unfortunately some of my fellow soldiers, who did not share my respect for the people, would make a game out of trying to hit them with the cans.

Dick Turner, *Boatswain's Mate Third Class, U.S. Navy, River Assault Squadron 15, River Division 152, Task Force 117, Dong Tam and My Tho, 1968–69*

The country itself was beautiful, it really was. The vegetation, the open spaces, and the rivers that we operated in were like canals; it was quite a beautiful spot. But at night you'd get this low-hanging fog over the water. It was really an eerie sight.

William Sullivan, *Lieutenant Commander, U.S. Navy, Fighter Squadron 213, U.S.S.* Intrepid, *Air Wing, U.S.S.* Kitty Hawk *(CVA-63), U.S.S.* Intrepid *(CVA-11), U.S.S.* Paul Revere, *and U.S.S.* Blue Ridge, *1965–68 and 1971–72*

The first time I flew off the carrier over Vietnam in the F-4 Phantom, I was struck by the immense jungles and wondered how were we ever going to find the enemy with all that underbrush and foliage below. I was also struck by the lack of metropolitan areas, like you see in the States.

Michael Toner Farrell, *Specialist Five, U.S. Army, 544th Replacement Company, Cam Ranh Bay, 1969–70*

We landed in Cam Ranh Bay. I looked out the window and the first thing I said to myself was, "Holy shit, there's nothing here." It was just barren land and sand for as far as the eye could see.

Ken Garthee, *Private First Class, U.S. Marine Corps, 3rd Battalion, 3rd Marines, 3rd Marine Division, Da Nang, Rock Pile, 1966–67*

The ride to my base camp was bumpy, dirty, and hot. I saw a lot of kids trying to sell soft drinks, bananas, coconuts, and melons. There were Vietnamese *mama-sans,* or peasant women, and prostitutes lining the road out of the city, offering a good time to all GIs and telling the marines they were "number one," which, I suppose, meant we were the best. No one was interested, and we immediately became "number ten." When going through the villages, you saw chickens, dogs, goats, and pigs in abundance.

The countryside was very picturesque: panoramic mountain ranges, green hills, open areas with rice paddies, and farmers with their water buffalo pulling a plow.

Betsy Wylie, *Lieutenant, U.S. Navy, Management Information Center, Headquarters, Naval Forces Vietnam (NAVFORV), Saigon, 1967–68*

The sights were interesting because I had never been in the Orient before. So from that perspective it was new and different and very interesting.

I really enjoyed my opportunities to get out of Saigon because South Vietnam is an absolutely gorgeous country! It's very, very pretty! I always thought, in retrospect, that if the North and South stopped fighting each other, they would have been better off building a lovely resort around Cam Ranh Bay. Cam Ranh Bay is beautiful, absolutely gorgeous! And there were other places like that. I did a lot of flying around Vietnam because that was basically how I traveled, and I took advantage of every opportunity I had to look at the countryside. It was just magnificent!

Yet you'd have to contrast that beauty with the small villages, where hunger was obviously constant, because they couldn't do the trading they needed to do on account of the war; where sanitation was, in many cases, almost nonexistent; where any kind of medical help was, in fact, nonexistent; where kids needed to go to school, yet they didn't get to go; where mothers and fathers needed to farm and they didn't get the chance. Fighting aside, in that respect, it was a land of contrasts.

Stephen Butler, *Lance Corporal, U.S. Marine Corps, 7th Marine Combat Engineers, Da Nang, 1966–67*

I was kind of amazed because we pulled into a full military installation.

It looked like an air base; I mean, it even had a paved runway. Then we got out of the plane, we were put in cattle cars, tractor trailer trucks with benches in them, and we got hauled down and broken up into these different buildings and tents, based on our military occupational series and where our units were.

When we went over, we were sent with our full packs of war gear; I mean, we had eighty pounds of junk with us, besides our full utility bags. Eventually, these two marines pulled up in a Jeep and picked me and one other guy up to take us to our new unit. Anyway, we were cruising down the road, just like we were in Island Park in Portsmouth! I was looking for foxholes and the war. It was like, "Where the hell is the war?"

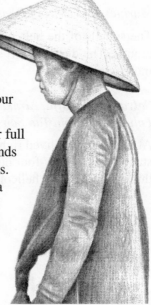

A Vietnamese mama-san

THE SOUNDS

For many veterans, the sound most often associated with Vietnam had to be that of the helicopter. It certainly was the most common one. When aloft, choppers had a distinct noise made by the rotor blades cutting through the air. The racket of the engine added to its uniqueness, and for those who served there, the noise would not be easily forgotten.

There were other distinct sounds—incoming rockets whistling overhead, the whoosh of mortars being fired from a tube, incoming rockets or mortars exploding as they struck, and the crack and echo of gunfire from friendly and enemy positions. These sounds would also always be remembered.

Thomas Finn, *Specialist Four, U.S. Army, Company A, 519th Military Intelligence Battalion, 525th Military Intelligence Group, MACV-J2, Saigon, 1966–67*

The Hueys (troop-transport helicopters) had their own distinctive sound. I'll never forget it!

Ken Garthee, *Private First Class, U.S. Marine Corps, 3rd Battalion, 3rd Marines, 3rd Marine Division, Da Nang, Rock Pile, 1966–67*

The sounds of the helicopters, roaring jets, and other airplanes were all around. The dust and dirt swirling around because of them made it even more unpleasant.

Salvatore T. Raffa, *Airman Second Class, U.S. Air Force, 377th Security Police Squadron, Tan Son Nhut Air Base, Saigon, 1967–68*

At the air base, I lived right next door to the heliport, and it was just constant noise, twenty-four hours a day, day after day, week after week. 'Til this day, if I hear a helicopter, I still get queasy.

The Universal Sound of the Vietnam War—a Helicopter

Doug Johnson, *Specialist Four, U.S. Army, 25th Infantry Division, 2nd Battalion, 12th Infantry, 1968*

The most persistent sound of Vietnam from the moment I arrived until I left was the sound of artillery or small-arms fire. That first night when we landed in Vietnam, it was scary to hear the sound of distant explosions because we didn't know whether it was incoming or outgoing. The incessant flares and flashes made it seem like each day and night was a bizarre celebration of the Fourth of July, but somehow I wasn't enjoying it. To this day, Fourth of July pyrotechnics remind me of the days when each explosion could lead to your demise. Learning to quickly assess the difference between incoming and outgoing rounds became an important skill—one which would ultimately save my life.

Another sound that permeated my tour of duty was the cadence of spoken Vietnamese and the plaintive, almost wailing sounds of the Vietnamese music on the radio. It represented to me a barrier in communication that I could not breach despite my feeble attempts to learn the basic words to communicate. Somehow this inability to communicate was almost a metaphor for our inability as Americans to understand the people, their struggle and how to solve the perplexing puzzle that was Vietnam.

Dick Turner, *Boatswain's Mate Third Class, U.S. Navy, River Assault Squadron 15, River Division 152, Task Force 117, Dong Tam and My Tho, 1968–69*

You didn't hear too many birds. I remember a lot of gunfire in the background. Also I remember hearing jets making bombing runs at night. Those pop-flares were something, too. When fired by hand, they made a *whop* sound, and as they gained altitude, you could hear a *whoosh* and a *pop* sound when the parachute finally opened on the flare.

Stephen Butler, *Lance Corporal, U.S. Marine Corps, 7th Marine Combat Engineers, Da Nang, 1966–67*

I remember more about the lack of sounds. It was pretty quiet where we were, out there in the field. But I remember more about the smells of the villages than anything else.

THE SMELLS

Due to the rotting tropical vegetation, stifling heat and humidity, and the lack of proper sanitation, the dominant sensation on one's arrival in-country was the foul odor. The jungle smell wasn't as bad as the odor of burning excrement, which became worse as the day grew hotter. To get rid of body waste, the unlucky person assigned to this very unpleasant detail had to pour diesel fuel or kerosene into a fifty-five-gallon steel drum (cut in half) containing the you-know-what, light a match, drop it in, stir it up with a large paddle, and stand back for an olfactory experience not soon to be forgotten. The odor lingered in the air all day, and for many, the mental stench lasts a lifetime.

Another penetrating odor was that of *nuoc-mam*, a pungent, highly concentrated fish sauce that the natives used to flavor rice meals. It was made from fish heads, which were placed in a pan full of water and left to ferment in the hot sun for several days. Once smelled it was never forgotten. *Nuoc-mam* made castor oil seem appealing.

Stephen Butler, *Lance Corporal, U.S. Marine Corps, 7th Marine Combat Engineers, Da Nang, 1966–67*

When I was working on produce farms back home, I can remember that when the crops died—like tomatoes and such—the mix of smells could really get to you. Vietnam, at times, was a lot like that.

Doug Johnson, *Specialist Four, U.S. Army, 25th Infantry Division, 2nd Battalion, 12th Infantry, 1968*

My first lasting memory about Vietnam is of the smell of the country. As soon as the doors to our jet were opened when we arrived, I recall the most pungent smell I had ever encountered in my life. It smelled like we had been dropped in the middle of a vast farmland, and the aroma was a mixture of manure and mildew that had been slowly baked over a steady fire.

Betsy Wylie, *Lieutenant, U.S. Navy, Management Information Center, Headquarters, Naval Forces Vietnam (NAVFORV), Saigon, 1967–68*

The smells in Saigon were overwhelming initially because I had never smelled mounds of garbage like that before. I got used to it after a while.

Thomas Finn, *Specialist Four, U.S. Army, Company A, 519th Military Intelligence Battalion, 525th Military Intelligence Group, MACV-J2, Saigon, 1966–67*

The smell of *nuoc-mam* will never leave me. And when a bus goes by me today and I smell spent diesel fuel, it instantly reminds me of Vietnam.

Dick Turner, *Boatswain's Mate Third Class, U.S. Navy, River Assault Squadron 15, River Division 152, Task Force 117, Dong Tam and My Tho, 1968–69*

Every river we were on, no matter if it was day or night, you could smell *nuoc-mam*. The odors of the rivers, too, were something to experience; the dank stench of raw sewerage was everywhere. Actually, the way people lived over there was filthy. It was all open ditches of sewerage.

It was nothing to see a body float down the river—people had been shot and just thrown in. You'd see animals, too; water buffaloes would float right by as we were on our boat.

Bill McCollum, *Sergeant, U.S. Army, 173rd Airborne Brigade, Charlie Company, 4th Battalion, 503rd Infantry, LZ-English, 1969–71*

The place definitely had its own distinct odor. No matter where they burned the shit, you could smell it. Even the ground had a distinct odor that seemed to linger in the red dirt.

Ken Garthee, *Private First Class, U.S. Marine Corps, 3rd Battalion, 3rd Marines, 3rd Marine Division, Da Nang, Rock Pile, 1966–67*

The odors were pungent. The smell of human waste and the gasoline used to burn it away was something I'll never forget. You could also smell food that had rotted and started to decay in the heat. Stagnant water from the rice paddies also reeked. Until that time, I had never smelled odors like that before. I then realized, this wasn't going to be fun!

Howard North, *Lieutenant j.g., U.S. Coast Guard, Coast Guard Squadron One, U.S.CGC Point Clear (WPB 82315), An Thoi and Cat Lo, 1967–68*

I couldn't believe it. I mean, I never smelled anything like it in my life. It was a combination of all the foul odors you could ever imagine—charcoal, excrement, the jungle—you name it.

Mike Pinksaw, *Specialist Four, U.S. Army, 60th Land Clearing Company, 62nd Engineering Battalion, 20th Engineering Brigade, Long Binh, Bien Hoa, Lai Khe 1968–69*

The first thing that hit me when they opened the door to that plane was the heat, but even more so was the smell—it was the smell of death! It was a rotten, stinking smell.

NEW AND GREEN

As early as 1965, most military personnel went to Vietnam as individual replacements rather than in units.* If going to Vietnam wasn't bad

---

* Stanley Karnow, *Vietnam: A History* (New York: Viking Press, 1983), p. 466.

enough already, the GI found himself not only a new replacement in a combat zone, but a lonely one at that. This feeling could be intimidating. Buddies who may have been assigned to Vietnam after advanced training in the States ended up anywhere in-country.

If you weren't called a FNG when you were new in-country, then you were referred to as a "cherry."

What was it like to be a new guy in Vietnam? Quite simply, a f—in' new guy in Vietnam stood out like a sore thumb, because the uniform was invariably a dead giveaway. The army called their work uniforms *fatigues*, while the marines called them *utilities*. Anyone who was there for a period of time wore uniforms that were badly faded by the sun and from repeated washings.

Ken Garthee, *Private First Class, U.S. Marine Corps, 3rd Battalion, 3rd Marines, 3rd Marine Division, Da Nang, Rock Pile, 1966–67*

You could tell the new marines from those who had been there a while. The new arrivals wore clean green utilities, while those who were going home had dirty, dingy utilities.

I will never forget the lack of expression on the faces or the look in their eyes of those who were going home. It was a stare, a look, and an attitude, or a combination of all three. Whatever it was, they looked at us but kept their distance, never saying a word. More shocking were the rows and rows of caskets I saw that were being prepared for loading on the same plane for return to the States.

We were in-country!

I was assigned to 3rd Battalion, 3rd Marines, 3rd Marine Division, Mike Company, located on Hill 22, northwest of Da Nang. As soon as I got there I was told to take off my white T-shirt because I made too good a target for the Viet Cong. I gladly obliged. Heck, it was hot anyway. It was so hot that I never wore any underwear again during the remainder of my tour.

Thomas Finn, *Specialist Four, U.S. Army, Company A, 519th Military Intelligence Battalion, 525th Military Intelligence Group, MACV-J2, Saigon, 1966–67*

You stood out with your dark green fatigues that hadn't yet been stone washed. You could tell immediately the new guys from those who had been in-country for a while.

Rob Roche, *Sergeant, U.S. Army, 101st Airborne Division, Da Nang, 1967–69*

We landed in Bien Hoa. Shortly after we arrived, we had to go through a week's worth of jungle training, crawling through swamps and getting shot at over our heads by friendly fire. It was just like basic training stuff, and it was mandatory.

At the end of training, an instructor had everyone stand in formation, and he began to issue orders. He said, "You three are going to the 1st Cav; you're going to the 173rd Airborne," and he looked at me and said, "You're going to the 101st Airborne," and so on, all the way down the line. That's when I first found out what unit I was assigned to and where I was going in-country.

I felt like a trainee going into basic training, like a new kid on the block. In a bar shortly after jungle training, I forget where, we met some Aussies who had been in and out of combat. They were kind of teasing us about our brand-new uniforms. But they turned out to be a bunch of hot shits. I liked those guys.

Stephen Butler, *Lance Corporal, U.S. Marine Corps, 7th Marine Combat Engineers, Da Nang, 1966–67*

When I got to my new unit, in the battalion area, they put us in tents that were sandbagged up about three feet, with plywood sides and a canvas top. It was pretty late in the day, and the guys in the battalion area had worked pretty much a ten- to twelve-hour day. They were all in their tents, awake, but racked out on their cots. Some of them were writing letters, and some were playing cards. The guy that would have been my bunkmate, the next-closest marine, he was just lying there looking up at the ceiling. And he didn't even acknowledge that I came through the door. So after I had been there a while, I started to unpack my gear.

After a short while, I said to him, "My name is Butler. How long have you been here?"

He just continued to stare at the ceiling, and after quite a while he finally said, "All day, baby, all day."

With that response, I got the idea what Vietnam was going to be all about.

Bill McCollum, *Sergeant, U.S. Army, 173rd Airborne Brigade, Charlie Company, 4th Battalion, 503rd Infantry, LZ-English, 1969–71*

At the replacement battalion, they lined us all up and started calling out names for assignments in-country. I said to myself, "I hope I get the

101st," which was an elite airborne unit. But I got the 173rd Airborne instead.

So I got to the 173rd base camp, and immediately they put us on half-tracks (trucks) and brought us out into the field. We were put in the main command post, which was surrounded by three companies.

While waiting at the CP, a guy came in and looked at me and yelled, "Hey, are you a blue leg or a red leg?"

I said to myself, "What the f— is this guy talking about?" So I said, "What was that?"

He yelled again, "Are you a blue leg or a red leg? Answer the question!"

I looked at this other new guy quizzically. Then I took a guess, remembering that blue was the color of the infantry and red artillery, so I said, "I'm a blue leg, I guess."

"Then get over there," he yelled at me. Then he looked at the other guy and said the same thing.

He responded, "I'm what he is," looking at me. He didn't have a clue what the guy was talking about, either.

The guy yelled back, "Then get over there!"

They were looking for infantry replacements, and I just happened to make a good guess.

So we were outside and a guy came down in a truck to pick us up. He got out of the vehicle and yelled at us, "Hey, you blue legs, come here. You guys are going to the first platoon. Now pair up with those guys, and we're out of here."

We were also given weapons, so I was feeling a little bit better. I said to the guy, "How far is this place?"

He said, "Just get in line."

I said to myself, "Now there's a friendly guy." Of course, I happened to be the last guy to fall in line, and the next thing I heard, the guy was yelling at me.

"Hey, blue leg," he said to me. He gave me a case of C-rations and some ammo. Then he said, "Pick up that bag." It was a fifty-pound bag of dog food.

"What the hell do I have to carry this for?" I figured he was screwing with me.

He said it again, "Pick up the damn bag and put it on the truck."

I did it this time, with a little bit of reluctance. Anyway, when we arrived at our destination, they actually had a dog. My sense of humor a bit warped after carrying the bag in the heat, I said to myself, "I hope the son-of-a-bitch gets it."

Mike Pinksaw, *Specialist Four, U.S. Army, 60th Land Clearing Company, 62nd Engineering Battalion, 20th Engineering Brigade, Long Binh, Bien Hoa, Lai Khe 1968–69*

When I first arrived in Charlie Company of the 62nd Engineering Battalion, I heard a guy yell, "Short!" I didn't know what that meant yet. Here I am, coming in with brand-new fatigues and all, and this guy catches a glimpse of me. I guess he wanted to send me a message that he was almost ready to go home, and I was just starting my tour.

Betsy Wylie, *Lieutenant, U.S. Navy, Management Information Center, Headquarters, Naval Forces Vietnam (NAVFORV), Saigon, 1967–68*

I think, for anyone in Vietnam, whether officer or enlisted, male or female, in one of the headquarters or out in the field, as a new person you were probably close to being overwhelmed and always concerned about your safety.

While I was the first navy woman line officer in Vietnam, I was by no means the first woman. There were already nurses there from other services. And in Saigon itself, there were woman officers from the army, air force, and marine corps. For almost the whole year that I was in Vietnam, my roommate was the first woman marine officer in Vietnam. She beat me to Vietnam by about three weeks. She had it all down and knew everything—what to do, where to go, and all that sort of stuff. She was just a lovely individual, and I was very lucky to have her as a roommate. She left, and for about the last three weeks that I was there, a marine captain was my roommate.

Dick Turner, *Boatswain's Mate Third Class, U.S. Navy, River Assault Squadron 15, River Division 152, Task Force 117, Dong Tam and My Tho, 1968–69*

When I was the new kid on the block, I was scared shitless. I mean, I didn't know what was up; all of us FNGs were considered fresh meat.

Salvatore T. Raffa, *Airman Second Class, U.S. Air Force, 377th Security Police Squadron, Tan Son Nhut Air Base, Saigon, 1967–68*

Everybody was very friendly to me. I had no problems making new friends; it was the place. I knew I'd never become accustomed to being in Vietnam.

Within a few hours after I got there, I was pulling guard duty at an ammunition dump somewhere. I was standing in the dark, holding an M16, without the slightest idea where I was. Seventy-two hours before, I was watching the *Price is Right.*

Peggy R. Zarek, *Lieutenant Commander, U.S. Navy, U.S.S.* Sanctuary *(AH-17), Coastal Waters off South Vietnam, Military Region 1, 1969–70*

I didn't feel different being new, because the navy nurse corps really takes care of its own. There were two nurses there to meet me when I got off the plane; and when I got to Da Nang at the hospital, there were other navy nurses there; some I knew from my days back in the States.

Michael Toner Farrell, *Specialist Five, U.S. Army, 544th Replacement Company, Cam Ranh Bay, 1969–70*

After arriving at the replacement battalion at Cam Ranh Bay, I anxiously awaited my assignment to another destination in-country. This major in-country personnel transient point served several functions. It handled in-country arrivals and departures from and to the states and troops leaving or returning from R & R.

My name was called, and I feared the worst. Surprisingly, I was selected to stay put right where I was. I was permanently assigned to the 522nd Replacement Battalion in Cam Ranh Bay. We were located in an annex facility at the tip of the island near the main base.

Our company was divided into two separate groups—it was lifers,* who drank, and the druggies. I mean, where we were, there was absolutely nothing else to do. There was no war, you didn't have to protect yourself or your buddy, so there was nothing really constructive to do in your spare time. You could drink or sit in your room and get high—my choice was to get high.

I was put in with guys who had been in-country for a while, and of course, there was this major mistrust. At first, I was looked upon as a plant, and no one wanted to give me any joints for fear they would be busted and end up in jail. My first roommate was black. I tried to be his friend, but he wanted no part of me. He had just lost his previous roommate, who had rotated back to the States. Of course, here I was coming in as the new white guy on the block. Needless to say, we didn't hit it off too well. As time went on, it became a little easier, but it never really

---

* "Lifer" was a derogatory term used to identify career enlisted soldiers.

ironed itself out. Not long after, he left for home also, and eventually, I was finally accepted. After that, I'd estimate that I smoked pot every day.

MENTALLY UNPREPARED

There were no psychology courses in the services which would have prepared individuals for what they were about to experience. Were the services deficient in not providing such training? Perhaps; perhaps not. The psychological aspect of combat and its aftereffects were just beginning to be seriously studied. Whether such training would have done any good, no one really knows for certain.

Just seeing Vietnam for the first time was a unique experience, if not a frightening one, for many. As one nurse described it,

> I have arrived in Vietnam! And I'm crying. I wasn't and
> still am not prepared for this place. I've seen pictures of
> the wire fences, wooden shacks and dirt roads, but no
> photo can realistically portray what one experiences
> when actually visualizing it for the first time.*

Peggy R. Zarek, *Lieutenant Commander, U.S. Navy, U.S.S.* Sanctuary *(AH-17), Coastal Waters off South Vietnam, Military Region 1, 1969–70*

I didn't feel prepared for what I was about to see—at least not mentally prepared for what the war was doing to these young men and the wounds that we saw.

Doug Johnson, *Specialist Four, U.S. Army, 25th Infantry Division, 2nd Battalion, 12th Infantry, 1968*

I am of the considered opinion that people who say they were prepared for the Vietnamese experience when they first arrived in-country should be instantly hooked up to a lie detector. If they pass the test, they should immediately be signed up to sell swampland and snake oil to unsuspecting customers. As for me, I was clearly not prepared for this experience. Until that time, I had never been further from home than Washington,

---

* Ann Thompson et al., *Another Kind of War Story: Army Nurses Look Back to Vietnam* (Lebanon, Pa.: Ann Thompson, 1993), p. 25.

D.C., and my life experiences had been mostly protected and uncomplicated. I had, on one occasion, fired a .22 caliber rifle at a rifle range in high school; but I had never been hunting or hiked in any terrain remotely resembling Vietnam.

Soon after arriving in-country—I believe it was probably on my first night of guard duty on the perimeter at Cu Chi—I inventoried the hardware in my arsenal and determined that there were a hell of a lot of ways one could meet his maker. In reflecting on the claymore mines, M50 and M60 machine guns, M16s, M79 grenade launchers, LAWs (M72 light antitank weapons), hand grenades, mortars and artillery

Doug Johnson, wearing his flak jacket. (Courtesy of Doug Johnson)

guns of various shapes and sizes, the Huey and Cobra gunships and Puff the Magic Dragon (those were C-47 up-gunned air force support aircraft), there was no doubt we were playing for keeps. Visions of land mines, booby traps, snipers, and the always fearsome rocket-propelled grenades made life, liberty, and the pursuit of happiness a perilous adventure indeed.

Thomas Finn, *Specialist Four, U.S. Army, Company A, 519th Military Intelligence Battalion, 525th Military Intelligence Group, MACV-J2, Saigon, 1966–67*

Our training prior to arriving in Vietnam was perhaps, at best, a good overview. Here I was going to an interrogation unit and I couldn't even speak the language. I had never experienced any ambush training other than at Fort Bragg, when we watched Green Berets simulate a North Vietnamese Army and Viet Cong attack. But we were just observers. I don't know if we lacked that training because we were a noncombat unit. If the shit really hit the fan, no way would we have been ready!

Dick Turner, *Boatswain's Mate Third Class, U.S. Navy, River Assault Squadron 15, River Division 152, Task Force 117, Dong Tam and My Tho, 1968–69*

I felt physically prepared for Vietnam, but not mentally. At the school, not too much emphasis was placed on the mental aspect of it. But the physical part, that was what the instructors really concentrated on. We ran a few miles each day, and on Fridays, we ran five miles through a gravel pit. They wanted to get us in top physical condition, so in case we lost a boat, we were physically fit to survive. But the mental part . . . Well, they taught us about intelligence, to be careful whom we talked to over there, because missions could be compromised, but that was about all.

Bill McCollum, *Sergeant, U.S. Army, 173rd Airborne Brigade, Charlie Company, 4th Battalion, 503rd Infantry, LZ-English, 1969–71*

A convoy took us out to this secure area for one week of jungle training prior to our being assigned to a unit. I remember being pulled into the back of a deuce-and-a-half (two-and-a-half ton truck) by a guy who had a weapon. And I was thinking to myself, "Why don't we have weapons yet?" I was already paranoid.

There we were in the back of this truck as we drove down this highway. I don't know if this guy with the weapon was trying to impress us, was whacked out, or if he was on something, but as we passed these peasants walking along the side of the road, he stuck out his M16 and spun this woman around. She was carrying two baskets suspended by a pole and slung over her shoulder for balance. I mean, he nearly spun her into the ground. I can see it like it was yesterday—the ugly American has arrived. I said to myself, "Oh baby, what are we in for here?" On the truck, all the way to the training area, I was hoping this guy wouldn't do something even worse. Fortunately, he didn't.

You know, I thought I was prepared for my Vietnam experience, but this incident told me otherwise. We were out in a village during the pacification program, and I was told to look for a person to combine my shelter tent with for the night.

I found a spot that looked pretty good, but the guy with me said, "You don't want to go there."

I said, "Why not?"

"Because we lost two guys there last night. They were looking through a starlight scope, and they took a direct hit with a rocket."

I said to myself, "Yup, I guess I don't want to bed down there!" Their poncho was still on the ground, and it was riddled with shrapnel and stained with blood. I said to myself, "Holy Christ!"

Salvatore T. Raffa, *Airman Second Class, U.S. Air Force, 377th Security Police Squadron, Tan Son Nhut Air Base, Saigon, 1967–68*

I was a Newporter. I was mama's little boy and had anything I ever wanted. No, even with the little training I had back in the States, I wasn't prepared.

Betsy Wylie, *Lieutenant, U.S. Navy, Management Information Center, Headquarters, Naval Forces Vietnam (NAVFORV), Saigon, 1967–68*

I was prepared as well as anyone could have been. Was it the best training? Probably not. Could it have been improved? Maybe, but I'm not sure how. One of the things that I had spent a lot of time working on was what I thought my job was going to be, which was to be in charge of the machine-card preparation. Remember, in those days IBM machines were still using punch cards. I was to be the supervisor of punch cards. As it turned out, I never did that because the equipment never arrived. It arrived about three months after I left. So when it became apparent after the second or third day that there wasn't any equipment on the horizon, they sent me to the Management Information Center, which was terrific. And that was fine. But I was not prepared for that. But that didn't make any difference, because I don't think anyone else there was prepared for it either. It was all on-the-job training.

Stephen Butler, *Lance Corporal, U.S. Marine Corps, 7th Marine Combat Engineers, Da Nang, 1966–67*

To do my job, I was prepared; frankly, I think I was overprepared. I had absolutely no concept at all that I wasn't there to do anything other than be the consummate marine, do my job, and go home.

VIETNAMESE CULTURE AND CUSTOMS

Several centuries of political domination by China significantly enriched Vietnam's culture. History has confirmed that Vietnam's achievements were directly enhanced and enriched by this intervention. Owing to French occupation and colonial rule in the early 1950s, until their defeat by the Viet Minh at Dien Bien Phu, Vietnam's culture, customs, and even some of the language were dramatically affected. As diverse as both countries were, it was an interesting amalgamation of European and Far Eastern culture, proprieties, foods, and language; one that surprisingly not only survived, but flourished. Food took on a French influence, architecture was of French design, and some of the Vietnamese language incorporated the use of French words or phrases. In fact, some French words and expressions would become part of the everyday American soldier's vocabulary. For instance, *beaucoup* (pronounced boo coo), meaning "many," would be used in English speech by many American military personnel throughout the war. Even some of the women in Saigon were of French descent, born during the years of French occupation—their mothers were Vietnamese peasants; their fathers, French soldiers.

For newly arrived American military personnel, adapting their way of life to those of the Vietnamese became a culture clash that, in numerous cases, continued unabated during their entire tour of duty. Having recently been abruptly removed from familiar, modern surroundings, young men and women were cast into this uniquely strange environment totally unprepared for what they were about to experience. Whereas proper sanitation was an established norm back in the States, it was virtually nonexistent in Vietnam. Americans chewed gum, while the Vietnamese chewed beetle nut. Observing the Vietnamese enjoying this habit must have left some rather strange memories for the Americans. It certainly left some cosmetic dental consequences for the Vietnamese, as it had a tendency to blacken teeth. When relaxing, Americans chose to sit or lie down, while the Vietnamese simply squatted. Back home, Americans walked hand-in-hand with their girlfriends, but in Vietnam, males who were best friends did the same.

Because they chose not to—or simply lacked the time between duty and rest—American military personnel never truly understood or appreciated the cultural differences. Others felt that for their own safety, it was better not to become too involved with the local populace.

Salvatore T. Raffa, Airman Second Class, U.S. Air Force, 377th Security Police Squadron, Tan Son Nhut Air Base, Saigon, 1967–68

Vietnam had some beautiful women, I mean gorgeous women, especially the ones with the mixture of French along with the Vietnamese, but when they smiled, their teeth were black from chewing beetle nut.

The other thing I remember is what little value they seemed to place on life. In Saigon, for instance, the streets were just loaded with trucks, Jeeps, and carts. It was unbelievable. I remember some people fell off a wagon one day, and everybody just kept going without offering any assistance whatsoever. Yet this first impression was proven wrong. The night after we got attacked once, they had a bulldozer bury hundreds of Viet Cong in this mass grave on base, and the next day I saw them digging it up again. I said, "What are they doing?" I was told that by mistake they had buried a South Vietnamese lieutenant along with the VC. They had to dig them all up again in order to find this guy.

Doug Johnson, *Specialist Four, U.S. Army, 25th Infantry Division, 2nd Battalion, 12th Infantry, 1968*

One day I was traveling through a village when I noticed a group of villagers gathered around what appeared to be some kind of barbecue pit on the ground. There was smoke billowing up from the fire and some object which I could not yet identify occupying the place of honor atop the fire. As I drew closer, my wondering eyes beheld a dog, fur and all, on the fire, being prepared for the feast. I had heard that dog was considered a delicacy in Vietnam, but had never had any reason to believe or disbelieve the rumor until that auspicious day. I was not invited for dinner and probably would have declined had the invitation been tendered. From that day forward, I never had any problem understanding why the dogs at our base camp always seemed to bark incessantly at the Vietnamese. Maybe they were mind readers, or perhaps they even caught a glimpse of one of the Vietnamese drooling at the prospect of a filling meal. To this day, I threaten my dog Chester when he gets on my nerves that I am going to donate him to a local Vietnamese family for holiday dinner.

Another difficult custom that it took a while for me to adjust to was the "portable bathroom" of the Vietnamese. To be blunt, they would squat by the side of the road or wherever they happened to be when nature called and relieve themselves in place. So much for privacy, modesty, and the sanitary habits to which we were accustomed in America. It gave the term "letting it all hang out" new meaning.

Another memory of a strange custom resulted from my volunteering to provide security for a medcap into one of the local villages. A medcap was when an army doctor and some medics would go into the local villages to attempt to render whatever medical assistance they could to the sick. I was along to provide protection in case the shit hit the fan while we were there. While I was sitting in the middle of the village at the temporary aid station, my mind started to wander and I began to daydream. I was torn from my reverie by a rather large red splash that landed near me on the ground. I looked up quickly, expecting to see someone bleeding profusely. What I saw instead was an elderly lady being examined by the doctor and chewing contentedly as a cow chews its cud. As I continued my observation, this slightly built old lady brought forth the biggest gob of red saliva I had heretofore observed, and spat it on the ground at my feet. I later learned that this lady was chewing on beetle nut, a nut which apparently had some medicinal and perhaps narcotic properties. Beetle nut went on my list of local delights, along with *nuoc-mam* and dog, none of which ever crossed my teeth or gums.

Rob Roche, *Sergeant, U.S. Army, 101st Airborne Division, Da Nang, 1967–69*

I didn't talk to the Vietnamese very much because of the possibility that they could be VC. That was always in the back of your mind.

I do remember them squatting all the time. To me it looked kind of uncomfortable to be in that position for so long.

Also, they were really thin people, mostly skin and bone.

David Rossi, *Specialist Four, U.S. Army, 1st Infantry Division and 25th Infantry Division, Di An, Tay Ninh, and Cu Chi, 1969–70*

I remember the Vietnamese civilians squatting all the time. They would rather do that than stand.

Betsy Wylie, *Lieutenant, U.S. Navy, Management Information Center, Headquarters, Naval Forces Vietnam (NAVFORV), Saigon, 1967–68*

I remember part of our SEER training before we went. There were certain things we shouldn't do, I guess that's the best way to put it, because while they were appropriate for us in this country, they were not appropriate in Vietnam. Two that stick with me were don't touch kids on the head—you know how we tend to pat kids on the head—and the other one was don't cross your ankle over your knee and show the Vietnamese the sole of your shoe. For some reason, that was inappropriate, and I don't know why.

Dick Turner, *Boatswain's Mate Third Class, U.S. Navy, River Assault Squadron 15, River Division 152, Task Force 117, Dong Tam and My Tho, 1968–69*

Many of the Vietnamese were Buddhists. In the afternoon, they would always find time to bow down and say their prayers. When saying them, it sounded to me like they were crying.

Bill McCollum, *Sergeant, U.S. Army, 173rd Airborne Brigade, Charlie Company, 4th Battalion, 503rd Infantry, LZ-English, 1969–71*

During our in-country indoctrination, we were told about things we should not do to the Vietnamese and things that annoyed them. Like, if I asked you to come here and I raised my hand and motioned you forward with my hand pointed upward while waving it, that would be considered an insult. The hand should be directly in front of you while pointing it down toward the ground while waving it, as you say *"den,"* which means "come."

When you first got there, the guys were pretty good in teaching you the local customs. You know, the *do*s and *don't*s, like, don't trust anyone.

Howard North, *Lieutenant j.g., U.S. Coast Guard, Coast Guard Squadron One, USCGC* Point Clear *(WPB 82315), An Thoi and Cat Lo, 1967–68*

When I first arrived in-country, I was picked up by a coast guard representative in Saigon. Instead of going through the camp for replacement personnel, they brought us to this hotel in the middle of the downtown area. I never saw anything like it in my life. All the trucks and mopeds, the stink from exhaust and diesel fumes, people with guns all over the place; I couldn't believe it. It was culture shock.

Once out of Saigon, I was amazed at the lack of sanitation practices by the civilians. People simply went to the bathroom no matter where they were. I remember them doing it off the back end of river boats, which were called *sampans*. They'd just pull up a floor board on the boat, squat down and do their business in the water. Coming from a Western civilization, it was difficult to get accustomed to.

Michael Toner Farrell, *Specialist Five, U.S. Army, 544th Replacement Company, Cam Ranh Bay, 1969–70*

Most Vietnamese lived at the basic level of subsistence, and the local nationals employed in the mess hall stole as many leftovers as they could.

They just didn't steal to take it home, they ate it immediately. Let me tell you, they loved American food.

The truth be known, they were good people, and I really liked them. Now, they could have been VC sappers* or the same ones dropping mortars and rockets on us at night, but while they were working with us, they were decent human beings. I remember that in a strange kind of way, they were a little like what we as low-ranking enlisted soldiers were. They were all too frequently mistreated by far too many Americans, and you couldn't blame them for doing what some may have done to us at night.

Stephen Butler, Lance Corporal, U.S. Marine Corps, 7th Marine Combat Engineers, Da Nang, 1966–67

I still remember a beautiful sunrise just after the monsoon season had ended. I was setting up a water purification unit near Pho Loc 6. It was situated in a small mountain range. I happened to look up the mountainside, and there were all these Vietnamese civilians going to work. That view and my thoughts at the time were: "God's people like us—different place, different culture, but surely God's people!"

Yes, I liked the people there. I didn't think they were strange at all. I mean, I knew they had a totally different culture, but I like people in general, and the more I interacted with them, the more I realized that they were good people.

Thomas Finn, Specialist Four, U.S. Army, Company A, 519th Military Intelligence Battalion, 525th Military Intelligence Group, MACV-J2, Saigon, 1966–67

The Vietnamese, like other Asians, didn't have much body hair to speak of. Sometimes, when we interrogated prisoners, they'd be looking at the hair on your arm, and they'd pick at it. They couldn't believe we were so hairy.

Males who were good friends used to walk hand-in-hand. It was nothing to see the South Vietnamese soldiers walking hand-and-hand with one another. A few times, we'd walk behind them and mimic them. Cruel, but what can I say? We looked like Bob Hope and Bing Crosby frolicking in one of their movies.

---

* Sappers were Viet Cong who performed suicide missions with explosives carried in backpacks.

Howard North, *Lieutenant j.g., U.S. Coast Guard, Coast Guard Squadron One, USCGC* Point Clear *(WPB 82315), An Thoi and Cat Lo, 1967–68*

We had this South Vietnamese officer working on the boat with us. His name was Nguyen Van Linh. We had a lot of fun with him and fooled around with him every chance we got. After being around us for a while, he became very Americanized. However, there wasn't much he or any of us could do about his lack of body hair. The Vietnamese, genetically, didn't have much body hair except on their heads. Linh had only one hair on his chest, which he was very proud of. We'd chase him around the boat all day and all night trying to pull that sucker off.

FIVE

THE WAR

So nigh is grandeur to our dust,
So near is God to man,
When Duty whispers low, Thou must,
The youth replies, I can.
—Ralph Waldo Emerson

JUST DOING MY JOB

REGARDLESS of one's branch of service, whether enlisted man or officer, everyone in the military had a military occupation, a job one was required to perform every day. Some service branches, such as the army, had primary and secondary military occupational specialties. This meant everyone was trained and/or qualified to perform in either capacity. The marines also called it MOS, while the navy called it a rating. The coast guard simply called it rates, and the air force referred to it as an air force specialty code.

Military occupations were as diverse as one can imagine—from cooks and supply clerks to more dangerous duties, such as artillery and infantry. An infantry soldier in the army carried the MOS code 11B10, which was commonly referred to by the troops as 11 Bravo.

Regardless of their MOS, all marines were trained as riflemen (infantry). In the army, this was not the case. A soldier could have two MOSs, neither of which had to be infantry.

Thomas Finn, *Specialist Four, U.S. Army, Company A, 519th Military Intelligence Battalion, 525th Military Intelligence Group, MACV-J2, Saigon, 1966–67*

For the first three months in-country, I worked at an intelligence center near Tan Son Nhut Airport. There, I worked in a section plotting B-52 targets in I Corps for the air force. I'd draw small circles on a map, and the air force would pick from them. Later, I was assigned to a prisoner interrogation unit.

We were kind of an oddball lot. Matter of fact, we wore civilian clothes more than we did our jungle fatigues. For some reason we were paid more money than the average soldiers in Vietnam. We also received a special clothing allowance and extra rations. Primarily, my job was to analyze information obtained from NVA and Viet Cong prisoners captured within the country. I only interrogated prisoners on a few rare occasions. Actually, my main function was to analyze the information obtained during the interrogation. After a while, I was able to converse a little bit in Vietnamese. In fact, I surprised myself as I became more proficient with the language.

Rob Roche, *Sergeant, U.S. Army, 101st Airborne Division, Da Nang, 1967–69*

My job was to do search and destroy missions. In the bush, we'd get up in the morning, go through jungles all day long looking for the enemy, stop to eat a lunch, and sweat. Because of the heat and humidity, we'd sweat constantly. It was like jumping into a pool of water, getting out, and never drying off. We took twenty to thirty salt tablets a day in order to replace the salt our bodies had lost. We also took malaria pills.

Sometimes we'd get so tired our muscles would cramp up from fatigue and from not drinking enough water. Anyway, we just couldn't walk. Sometimes we were in the bush for a month and a half, sometimes two months at a stretch. The helicopters would drop us in there, and that would be it. We were virtually on our own.

Mike Pinksaw, *Specialist Four, U.S. Army, 60th Land Clearing Company, 62nd Engineering Battalion, 20th Engineering Brigade, Long Binh, Bien Hoa, Lai Khe, 1968–69*

I was a 62E20, heavy equipment operator. My job, and the job of guys in my battalion, was to level and clear jungles to prevent enemy sanctuaries.

When I first got to my company, I thought I'd be operating a D-7 bulldozer, like I learned to operate back in the States. No way! They just put me on all these details instead. You know, filling sandbags and the whole bit. Finally, they put me on what we called a 290; it was like a big-wheeled tractor, but nothing compared to a D-7. It was used to push soil.

You'd get behind an earth scraper and just push dirt around all day. Eventually, I did get to operate the D-7s.

A few months later our battalion was broken up, and we became the only land-clearing battalion with such heavy equipment in the entire country.

Michael Toner Farrell, *Specialist Five, U.S. Army, 544th Replacement Company, Cam Ranh Bay, 1969–70*

In Cam Ranh Bay I was assigned as a cook in the only mess hall on the island. I'd work in there from midnight to six A.M. with a great group of guys. Every night for KP, we were given forty new troops who had just come into Vietnam, and they helped us prepare about six thousand meals a day, which consisted of two thousand breakfasts, two thousand lunches and two thousand dinners. This went on seven days a week for my entire tour of duty.

Howard North, *Lieutenant j.g., U.S. Coast Guard, Coast Guard Squadron One, USCGC* Point Clear *(WPB 82315), An Thoi and Cat Lo, 1967–68*

Just prior to the time I had enlisted in the summer of 1965, it became apparent that there was a problem with smuggling off the coast of South Vietnam; therefore, twenty-six patrol boats were sent over. At the time, the navy didn't have such small boats to perform this type of duty. So they enlisted the coast guard.

These boats were the 82-foot class WPBs. The W stands for "coast guard" and PB stands for "patrol boat." They were steel-hulled boats with an aluminum superstructure. Prior to my arrival in-country, these boats were already in South Vietnam. They were performing in an exercise called "operation—market time." The idea was to stop the infiltration of weapons into the hands of the enemy via the coastal waterways of South Vietnam. What supposedly was happening was communist boats would leave North Vietnam and head out to international waters and then come in any place along the coast of South Vietnam, even as far around as the Gulf of Thailand down south, in order to drop off their illegal cargo of weapons.

When the winds shifted during the monsoons, the coast guard patrol boats would travel around the coast of South Vietnam and patrol in the South China Sea as far up as Cam Ranh Bay.

When I arrived in South Vietnam, I became an executive officer on one of these boats. I was the navigator, the guy who took care of the personnel records, and had a watch standing for eight hours a day. We had a crew of eleven, and sometimes a South Vietnamese liaison officer would patrol with us. Our mission was to provide gunfire support to troops on the shore, as well as search for contraband while in the waters off the coast. When searching a boat, one guy would board; I would be up in the pilothouse with an M16; either the engineer or the helmsman would stand on the bow with a shotgun.

Salvatore T. Raffa, *Airman Second Class, U.S. Air Force, 377th Security Police Squadron, Tan Son Nhut Air Base, Saigon, 1967–68*

Our unit was the sole military police force for all of Saigon. We were also responsible for flight line security at Tan Son Nhut Air Force Base, plus we had Military Assistance Command, Vietnam, 7th Air Force honor guard.

Peggy R. Zarek, *Lieutenant Commander, U.S. Navy, U.S.S.* Sanctuary *(AH-17), Coastal Waters off South Vietnam, Military Region 1, 1969–70*

The main purpose of our ship was to take care of the wounded. I was on it when we had our ten-thousandth medevac helicopter landing.

Vietnam was different from any other previous war. The helicopter

The hospital ship U.S.S. Sanctuary *AH-17. (Courtesy of Peggy R. Zarek)*

would get the wounded right out of the field, right out to our hospital ship, and land on the helo decks, all within a short period of time.

There'd be an announcement over the ship's intercom: "Stand by for helo-ops." If they were on litters, we knew they were most likely going to be intensive-care patients.

I'm not sure exactly how many medical personnel were on our ship, but I do know there were twenty-nine nurses. There were two commands on the ship: the hospital ship and the ship's company.

I was in charge of the ship's intensive-care unit. I had to make sure the patients, who were mostly marines, both sick and wounded, got the proper care they were supposed to receive. We had the equipment to treat almost any situation. For example, in the unit we had two kidney machines.

I also had to supervise the nurses under me as well as the corpsmen. We had to give classes to the corpsmen because they were just nineteen-year-old kids. Today, I can't give them enough credit, because mentally it had to be as difficult for them as it was for us.

William Sullivan, *Lieutenant Commander, U.S. Navy, Fighter Squadron 213, U.S.S.* Intrepid, *Air Wing, U.S.S.* Kitty Hawk *(CVA-63), U.S.S.* Intrepid *(CVA-11), U.S.S.* Paul Revere, *and U.S.S.* Blue Ridge, *1965–68 and 1971–72*

I was a naval flight officer serving in squadrons and as a member of ship's company aboard four different ships. All were deployed in the Western Pacific. My primary mission was to perform bombing runs over North and South Vietnam, as well as to fire air-to-ground missiles. I also flew observation runs looking for the enemy. As a forward air controller, I deployed ashore on several occasions with members of the 9th Marine Amphibious Brigade.

INCOMING

Seventy-six percent of the American troops serving in South Vietnam would experience mortar or rocket attacks at least once during their tour, and 56 percent would witness the death or wounding of a fellow soldier.*

Perhaps no other single word in South Vietnam sparked more of a reaction then when someone shouted, usually in a blood-curdling yell,

---

* John S. Bowman, *Vietnam War, Day by Day* (New York: Mallard Press, 1989), p. 202.

INCOMING! It meant the area was being shelled by the enemy. The message was understood by all: Take cover as quickly as possible. Everyone ran for the protection of sandbag bunkers strategically located throughout the compound. In these, an individual was less likely to be injured than in wooden barracks or other less protected areas. The bunkers were meant to block shrapnel, but they were not totally bombproof. A direct hit by a rocket could destroy such a fortification in an instant and kill whomever was in it.

To a much lesser extent, some soldiers used the signal *incoming* to indicate small-arms fire.

Stephen Butler, *Lance Corporal, U.S. Marine Corps, 7th Marine Combat Engineers, Da Nang, 1966–67*

It was . . . it was scary. It was the kind of thing that was just a crapshoot, and you didn't know where it was going to go. All this bullshit on television, that if you can hear 'em, they've passed you; that's all crap.

When we first got there, the Viet Cong had a bunch of old junk; but as the war went on, the stuff they threw at us got more sophisticated. Some of it was Chinese stuff.

The land missile station we had was a big target for incoming rounds.

Thomas Finn, *Specialist Four, U.S. Army, Company A, 519th Military Intelligence Battalion, 525th Military Intelligence Group, MACV-J2, Saigon, 1966–67*

I was at my center of operation for only a few days when some rounds were fired at our compound, rat-tat-tat-tat, hitting gravel on the ground about twenty feet from where a group of us were sitting. This happened right after lunch while we were minding our own business. We had no idea where it came from. It kind of startled all of us. We looked at each other, and our eyes were saying, "What was that?" Then we realized, that was it; we've just been shot at. Nobody moved—we were like frozen—there was absolutely no reaction. In all, perhaps no more than three or four rounds were fired, but it got our attention.

David Rossi, *Specialist Four, U.S. Army, 1st Infantry Division and 25th Infantry Division, Di An, Tay Ninh, and Cu Chi, 1969–70*

I had been in-country for approximately eight to nine months before I saw my first incoming rounds. We got hit with both mortars and rockets.

At that time I had been transferred to the 25th Infantry Division. I was lucky. As a medic I had no really bad cases. Most of the injuries that I treated were minor shrapnel wounds.

Ken Garthee, *Private First Class, U.S. Marine Corps, 3rd Battalion, 3rd Marines, 3rd Marine Division, Da Nang, Rock Pile, 1966–67*

When we returned from patrols, we'd be busy filling sandbags and building bunkers higher and wider to protect ourselves. Almost every night there would be some kind of contact with the VC. We'd get shot at while manning our perimeter bunkers, or worse, they would launch mortars at our position.

It seemed that during the day the Vietnamese, even the children, who happened to be in our compound—to do laundry or give haircuts—would remember where our bunkers were situated. At night, rockets would be launched on those locations.

The scariest sound was the sound of rockets whistling overhead, not knowing where they were coming from or where they were going to land and explode. Even to this day, I still don't like loud noises or sudden bangs.

Mike Pinksaw, *Specialist Four, U.S. Army, 60th Land Clearing Company, 62nd Engineering Battalion, 20th Engineering Brigade, Long Binh, Bien Hoa, Lai Khe, 1968–69*

One day I was climbing on the deuce-and-a-half to get my weapon, and all of a sudden, I heard this sound, and I looked in that direction and heard a loud explosion. I jumped off the truck and crawled into the nearest bunker. They threw four rockets at us that night. The following day, we located the weapons in the jungle. We captured a number of unexploded rockets and mortars.

Michael Toner Farrell, *Specialist Five, U.S. Army, 544th Replacement Company, Cam Ranh Bay, 1969–70*

There were five guys in my room one night, and all of a sudden we heard the first explosion. I remember there was this explosion first, but no whistle. Next you heard the whistles and the rounds started hitting and exploding in the distance. Then the sirens went off for the alert. It was terrible. I thought to myself, "This is it. I'm dying!" I mean, I had been there for six months, and nothing like this had happened to me before. Fortunately, no one got hurt in the whole incident.

I was stationed in a tower during the attack and had a grenade launcher for protection. Looking across the water, I could see red tracers coming across the water. The sky was literally red with tracers.

Being naive, I said to the guy next to me, "What are those red things in the sky?"

"Those are tracer bullets, and in between each one are six more bullets."

In the eighteen months that I was in Vietnam, we were attacked only four times. Some were mortars and rockets only; some were incoming rounds taken after enemy sapper attacks. Unfortunately, in one incident, sappers blew up part of the hospital and caused considerable damage to the facility. I don't remember what the extent of the injuries were, but there must have been some.

Dick Turner, *Boatswain's Mate Third Class, U.S. Navy, River Assault Squadron 15, River Division 152, Task Force 117, Dong Tam and My Tho, 1968–69*

It was scary. We were in Dong Tam with the boat for a yard overhaul to have the engine changed. The boat was also lifted up and put on a barge so we could paint it. That night the place was overrun. It was mortared and the VC blew up the ammo dump. I've never seen so many explosions! They hit the bunker full of white phosphorus, which we called willie peter. Once that gets on you it really does a job. It's like napalm. It has a jelly-like consistency. It blew up tin buildings and leveled them; I mean, it was a mess. There were a lot of casualties that night from all the explosions.

Salvatore T. Raffa, *Airman Second Class, U.S. Air Force, 377th Security Police Squadron, Tan Son Nhut Air Base, Saigon, 1967–68*

Horrible, that's what it felt like being in a rocket attack. I remember guys telling me, "Worry about the ones you don't hear"; and, in a way, I guess they were right. 'Til this day, I still can remember how they sounded. It was like a real loud slap, and the ground and everything else would shake.

One night I was all alone in my barracks. I lived right next to the base exchange, a huge complex with pallets and pallets of every commodity imaginable. They had everything there. Anyway, a rocket came in and hit a pallet loaded with cans of aerosol shaving cream, which started to explode. To me it sounded like gunfire. I jumped under my bunk with my M16 on full automatic, just shooting at nothing.

A sergeant ran into my room and yelled, "Raffa, what the hell are you doing?"

When I calmed down, he told me what was going on. To me it sounded like an entire Viet Cong unit was coming through.

Betsy Wylie, *Lieutenant, U.S. Navy, Management Information Center, Headquarters, Naval Forces Vietnam (NAVFORV), Saigon, 1967–68*

When I was finishing up my tour, my roommate was a marine corps officer who had recently arrived in-country. It was just after we had turned the lights out, about ten-thirty at night, when we heard a couple of errant mortar rounds exploding. One of them came very, very close to our quarters. Someone later told me it had landed in the backyard where we were living. Our beds were on opposite sides of this pretty decent-sized room. I had barely been awakened by the first sound; after the second one hit, Elaine made the leap from her bed to the edge of my bed, and I don't think her feet ever touched the ground. She was just sitting there, very straight and very proper, with her hands folded in her lap, looking at me lying there, and she said, "Now Betsy, what do you think that was?"

WHO'S THE ENEMY?

In Vietnam, the enemy could be anyone. An extremely small percentage from one's own side was suspect, but not in the way one might envision. They weren't spies. They were simply immature young men who either had too much to drink, fell victim to drugs, or just couldn't handle the stress of being in a combat zone. Some were already serious delinquents before they became part of the military.

As for the Vietnamese nationals, it was nearly impossible to determine where their allegiance lay. In the daytime, they could be seen working as common laborers on American compounds, performing such menial jobs as filling sandbags, cleaning latrines, or swabbing floors in the mess; but at night, they could become the enemy, the Viet Cong, lobbing mortar rounds into your compound. It wasn't unusual for an American soldier to wake up in the morning to find that the Vietnamese civilian he or she used to see regularly on the compound was killed the night before in a Viet Cong sapper attack. Not surprisingly, the Viet

Cong weren't always men. Take, for example, this account by a marine captain:

> They all looked alike. They all dressed alike. They were all Vietnamese. Some of them were Viet Cong. Here's a woman of twenty-two or twenty-three. She is pregnant, and she tells an interrogator that her husband works in Da Nang and isn't a Viet Cong. But she watches your men walk down a trail and get killed or wounded by a booby trap. She knows the booby trap is there, but she doesn't warn them. Maybe she planted it herself. It wasn't like the San Francisco Forty-Niners on one side of the field and the Cincinnati Bengals on the other. The enemy was all around you.*

Thomas Finn, *Specialist Four, U.S. Army, Company A, 519th Military Intelligence Battalion, 525th Military Intelligence Group, MACV-J2, Saigon, 1966–67*

I spent both my twenty-first and twenty-second birthdays in South Vietnam. I had only been in-country for a couple of days when I celebrated my twenty-first birthday on June 11, 1966. At the time, I was situated at the Parker Compound in Gia Dinh, near the Binh Loi Bridge. Just outside the compound gates was a building we called the Two Story. The building got its name because it was the only structure in the area that had two levels. The Two Story was nothing more than a local bar for the Vietnamese and an occasional group of American soldiers out on a frolic.

On Saturday, June 16, 1966, it was to be our first off-post trip. As an excuse to have a beer or two, the boys chose my birthday as a reason to celebrate. First we had a few beers at the enlisted club in order to build up our courage. After downing a few, we were brave enough to make our first excursion outside the front gates and into the jungle, as we called it at the time. It was approximately ten P.M. and curfew was set for eleven P.M. Because we were already close to curfew, we had time for only one quick beer before we had to make it back to the compound. We figured we had enough time.

Heading out the compound and toward the Two Story, we said good-bye to a private and the sergeant-of-the-guard, who were stationed that

---

* Stanley Karnow, *Vietnam: A History* (New York: Viking Press, 1983), p. 467.

evening at the guard shack. As we walked up the street, everything seemed quiet and eerie. I was certain my heart was beating so loud that it could be heard a mile away. Fearing the worst, we kept looking off the side of the road into the jungle to see if we could see the Viet Cong looking at us. We all felt they surely must be. At least on one occasion, I thought I'd never see the light of day. I was convinced the others felt the same.

As we crossed the halfway point, approximately two hundred yards away from the main gate, what could be considered as the point of no return, I really became apprehensive. I said to myself, "Do I really want to have a birthday beer this bad?" As we got closer and closer, it became more and more eerie. The road, which was narrow and dark, made it feel even worse. When we finally arrived at the front door, we all breathed a sigh of relief. We bellied-up to the bar and each of us ordered a beer from the Vietnamese bartender.

The Two Story was an extremely small house by our stateside standards. It had one or two rooms downstairs and maybe one room upstairs, which was most typical for the Gia Dinh area. As I remember it today, I couldn't see into the corners of the room because of the darkness. I did, however, see a few Vietnamese in the bar, also having a beer. Overhead, I observed a slow-moving, Casablanca-type paddle fan, which wasn't very effective, just moving the hot air from one side of the room to the other.

Besides the bartender and a few Vietnamese customers, there were two Vietnamese barmaids dressed in their country's native dress, the *ao dai*. The *ao dai* had a high collar with a long, brightly colored gown made of silk and was usually worn with white or black slacks. I still think these very petite women in their *ao dais* looked extremely beautiful.

In the background, we could hear Vietnamese music. The music was very high-pitched. We also detected what was to become for us the ever-present smell of *nuoc-mam*.

Although I was the new guy on the block, I felt like I quickly fit in. Standing next to me, my friends seemed to be enjoying themselves. The girls were just starting to tell us about Saigon Tea, an extremely watered-down, overpriced Vietnamese alcoholic drink. I hadn't a clue what any of them were talking about. Suddenly, the calm of the night was broken by the distinct sound of automatic rifle fire, *rat-ta-tat, rat-ta-tat, rat-ta-tat*, coming from the direction of our compound. It's been nearly thirty years since that night, but I can still remember everything going on in slow motion, just like it was yesterday. Both we and the Vietnamese kind of froze in place, each asking one another what they thought was going on. The Vietnamese kept saying over and over that it was the VC, the VC, the VC. If I had thought my heart was pounding before, it really was pounding now. It seemed like a terrifyingly long period of time, when in actuality, from the first shots fired to the final sound of a single shot, less than a minute had elapsed. We found out later that twenty rounds from an American-made M14 rifle were expended.

It now dawned on us that we were all unarmed. Between us, we didn't even have a pocket knife. Within seconds, we decided to get back PDQ to our own lines, going back in the direction we had previously traversed less than an hour earlier. With the Vietnamese in the lead (for some unknown reason they wanted to go back to the compound with us), we made our way out the back door of the bar. Doing a low crawl, we paralleled the road about a hundred feet in from where we previously walked, going in the direction of the gate. We came to a small opening near the road. As we lay on the ground, we could see the compound and gate all lit up like high noon. By this time, there was a considerable amount of commotion going on. When we saw the MPs, we decided to make a run for it. At about the same time, the Vietnamese turned an about-face and hightailed it back to the bar. They must have surmised what was up faster than we did.

We still were under the misconception that the compound had been attacked by the VC. As we got closer to the gate, we could see the sergeant-of-the-guard. He was lying dead on the ground. We all but had to step over him to get inside the compound. Those at the gate never asked us where we were, even though it was apparent that we were past the curfew. Quickly, we hustled back into the safety of our compound.

Once inside, I turned around and saw another sergeant leaning against the guard shack. It was obvious that he had also been wounded. In the distance I could see a private looking really pale as he was being surrounded by MPs and officers. We asked what had happened. After a few minutes of discussion with the MPs, we got to the bottom of the story. The wounded sergeant, who had been drinking heavily, had wanted to go to the bar for one last drink that night. The sergeant of the guard said to him, "You've had too much to drink tonight, so go back to your bunk and sleep it off." Not liking the answer, the drunken sergeant went back to his bunk and got his M14, with a magazine clip of twenty rounds, and proceeded to go back outside. Undetected, he came within a few feet of the guard shack where the sergeant-of-the-guard and the private were standing watch. He then pointed the gun at the sergeant-of-the-guard and nearly emptied the entire clip into him, killing him instantly. The private immediately swung around and demanded that he drop his weapon.

The sergeant said, "If I drop the gun, you'll kill me."

The private replied, "If you don't let it go, I'll kill you."

The drunken sergeant went to jerk the rifle away, and it accidentally discharged. The drunk was wounded in the arm and leg simultaneously from the same round.

After a brief period of time, the drunken sergeant, now under MP custody, was taken for medical treatment. The shaken-up private was taken to the 525th Headquarters, just up the street from where the incident happened, where he was questioned all night about the unfortunate happening.

After all the pandemonium died down, everyone was told to hit their bunks. Well, I for one didn't get much sleep that night. As for the drunken sergeant, he was taken under guard to Tan Son Nhut Air Base and within a few months was tried for the crime.

The prosecution in its closing argument said that the sergeant had "snuffed out the life of an innocent soldier in a cold-blooded act of animal cunning." The sergeant was found guilty, sentenced to life imprisonment, and eventually ended up at Fort Leavenworth, a federal prison in Kansas.

For me, the memory of that night will always remain crystal-clear in my mind. Sometimes it seems like it just happened yesterday.

The following evening, I pulled guard duty on the back tower. I thought about the fact that it could have been me pulling guard duty the night before. Alphabetically, I missed the assignment by one day. Even though I got very little sleep the night before, I don't think my eyelids closed once that entire night while pulling guard.

Oh yeah! As for going out with the boys for my birthday, I'm still not crazy about it, even today.

Salvatore T. Raffa, Airman Second Class, U.S. Air Force, 377th Security Police Squadron, Tan Son Nhut Air Base, Saigon, 1967–68

One of the Vietnamese barbers that used to cut our hair was found on our perimeter one night. During the day, he cut the hair of American soldiers, but at night he was a Viet Cong sapper. You never knew whom to trust.

Dick Turner, *Boatswain's Mate Third Class, U.S. Navy, River Assault Squadron 15, River Division 152, Task Force 117, Dong Tam and My Tho, 1968–69*

I used to call the Vietnamese farmers by day, soldiers at night. You used to see them out in the daytime, and you knew damn well they were the enemy; that they were VC. At night, many of the civilians became soldiers and wore the black pajamas and the whole works. It seemed like they were so heavily infiltrated into the area of South Vietnam that I was in that it was probably impossible to get them out of there.

Bill McCollum, *Sergeant, U.S. Army, 173rd Airborne Brigade, Charlie Company, 4th Battalion, 503rd Infantry, LZ-English, 1969–71*

In terms of determining who the enemy was, or finding him for that matter, you normally didn't think about that because he usually found you first. I've got to give them credit. They were smart unless you caught them off-balance. They could sit there forever. You've got to remember that we were in their backyard. They'd just sit there and wait and smell you approaching. Those snipers could just spoil your whole day!

When we went down into the valley, it took maybe twelve days to clear the area we were going to work in. In those twelve days, we lost ten guys because of one sniper. He didn't give a shit if he killed you, he just wanted to hit somebody, and in this way he'd disrupt the entire mission for that day. It was impossible to tell where he was hiding. You know, I don't think we ever got him; we may have, but I know for the first twelve days we didn't.

During the same time, we also lost two guys because of booby traps. They were investigating a pagoda-type building. One guy walked through the front door, hit a trip wire, and set off an explosion. The other guy, hearing the explosion, went in the back door of the same structure, and *boom*, the same thing happened to him. You would have thought the other guy would have learned.

Michael Toner Farrell, *Specialist Five, U.S. Army, 544th Replacement Company, Cam Ranh Bay, 1969–70*

It had been over a year since I had been in Vietnam, and I had just come back from my R & R. I was heading toward my barracks. No one had told me there was a different kind of war going on, the one between the lifers and my own kind, the low-level enlisted soldiers. Anyway, the new supply sergeant called me over and shook my hand as we walked down the hallway to my barracks. He invited me to his barracks, which was in an adjacent building, to have a beer with him in his room.

As I walked in, he turned off the lights and said to me, "You're f—in' dead!"

I suppose that since they hadn't won the war on drugs while I was gone, I was again considered Public Enemy Number One. He started to beat the shit out of me. I just screamed for help because this guy was so much bigger than I. My friend Dan, who was also a large and well-proportioned guy, knocked the door down. I mean he literally kicked the door right in to rescue me. We called the MPs, but we initially got in trouble for calling them without going through the proper chain of command. Everything was eventually swept under the rug. From then on, I knew I had to be on constant alert.

Thomas Finn, *Specialist Four, U.S. Army, Company A, 519th Military Intelligence Battalion, 525th Military Intelligence Group, MACV-J2, Saigon, 1966–67*

Next to our compound was a Vietnamese laundry operated by a Vietnamese gentleman who kept a low profile and quiet demeanor. My clothes were cleaned by him and his staff regularly. Amazingly, he proved to be an intelligence officer of the NVA. He held the rank of colonel. I had already left Vietnam by the time his cover was discovered. His allegiance to the NVA was actually discovered during the Tet Offensive. His laundry helpers were also proven to be either NVA or VC. I can't remember if he or any of his men were captured or killed.

Although we had no clue at the time, our compound was probably one of the safest from mortar and rocket attacks because if we were fired upon, his building, being adjacent to ours, could have also been severely damaged. What was incredible, however, was that this laundry was a major intelligence center for the enemy. It had survived for more than a year, right next door to our intelligence unit. Here we were, an American intelligence unit, and we didn't even know the enemy was our immediate neighbor.

Doug Johnson, *Specialist Four, U.S. Army, 25th Infantry Division, 2nd Battalion, 12th Infantry, 1968*

The enemy had many faces, but most often, he had no face at all. The battle lines shifted from day to day, perhaps even hour to hour, with no clear beginning and no end. After that first experience of being shot at, I never again felt secure or safe, and any illusion of immortality I had was replaced by terrifying feelings of vulnerability and mortality. For the first time, I realized that there was indeed a war going on, and there was an enemy that was out to kill me.

I thought that the enemy was a very disciplined, well-trained, fanatical, resourceful, and motivated group of soldiers. I would attribute this to the fact that they, unlike the American soldiers, had a clear sense of mission and were willing to die for a cause in which they truly believed. To me, the VC and NVA had a very different view of the value of life and had what seemed to be a rather cavalier attitude toward death.

I vividly remember that within a week or two of arriving in-country, while I was still in the base camp at Cu Chi, there had been an attack on one part of the perimeter. The morning light revealed that one of the dead enemy soldiers on the wire was a Vietnamese man who had been a barber in the base camp. This was an early lesson to me that this was a war without any distinguishable battle lines, and we didn't know who was really the enemy. It also demonstrated to me that the VC had no problem biting the hand that fed them. At any rate, some of the guys in my unit went down to the wire and took some Polaroids of this dead VC barber. I considered going with them, but decided that, being new in-country, I would probably have plenty of opportunities to see dead VC. The rather gruesome photos that I was later shown demonstrated that the barber's hand had been blown off and was lying near him on the ground. It was obvious that these pictures had been posed, as a cigarette had been unceremoniously placed in his cold lips in what I am sure was an attempt to mock and dishonor him. I was quite surprised that I was not particularly upset or sickened by these photos.

As my tour of duty continued, I had the opportunity to witness other wounded or dead enemy soldiers. I must admit that as time progressed, I

THE ENEMY IN YOUR HANDS

AS A MEMBER OF THE US MILITARY FORCES, YOU WILL COMPLY WITH THE GENEVA PRISONER OF WAR CONVENTIONS OF 1949 TO WHICH YOUR COUNTRY ADHERES. UNDER THESE CONVENTIONS :

YOU CAN AND WILL

DISARM YOUR PRISONER
IMMEDIATELY SEARCH HIM THOROUGHLY
REQUIRE HIM TO BE SILENT
SEGREGATE HIM FROM OTHER PRISONERS
GUARD HIM CAREFULLY
TAKE HIM TO THE PLACE DESIGNATED BY YOUR COMMANDER

YOU CANNOT AND MUST NOT

MISTREAT YOUR PRISONER
HUMILIATE OR DEGRADE HIM
TAKE ANY OF HIS PERSONAL EFFECTS WHICH DO NOT HAVE SIGNIFICANT MILITARY VALUE
REFUSE HIM MEDICAL TREATMENT IF REQUIRED AND AVAILABLE

ALWAYS TREAT YOUR PRISONER HUMANELY

A Geneva Convention card, which was given to all troops serving in Vietnam. (Property of Frank Grzyb)

became numb to this spectacle and no longer viewed them as part of humanity. I realized after the war that this is one of the many troubling and ugly realities of war. We learn to dehumanize our enemy over time and instead of seeing a fellow human being with family and loved ones, we see nothing more than a wax figure, a cipher, devoid of humanity and no loss to the human race.

FIRST EXPERIENCES IN COMBAT

There aren't too many veterans who don't remember their first combat experience, whether it was brief or lengthy, tolerable or intolerable, scary or not. Later combat experiences were sometimes worse, but the first one was never forgotten. In some cases, an individual who experienced enemy fire for that first time was almost dumbfounded. Some froze in shock, while others were in a state of absolute disbelief.

"This really can't be happening to me!" or "What do I do now?" were often the first thoughts that came to mind while being shot at. It was a time of confusion, to say the least. It was possible to go through live fire exercises in basic and advanced training without being nervous or apprehensive, but once you realized someone was actually trying to kill you, a new ingredient was added to the formula—pure, unadulterated fear.

Regurgitation of breakfast, lunch, or dinner and a loss of bowel control were more frequent than one could imagine. No one really wanted to admit it or talk about it. Fear did amazing things to the mind and body during such stressful and traumatic situations.

Rob Roche, *Sergeant, U.S. Army, 101st Airborne Division, Da Nang, 1967–69*

My first combat experience is very easy to remember. When I left Ben Hoa, we were flown up to Da Nang, and that became my home base. At the time, it was all tents, not the wooden buildings you would see later in the war. It was just tents. I remember seeing helicopters flying in and out and sandbag bunkers all over the place.

I reported to the CO for my assignment. Because my MOS was supply clerk, I thought that was what I was going to do in Vietnam. However, they had guys in the supply tent that had already been wounded in combat. In the 101st, after you were hit twice, if you recovered well enough to stay in-country, you were usually reassigned to the rear.

The CO said to me, "You're going out into the field. You've got to go and pack your backpack; get your canteens, get your rifle and ammunition and the rest."

So I did all that. Remember, back in the States, I wasn't infantry trained, even though I did go to jump school. I was a little out of my element.

After I was all suited up and ready to go out into the jungle to meet my new outfit, I and the other guys walked down to the landing zone. A helicopter picked us up and flew us out into the jungle. As I remember it, there were a bunch of helicopters loaded with soldiers. What happened next was something I'll never forget. The area we were about to land in was a hot landing zone. In other words, the enemy was present. I could see red smoke from American smoke grenades on the ground, which marked the landing zone for the helicopters.* When we came in, we were under immediate fire. The helicopter hovered about ten feet off the ground, and we had to jump because the pilots wanted to get out of there. We jumped out and lay in the grass. The helicopter quickly took off. Now we could hear gunshots going off, the pop-pop sound of rifles, but we just didn't know which way to crawl. I mean, we were seriously disoriented. Finally, a sergeant crawled out and got us and brought us in.

As compared to other firefights that I had been in, that one wasn't all that bad, but it was the first, and you always remember your first real experience under fire. You're brand-new, and you don't know what the hell is going on. I'm sure you've heard the story that when you're under combat for the first time you almost shit in your pants. Well, let me tell you, you almost do!

All this happened in less than two weeks from the time I first arrived in-country.

Stephen Butler, *Lance Corporal, U.S. Marine Corps, 7th Marine Combat Engineers, Da Nang, 1966–67*

We were about twenty-five to thirty miles south of Da Nang at a water point off Highway 1. I and a buddy of mine had two jobs out there. The first was to purify water, and the second was to sweep roads with the infantry in a really hot area. The enemy was well entrenched there, with Russian advisors, hard-core NVA, and Viet Cong. They also had an R & R

---

* Green smoke grenades were used to signify a cold (safe) LZ.

center in the immediate vicinity. I mean, it was a strong position for them. This is where my first encounter was.

They came to our hill one night. We had two platoons of grunts with us who helped us sweep roads, while we had a company of grunts south of our position. These guys ran patrols. Basically, the grunts took control of the situation and got us out of the picture. We were relegated to our tents. I was terrified. It left me with vivid impressions of what combat really was all about, even though I was in a tent. Also, it was the first time I saw a claymore mine go off. The flash was so bright that I actually saw the silhouette of a marine in the distance through the canvas fabric. Then the enemy really started kicking our butt. They came at us from different sides of the hill. We had these land radar and surface-to-air missile guys, who were a bunch of draftees, as well as college graduates. They kind of stuck to themselves. Anyway, with the help of these guys and the grunts, we made it through the night. Basically, all we did was hide.

Dick Turner, *Boatswain's Mate Third Class, U.S. Navy, River Assault Squadron 15, River Division 152, Task Force 117, Dong Tam and My Tho, 1968–69*

My first combat experience was in an area called Twin Rivers, right near Dong Tam in the Can Tho Province. It was actually a three-boat operation. At the time, we supported the 2nd Brigade, 9th Infantry Division. We were going to insert these groups of soldiers and then run gunfire support for 'em. Well, we got in there and one of the boats, right off the bat, took a B-40 hit, right in the side—a couple of guys were wounded. It got to be more than three boats could handle, so they pulled us out of there real quick.

The next time we went back there, it was a thirty-five boat operation. We really went in there and kicked butt. I mean, we cleaned the area up, but it was scary, especially the bullets going back and forth. At night you could see the tracer rounds going every which way. It scared the livin' shit out of me, you know. It's hard for me to think about it 'cause it brings up a lot of . . . .

Ken Garthee, *Private First Class, U.S. Marine Corps, 3rd Battalion, 3rd Marines, 3rd Marine Division, Da Nang, Rock Pile, 1966–67*

We were on patrol in the middle of the day, looking for the VC, walking along the bank of a rice paddy. We were in the middle of nowhere. Suddenly, I heard several cracking sounds, like the shooting of a rifle. The sounds were coming from a tree line in the distance. Dirt was being kicked up by the rounds hitting just in front of us. It was the first time I experienced being shot at. Like an inexperienced marine, I just stood there looking for the location of the enemy. As my squad leader was lying there returning fire, someone pulled on my sleeve.

"Get down and shoot back," demanded my sergeant.

I did get down, but I didn't shoot back, because I didn't see anything to shoot at. All my squad was shooting at the tree line in the distance, but I still didn't see anything. I never returned a shot. Fortunately, no one was injured in the incident, and we were able to continue on our way.

My sergeant later said to me, "Shoot back the next time."

And I thought to myself, "But at what?"*

Doug Johnson, *Specialist Four, U.S. Army, 25th Infantry Division, 2nd Battalion, 12th Infantry, 1968*

When I arrived in-country, I was assigned to Headquarters Company, 2nd Battalion, 12th Infantry (known as the White Warriors), which was attached to the 25th Infantry Division, with its base camp in Cu Chi. It was a huge base camp and was said to be very well protected and defended. Unfortunately, this myth was to be exploded soon after my arrival in-country.

About three weeks after I arrived at Cu Chi, I was sent out to a place called Fire Support Base Stuart. I didn't know at first why I had been sent out to Stuart but soon found out that there were some intelligence reports suggesting that the Viet Cong and the North Vietnamese Army were mounting some kind of offensive, and they were going to try to overrun FSB Stuart. We were sent out to help beef up the defenses. Being a FNG and not knowing shit from shinola, I was not overly thrilled about this assignment. FSB Stuart was a rather ominous place because it was literally set up in a cemetery. There were huge headstones in the middle of the encampment, most likely left over from when the French were there. I can't begin to describe to you how spooky it was to be surrounded by these huge monuments to death as they cast their eerie shadow over our camp in the dead of night. On the outskirts of Stuart was the city of Trang Bang, which was a known Viet

---

* All too often, combat in Vietnam meant shooting at shadows or ghosts. That is to say, you never actually saw what you were shooting at. When you took fire during the daytime, you returned it by shooting into a suspected enemy position. At night there was no way you could see what you were shooting at unless you used a starlight scope.

Cong stronghold. Trang Bang was the kind of city that you would not want to visit alone during the day and definitely not at night.

When I arrived at Stuart, I looked around and decided that I wanted to move into a big bunker at the corner of the camp with a rather sizable observation tower on the top. After making my choice of living accommodations, I was horrified to discover that the sandbags on the bunker had huge chunks missing, and several of the sandbags looked like Swiss cheese. Upon further inquiry, I learned that my new home had been rather regularly hit by increasingly accurate rocket and mortar fire. In fact, within the past few days, a soldier had been seriously wounded in the doorway of the bunker. It seems that this bunker was one of the enemy's favorite targets, and having successfully zeroed in on the co-ordinates, they engaged in some really accurate target practice.

One of the very first nights at FSB Stuart, while I was pulling guard, we began receiving sniper fire. It was the first time I had actually been shot at, and I remember vividly the tracer bullets from the sniper rounds passing over my head and perilously close to my position as the sniper or snipers attempted to zero in on our positions. Despite the training I had received prior to arriving in-country, my first reaction was panic, and I froze in place. Just as I was moving to safety, I witnessed one of my friends dive headlong off the top of the bunker and hit the ground with a thud. His eyes were as big as saucers, and he was speaking in some incomprehensible language—perhaps the language of sheer and utter terror. It wasn't long before the shooting stopped, but at the time, it was one of those slow-motion events that seemed to last a whole lot longer than it actually did. For the remainder of the evening, I seemed to be fixated by the Bao Dai Temple, not far off in the distance from our perimeter. It appeared like someone was walking throughout the temple with a candle or a flashlight, and I would catch the reflection every time the light passed by a window. I wondered if our sniper was using this temple as his sniper's perch or perhaps just an area of operation.

Within a day or two of my encounter with the sniper, I was again pulling guard at FSB Stuart. Suddenly my radio was buzzing with news that our radar was picking up huge movements of personnel near our perimeter. I became convinced that this was the anticipated attack by the VC and NVA that our intelligence had suspected was going to occur, and that tonight was going to be my version of D-Day. Preparing mentally for the worst, I listened intently to the reports that this large force was moving closer to our camp. At one point during this vigil, our artillery and mortars opened up with a steady barrage of rounds, hoping to discourage our visitors. I recall that we were told to get down as the barrage picked up, and the artillery and mortar barrels were lowered to fire almost directly outside our perimeter. As I squatted low in my position, I could hear the fleshettes from our mortar rounds whizzing through the air and I recall that this was one of many occasions when I was glad to be on our side. Almost miraculously, the radio reports indicated that the movement approaching our perimeter was disappearing, and we all waited in relieved but tense silence. For what seemed like an eternity, the only chatter on the radio was the periodic requests by the tactical operations center to report from our various positions throughout the camp *if sitrap* (situation report) *negative, break squelch twice,* to which I dutifully responded several times. At about three or four o'clock in the morning, a report came over the radio that *Charlie Charlie* (Cu Chi) had been overrun. It seemed incomprehensible to me that a base camp as large as Cu Chi had been overrun, but that's exactly what had happened. Apparently, the movement we had picked up that evening was part of a enemy force headed to attack Cu Chi. The wire had been cut and many throats had been slashed on the perimeter, and sapper squads went in and blew up loads of helicopters and killed many of our soldiers.

I was sent back to Cu Chi with the troops from FSB Stuart to help locate any VC or NVA sappers who had not been killed or captured. I must admit that I didn't rest comfortably until I was sure that the base camp was safe. It was ironic that while I awaited what I thought would be a fierce battle at the little outpost of FSB Stuart, Charlie decided to attack the large, heavily defended base camp at Cu Chi. It taught me a lot about being at the wrong place at the right time and the fickle finger of fate. It also gave me my first glimpse of the enemy we were up against—well-trained, disciplined, fanatical, and ready to die for a cause in which they believed. I learned that the sappers had entered Cu Chi with only the explosive sapper charges on their backs and no weapons. They knew they were not coming back, and it made a real impression on me that they were willing to risk it all in defense of their beliefs. I began to realize that I was in this war for the long haul and our enemy was definitely playing for keeps.

Bill McCollum, *Sergeant, U.S. Army, 173rd Airborne Brigade, Charlie Company, 4th Battalion, 503rd Infantry, LZ-English, 1969–71*

Before I'd seen any real action, I was out on one of my first patrols. All the new guys got stuck in the rear of the column. We were going up the side of a hill when all of a sudden, everything kind of came to a stop.

The word filtered back: "Send that FNG up here."

The guy in front said to me, "Hey, they want you up front."

I said, "Where do I go?"

"Keep following those guys right up there."

So I started up the hill, sore from sunburn, carrying all these canteens in the heat and humidity; and it seemed like I was never going to find the point man. I saw a creek, and since I was running out of water, I dunked my canteen in the water and filled up. I treated it, took a swig, and then continued walking till I got to the point.

I said, "What's up?"

"Check this out!"

I look down, "Oh, Jesus Christ, man," I muttered under my breath, and I started throwing up. There's these two dead dinks, two of the enemy, lying in the same water I had just filled my canteen from downstream. They were VC, killed by a previous patrol and left to decompose where they had fallen. Their ears were cut off, and each had a 173rd Airborne patch pinned to their lips.

The point man looked at me and said, "So what do you think about this country?"

I couldn't answer. I was still throwing up.

I don't know if you could consider this next story a combat story or not, as the poor guy didn't have a chance. There was this guy walking down a trail in this village, and the lead element spotted him.

As usual, "Get that FNG up here, now," were the platoon leader's words.

As I moved up to the front, they were watching this guy, a VC, just walking toward us. All he had on were Ho Chi Minh sandals, a GI sock tied around his waist (which we opened up later and found rice in), a loincloth, and a small weapon.

Now our platoon leader whispered instructions to us, "Nobody fire until I say fire."

I was thinking, "Holy God, here we go!"

Bill McCollum with his M16 rifle. (Courtesy of Bill McCollum)

The VC got within range—perhaps more than within range; I'd say as close as fifty meters—and the next thing I heard is, "Fire!" Everybody in the squad fired on him, and I couldn't believe the amount of bullets a body could take. The guy never knew what hit him.

That night, when I was lying down, I starting thinking to myself, "I just took part in this killing." But surprisingly, it didn't seem to bother me that much. It was like, "Here we go, I'm here; that's cool!"

Afterward, the guys told me, in a way that only a GI could tell another GI, "You just got your cherry broken."

It was their way of saying that I was no longer a combat virgin.

William Sullivan, *Lieutenant Commander, U.S. Navy, Fighter Squadron 213, U.S.S.* Intrepid, *Air Wing, U.S.S.* Kitty Hawk *(CVA-63), U.S.S.* Intrepid *(CVA-11), U.S.S.* Paul Revere, *and U.S.S.* Blue Ridge, *1965–68 and 1971–72*

The first time I experienced enemy fire was on my third or fourth mission after arriving in the Tonkin Gulf for my first tour of duty. We were on a night mission when all of a sudden the sky lit up like the Fourth of July.

I said to the pilot, who had former combat experience, "Look at the fireworks."

He replied, "Those aren't fireworks; those are tracer rounds from the ground."

The effect was like what you saw on TV when Baghdad's guard was firing all those rounds in the air during the Persian Gulf War. The sky was all aglow.

In my opinion, though, the last tour was far more dangerous than the first three. Serving with the marines and being on the ground with them on at least seven missions in-country gave me a different perspective of the war and certainly gave me a deeper appreciation for the greater dangers ground soldiers face in combat.

When you're flying in an aircraft, you're very detached, and it's a very impersonal type of war for you. You're simply dropping a bomb or shooting an air-to-ground missile at the enemy. It's not the same when you're down on the ground, face-to-face with the enemy.

Howard North, *Lieutenant j.g., U.S. Coast Guard, Coast Guard Squadron One, USCGC* Point Clear *(WPB 82315), An Thoi and Cat Lo, 1967–68*

We were in the Mekong Delta near a special forces camp in a village called Song On Doc. This place was fifty to sixty miles from the nearest friendly hamlet. It was desolate! The village stunk to high heaven, as that's where they made *nuoc-mam* on a large scale. The village population was approximately one thousand natives.

Song On Doc used to get raided by the VC virtually every night. At least it seemed that way. At night, we'd end up firing our weapons into the jungle. Basically, we were the villagers' artillery support while we were anchored offshore.

I remember once, early in my tour, we were called in for artillery support. Our mortars could be fired at a somewhat limited range, and therefore, we would go closer to shore. One night we got so close that the waves were breaking over the stern of the boat. We were afraid we were going to go aground.

What scared us even more was the sparks that started to come out of our mortar tube; it looked kind of like a Roman candle. We fired, but the $64,000 question was, Where did the round hit? We had no idea. Now, we had guys on land screaming over the radio to fire more mortars. We had to do something. So one of our chiefs looks down the tube with a flashlight, but he couldn't see because it was all smoky. Finally, someone picked up the tube, which was on a pivot, and shook it to see if the supposed dud was caught there. Finally, we realized that the round had been fired out of the chamber, but we still had no clue where it had exploded.

A few weeks later, we had the same thing happen. This time we figured it out. The bottom of the mortar, near the propellant, must have gotten wet, which significantly cut down on the distance it could be fired. In fact, the rounds were landing in the water some two hundred yards out from the boat, just far enough so we never saw it hit the water at night, yet never coming close to the targets in the jungle. The VC were lucky those nights.

Speaking of lucky, that's just what I was on my boat. The whole time we were there, we never got fired at. The boat took rounds a week before I got there and when I went on R & R.

Betsy Wylie, *Lieutenant, U.S. Navy, Management Information Center, Headquarters, Naval Forces Vietnam (NAVFORV), Saigon, 1967–68*

When the Tet Offensive started, I was still at work in the office, and somebody came around and said, "If you want to get back to quarters, you better get out now." He then told us that they were going to shut down the city, which meant you couldn't travel.

Later, the admiral's aide came around; and because Vera and I were living in quarters that were considered to be in a particularly dangerous area, he said, "We don't think you should go home."

We were allowed to go back quickly to get some overnight items, and we grabbed some toothbrushes and stuff, but didn't have time to get any clean clothes. We could hear some gunfire in the background, but at the time it didn't seem any different from some of the other stuff we used to hear.

There were about ten of us that were rounded up, in effect, and we were taken to the admiral's quarters, which was a villa in another part of town. We were told that there were South Vietnamese guards all around the villa.

That night we had a very nice dinner. Of course, when it came time for bed, none of us had any nightclothes to wear. We were then assigned our various sleeping rooms, and the admiral had some extra pajamas. Now, I'm 5 feet 7½ inches, but he was 6 feet tall. So I put on these lovely silk pajamas, rolled the sleeves up six times, and the legs up six times. Before we went to bed, the aide came back and gave us our defensive assignments, should anything happen. I was supposed to go up to the second deck, where there was a balcony, and I was supposed to defend that end of the balcony. My weapon was a .45. The person assigned to the other end of the balcony was the admiral.

About two in the morning, we were rousted out of bed, and I grabbed my weapon. I got out on the balcony, and it was total darkness up there.

Then I heard from the other end of the balcony, "Betsy, can you see anything?"

And I said, "No Admiral, I can't see anything."

So we were sitting up there, peeking over the edge every once and a while to see what was going on. Every now and then, you'd hear a mortar round go off.

After about five minutes I said, "Admiral, you know, I'd give a thousand dollars to have a picture of the two of us up here like this."

Out of the darkness at the other end of the balcony came his response: "I'd give a thousand dollars for no picture."

Shortly after the Tet, MACV put out all kinds of directives, like we all had to be armed all the time and that we had to wear camouflage clothes. Up until then the male navy officers had been wearing khakis, and I had been in service dress light blue, which was a two-piece outfit with a skirt. Before that directive I wore heels and a skirt to work everyday. After, I had to wear combat boots—those things were heavier than lead.

As far as being armed, I always thought it was a very dangerous thing to arm a sailor. I mean, anything less than a .50 caliber on a front end of a destroyer is probably not a good thing to give a sailor.

Salvatore T. Raffa, *Airman Second Class, U.S. Air Force, 377th Security Police Squadron, Tan Son Nhut Air Base, Saigon, 1967–68*

It was early evening and I was on perimeter patrol in a Jeep with a .50 caliber machine gun mounted to the back. Just outside the base at Tan Son Nhut was this large bunker we called 051, and it faced Highway 1, which led into Saigon. There was this little shanty in front of the bunker, and some South Vietnamese lived there.

On January 31, 1968, at around five o'clock at night, people started visiting this house. The four air force security guards in the bunker called into Central Control that there was some activity outside the house near the bunker, and that all these people were going in the front door. The security guards were told it was the Tet Lunar New Year, and that it was to be expected for people to visit.

Salvatore Raffa holding a captured Russian-made AK47 rifle near Tan Son Nhut Air Base shortly after the Communist Tet Offensive of January 1968. (Courtesy of Salvatore Raffa)

About an hour later, the guys in the bunker called back in and said that people were still going into this house.

They were told, "No problem, just keep an eye on the house."

They said, "Okay!"

About an hour later, they reported in again, "Listen, something's going on here. There's people going into this house, but there are more going in than this house can hold."

It finally dawned on everyone what was going on. The so-called guests had to be going underground.

Of course, in our situation,you always followed the MACV Rules of Engagement. You kept watching and waiting; you could never just shoot. There were these rules we all had to follow.

The guys in the bunker were again told, "Keep an eye on it and we'll check into it."

Then a taxicab pulled up in front of the bunker, and out stepped a couple of Vietnamese (come to find out later, they were Viet Cong), who proceeded to fire a hand-held rocket into the bunker. Bunker 051 was destroyed, and three security guards in it were either killed immediately or died a short time later. One survived. That was about the time that the Viet Cong started coming through our perimeters. For us, it was the start of the Communist Tet Offensive.

When I first got to Vietnam, I was told not to worry about the perimeter around the air base because there were so many mines out there that nobody could get through. The French mined the area, and then we did the same. Well, they just came marching through. At the time, we had nine hundred troops and were considered the sole support for Tan Son Nhut Air Base. Right after the initial attack, we were told that one of the airborne divisions (the 101st or the 173rd) was coming up Highway 1 to offer support. Well, they got detained because they started to get their butts kicked, too, by the enemy.

These were nine hundred guys just like me, who really didn't have the necessary training, trying to hold off I don't know how many Viet Cong. This is how we earned our Presidential Unit Citation. We held them and held them some more. In fact, we did a pretty good job on the Viet Cong in that battle.

I can remember just getting behind the .50 caliber on the Jeep, ducking down and firing into the darkness, not knowing what or whom I was shooting at. Later on I was in a foxhole and you could see the VC in the distance. But I was no hero. I just picked up the M16, put it over my head, and fired. I might have killed twenty, I might have killed one, maybe I killed none. I didn't care, and I didn't look to see. The battle went on this way for a few days, and I would never experience combat again like that for the remainder of my tour.

I know we tried to get the guys out of the bunker, and we came close to doing it until we realized that the bodies may have been booby trapped. Initially we still weren't sure they were dead but later realized that three of them were. If we had touched them, we would have been blown away ourselves. Finally, we found someone to come in and check for booby traps on the bodies and were able to remove two of them. I don't remember how or when we got the other body out.

I can remember, not long after the firing stopped, walking by a Viet Cong who had both legs blown away. He was still alive, and as I was walking past him, he looked up and said to me in perfect English, "GI got a cigarette?" He was so doped up. All of them had to be to do what they had just done.

When it finally ended on February 2, 1968, it was determined that an estimated seven battalions of VC and NVA troops, supported by additional companies of an NVA division located in the

Bunker 051, outside Tan Son Nhut Air Base, which was overrun and destroyed by the enemy during the Tet Offensive. Three men were killed, including a close boyhood friend of the editor. (Courtesy Salvatore Raffa)

Saigon area, had taken part in the attack. Enemy losses were listed at over 950, of which 157 were counted inside the west perimeter near the air base. Our security police losses were four killed in action, three of whom were in the bunker, and at least ten who were listed as wounded.

THE UNEXPECTED HAPPENS

Life is, and will always be, unpredictable. Yet in a war zone, normal everyday happenings seemed to be magnified even more so in intensity. Physical and mental fatigue, emotional stress, lack of control, and outright fear were all contributing factors.

Sometimes soldiers received disturbing news from home and at other times individuals would be called upon to provide support in dangerous situations where they lacked properly training.

For Mike Pinksaw, it didn't take combat to trigger the unforeseen. The event Mike would have to encounter was made even worse because it was taking place back home, thousands of miles away from where he was stationed. The initial feelings of hopelessness, coupled with the urgency of the situation, must have been overwhelming. Fortunately in this instance, all worked out for the best. Early in his tour, Mike flew home to be with his family and returned to Vietnam a month later. Within a short time he, too, would experience his own life and death struggle.

As for William Sullivan, being forced into a ground combat role, something totally unfamiliar to a naval aviator, must have been his own personal hell on earth. Having little choice but to react, he quickly had to rely on his own basic survival instincts. William would survive the ordeal, only to face another harrowing experience while flying over Vietnam.

Mike Pinksaw, *Specialist Four, U.S. Army, 60th Land Clearing Company, 62nd Engineering Battalion, 20th Engineering Brigade, Long Binh, Bien Hoa, Lai Khe, 1968–69*

I got there in July. In October, when I had been in-country for only about three months, I was called out by the first sergeant.

He said, "Go to the Red Cross; they have got some information for you."

When I got there, they told me my father had had a bad heart attack, and I had to go home.

My father eventually survived. However, at the time, my family was

Mike Pinksaw with an M50 machine gun. (Courtesy of Michael Pinksaw)

concerned that he wasn't going to make it, and they wanted me home. The one thing that stuck out in my mind about this entire episode was how the Red Cross handled it.

"We'll give you some money to get you home," they said as they handed me a voucher.

I said, "What's this about?"

"So you'll pay us back when you return."

I was not very happy about this. The money was deducted as an allotment from my check every month thereafter.

I was given a thirty-day emergency leave. Upon my arrival home, I immediately went to see my father in the hospital. He was amazed when he saw me walk through the door of intensive care. By the time I was ready to go back to Vietnam, my father had been released from the hospital.

William Sullivan, *Lieutenant Commander, U.S. Navy, Fighter Squadron 213, U.S.S.* Intrepid, *Air Wing, U.S.S.* Kitty Hawk *(CVA-63), U.S.S.* Intrepid *(CVA-11), U.S.S.* Paul Revere, *and U.S.S.* Blue Ridge, *1965–68 and 1971–72*

It was during my fourth tour of duty in 1972, when I was ashore near Hue City with the marines, that this incident happened. Hue City was being threatened quite a bit by the Viet Cong, and one night we came under sapper attack. The marines, needing all the able-bodied men they could muster, decided to use me. Not being trained in ground combat, I was stationed in a trench alongside a young marine whom I had never met before. My duty was to help him load his automatic weapons.

As I was loading one of the two weapons he had, I happened to look up and saw that he was slumped over, with blood pouring from his head. So instead of just loading, I had to start shooting.

Quickly, I pulled him down off his weapon and cradled him in my arms, but it was apparent that he was already dead; the bullet had entered behind his right ear and caused a massive wound on the side of his face. That was the first time that I had been up close and personal to seeing someone killed. Like I said earlier, when you're flying, you're very detached from all that; but when you're on the ground, that's different. I thought for sure I was going to get it next. The fighting went on for another hour or at least what seemed like an hour, when three or four marines moved up the trench right next to me. I felt a little more secure after that. Occasionally, I would fire a few rounds off and duck down for cover. I can still remember the bullets hitting around me. The entire attack lasted a total of three hours.

In the morning, the toll was high. We had eleven of our guys killed and eighteen wounded.

SIX

WAR IS NOT ALL BAD

What should a man do but be merry?—Shakespeare

FRIENDS

E ARLY in the war, troops normally shipped out to South Vietnam in groups. Friendships were already established back in the States, and they usually continued during the entire tour of duty. As the war progressed, this practice became less prevalent. More and more troops were being sent to South Vietnam as individuals; and when they arrived in-country, they had to prove themselves all over again.

It was considerably easier for those serving in the rear to form friendships than it was for those in the infantry. For support troops, the probability of losing a friend to enemy fire was far less likely. In support units, forming a bond was relatively easy. This was not the case for the infantry soldier. In forming a friendship, an individual made an emotional commitment. If a soldier lost that friend in combat, it was devastating. Now he had to add grief to the arsenal of negative feelings already being shouldered.

Salvatore T. Raffa, *Airman Second Class, U.S. Air Force, 377th Security Police Squadron, Tan Son Nhut Air Base, Saigon, 1967–68*

I had a lot of really good friends there. We'd go to the airmen's club together and drink screwdrivers, which cost about fifteen or twenty cents apiece. You could down those suckers all night long at that price; but that god-awful alarm would go off all over the air base, which would warn you that rockets were coming in. I mean, you'd just sober up in a heart-beat. You'd have to run back to your barracks to get your weapon be-cause you never carried them everywhere you went.

I had a good friend over there who was from Newport, and like me, he still lives in this area. He was a member of the MACV 7th Air Force elite guard, which provided security to the headquarters where General Westmoreland and his staff were stationed.

I had a friend from Kentucky, Gary, who was my best friend while in Vietnam. Every now and then, we still talk to each other on the phone. We all had some good times over there.

Peggy R. Zarek, *Lieutenant Commander, U.S. Navy, U.S.S.* Sanctuary *(AH-17), Coastal Waters off South Vietnam, Military Region 1, 1969–70*

Our ship used to go into Subic Bay in the Philippines for upkeep every three months, and we met some guys from an aircraft carrier, the U.S.S. *Oriskany.* And in those days . . . well, women weren't normally seen on carriers. Now they're everywhere. There were three of us—me, a lieu-tenant, and a j.g. We spent twenty-eight hours on this carrier. A photogra-pher on board the *Oriskany* took pictures of us climbing aboard and at several other locations during the day. It was an experience. They had us stay in the captain's quarters, with a marine guard outside the door. Some time during the day, another ship came alongside the carrier for refueling; and because I was the senior officer of the three, they had me announce it, and you could hear it echo over the South China Sea. Afterward, we sat in on a flight briefing for pilots, and we also got to see jets landing on the car-rier deck. When our visit ended, we left the carrier by jet and were cata-pulted off the flight deck. It was quite an experience!*

I remember on St. Patrick's Day we all got together and dyed white sheets green. One of the line officers dressed up as St. Patrick, and we all stood around and sang songs. We all dressed up in green, and then went parading through the wards. Of course, the Vietnamese had no idea what we were doing; they thought we were all nuts!

The camaraderie on the ship, among the crew, was wonderful. When I came back, people asked me, "How could you stand it?" It was an ex-perience I certainly didn't want—I mean, I wanted to take care of the

---

* It must have been as much of an experience for the sailors as it was for the nurses. More than likely, the nurses' visit to the carrier was a morale builder for both.

wounded, but that war was . . . But the camaraderie was great; I never experienced it before or since.

Peggy Zarek, second from right, standing next to entertainer Martha Raye. This photograph was taken in 1970 at the Third Marine Air Wing in Da Nang. (Courtesy of Peggy R. Zarek)

Mike Pinksaw, *Specialist Four, U.S. Army, 60th Land Clearing Company, 62nd Engineering Battalion, 20th Engineering Brigade, Long Binh, Bien Hoa, Lai Khe 1968–69*

I didn't have as many friends in the construction battalion as I did with my own land-clearing battalion. We got pretty close. One of these guys lives in Warwick, and I see him occasionally.

We'd spend ten hours a day together, ripping out the jungle; and when we finished, there wasn't much to do but drink. Somehow, we always managed to get alcohol out into the field. Drinking and writing letters were our main forms of entertainment.

Doug Johnson, *Specialist Four, U.S. Army, 25th Infantry Division, 2nd Battalion, 12th Infantry, 1968*

I don't think my experience was much different from that of most GIs in that most of the time I was bored to death, and the remainder of the time I was scared to death. We spent a lot of time in base camp swapping stories about where we grew up, what we did back in the world, the things that we really missed, like certain kinds of food and of course our girlfriends, fiancées and wives. The most interesting aspect of getting to know the guys in my unit was the variety of backgrounds that were represented, not only in our unit but throughout the army. We had men from all over the United States, representing every ethnic, racial, economic, and religious background that you could possibly imagine—and probably a few I wouldn't have imagined or become familiar with without having been there. There were soldiers in the infantry with educational backgrounds that varied from elementary school dropouts to Ph.Ds. We had representatives from areas as diverse as the hills of Tennessee to the concrete jungles of New York and the barrios of Los Angeles. Vietnam was a real melting pot, and it was a good lesson in how people of such diverse experiences could work, fight, and even die together in the pursuit of a common goal.

I was always a little jealous of the guys from the south or the hills and those who had done a lot of camping and hunting when they were growing up. Somehow I felt that they were better prepared for the life and duties in Vietnam because they had had these experiences.

Stephen Butler, *Lance Corporal, U.S. Marine Corps, 7th Marine Combat Engineers, Da Nang, 1966–67*

One of the guys I ran with was a plumber from Stamford, Connecticut. He and I worked together. Then there was another guy who was a water supply man.

The marine corps is broken down into squads, platoons, and companies, same as the army. There were nine guys in my squad; four of us went to the field, while the other five stayed at battalion headquarters. Obviously, that is what they preferred to do. Staying in the battalion usually meant doing details like filling sandbags. That wasn't my idea of fun. I wanted the field.

Today, I still see one of the guys from Connecticut when he stops by my house each summer on his way to Cape Cod.

Betsy Wylie, *Lieutenant, U.S. Navy, Management Information Center, Headquarters, Naval Forces Vietnam (NAVFORV), Saigon, 1967–68*

Our normal workday lasted about eleven or twelve hours a day. We generally worked six-and-a-half or sometimes seven days a week. But what we did for local recreation was go to dinner once or twice a week—there were some very fine restaurants in Vietnam—it was usually a group thing. Three, four, or five of us would go out. There were also occasional cookouts at the bachelor officers' quarters, and we'd go to those. And then I had three or four trips to Honolulu for personnel matters. These trips usually lasted three to four days. But I was always anxious to get back, as every time one of us women went to Hawaii, we usually went with a shopping list of personal items for the others. So we'd bring back a pair of stockings or a blouse another women wanted from the Sears catalog, or whatever it was. While the PX made an effort to stock basic items for the few American women that were there—like those in the Red Cross and the USO, who were so very necessary—a lot of the stuff used to disappear before it got to the shelves. You could tell it had come in because you'd find it on the sidewalks from the local vendors.*

Howard North, *Lieutenant j.g., U.S. Coast Guard, Coast Guard Squadron One, USCGC* Point Clear *(WPB 82315), An Thoi and Cat Lo, 1967–68*

On the boat, we were eleven guys who were squeezed into an area not much bigger than the average living room. It was a sleeping area, a dining area, and anything else you could think of. We all became real tight, like a family.

The first-class quarters were right off the mess deck. Three guys lived in an area about as big as an average picture window. There were three bunks high. The officers lived in the cabin. It was relatively spacious compared to other quarters on the boat, yet still small by anyone's standards. There were four bunks located here. White phosphorous mortar rounds, which were used to mark a location or burn an area, were stored in the cabin with us. They'd melt in the heat, which would make them out-of-true, so they were kept in an air-conditioned area—our cabin.

William Sullivan, *Lieutenant Commander, U.S. Navy, Fighter Squadron 213, U.S.S.* Intrepid, *Air Wing, U.S.S.* Kitty Hawk *(CVA-63), U.S.S.* Intrepid *(CVA-11), U.S.S.* Paul Revere, *and U.S.S.* Blue Ridge, *1965–68 and 1971–72*

We were in Fighter Squadron 213, which was called the Black Lions, and it was a unique group. We had won the Aviation Safety Award and

---

* The black market was a thriving business. Better-tasting beers and more popular brands of cigarettes were found more frequently in the Vietnamese markets than in the PXs.

the Aviation Efficiency Award. We thought we were the "best in the west," and our skipper had encouraged that camaraderie and esprit de corps by having us wear black T-shirts with our tan flight suits, fancy leather cowboy holsters for our pistols, and helmets which were painted bright orange with black lines on the front. We thought we were a special group, and we were very close.

William Sullivan (standing directly below the aircraft star) when he was a member of the Black Lions squadron. (Courtesy of William Sullivan)

Bill McCollum, *Sergeant, U.S. Army, 173rd Airborne Brigade, Charlie Company, 4th Battalion, 503rd Infantry, LZ-English, 1969–71*

For the first six months, I stayed close to the guys; however, when my friend Ralph got killed and a few guys got wounded and had to leave the field, it was different. When Ralph got killed, it really bothered me. Matter of fact, it'll be twenty-seven years tomorrow since his death. It's difficult to get close to someone again after seeing your best friend get killed.

BEER, CIGARETTES, AND OTHER VICES

Everything in Vietnam was cheap—wine, women, and song—not to mention cigarettes and drugs. Staying alive to enjoy these vices on a regular basis (for those who indulged) was an altogether different concern.

Liquor and cigarettes were easily obtainable at the local PX, but not always the brand names one desired. Some unscrupulous supply sergeants and other black-market profiteers diverted the more popular brands to other locations, or for that matter, to the Vietnamese, who sold it back to the American troops at exorbitant prices. Coke, which sold for ten cents a can in base camp, cost a dollar when purchased from a local villager.

Marijuana could be found on every street corner and in every hamlet or city in Vietnam, sold by Vietnamese as varied as an aged *papa-san* or *mama-san* to a child no older than eight. Joints of marijuana were as commonplace as soft drinks and cost almost as little.

Prostitutes were usually abundant on street corners. It was nothing to see a prostitute peddling her wares for several hours and then later see the same individual setting up an altar near her hooch in order to pray to Buddha. The practice of a woman selling her body was frowned upon by the Vietnamese, but for some women was their only means of subsistence.

Salvatore T. Raffa, *Airman Second Class, U.S. Air Force, 377th Security Police Squadron, Tan Son Nhut Air Base, Saigon, 1967–68*

I did a lot of drinking over there, normally screwdrivers; and at the time, I was also a cigarette smoker. God, I must have smoked what seemed like a carton a day, but I didn't care 'cause I didn't think I was coming back anyway.

Dick Turner, *Boatswain's Mate Third Class, U.S. Navy, River Assault Squadron 15, River Division 152, Task Force 117, Dong Tam and My Tho, 1968–69*

I'll be honest, I actually tried marijuana. I didn't get anything out of it.

Doug Johnson, *Specialist Four, U.S. Army, 25th Infantry Division, 2nd Battalion, 12th Infantry, 1968*

Beer was not one of my favorite beverages, and I can't say it tasted much better in Vietnam, but it sure does quench a healthy thirst better than just about anything I know. It sure beat the hell out of that wonderful potable water in Vietnam, which is indescribable. Like liver, it is a taste that cannot be disguised, even with abundant resupplies of Kool-Aid from the States. I recognized early in my tour that that pleasant "buzz" or complete state of incomprehension that could be attained by consuming enough beer was short-lived. What was certain to follow was awakening with a horrible hangover and realizing that yes, I was still in Vietnam, and no, the booze had not made it any easier to bear.

One day, I awoke on my bunk completely dressed in my jungle fatigues and jungle boots, completely caked in mud. I didn't have a clue where I was or what exactly I had been doing and realized that in a place like Vietnam this was a very, very bad idea; in fact, really stupid. Fortunately, on most occasions, I was able to be moderate in my consumption of beer, mostly out of fear of doing something stupid and getting myself killed.

I didn't smoke, either cigarettes or joints, before I went to Vietnam. On a few occasions, I did smoke a cigarette when I was on guard duty, mostly out of boredom or curiosity. Every package of C-rations would contain two or three smokes, and I'm certain that the first time I had a cigarette was for no better reason than I've heard people give for climbing Mt. Everest—it was there. I certainly didn't do it because I liked the taste because, quite frankly, if I want to choke myself to death I'd choose some other way to do it. As for smoking grass, that was a big no-no for me. I was amazed at how easy it was to get marijuana in Vietnam. It also seemed like smoking joints was tolerated—not condoned necessarily—but tolerated by those in charge.

My decision not to smoke grass was a conscious one. It was not based on fear of getting caught or fear of any particular health hazard. It was based on a realistic decision that I was going to do whatever was within my power to see that I made it out of Vietnam alive and in one piece. Covering my ass and my buddies in every way conceivable was my responsibility, and I was not going to be smoked up at a time when I needed every instinct for survival—which was at all times. It was no guarantee for survival, but in my mind it might increase the odds that I would someday walk out the same way I had walked into Vietnam.

Mike Pinksaw, Specialist Four, U.S. Army, 60th Land Clearing Company, 62nd Engineering Battalion, 20th Engineering Brigade, Long Binh, Bien Hoa, Lai Khe 1968–69

I smoked a little dope a couple of times, nothing much, although in my unit we had some heads. You could pick up the stuff very easily, normally when we went through villages. I remember a *mama-san* one day trying to sell me a bag of grass for five dollars. With the size of this bag, you could have smoked a lot. As for cigarettes, I never smoked them.

Usually, we had no problem getting alcohol, but there was this one time when we couldn't get it. We had this old guy in our unit named J. B., who died something like three years after he got back from Vietnam of pneumonia, God bless his soul. He was from Georgia, and we nicknamed him Horse-collar. Anyway, as an old hillbilly, he got to mixing and after a few days of brewing, we all got drunk on his moonshine. I can't remember what he put in it, but boy, it was good! I'm surprised we're not all blind today!

Stephen Butler, *Lance Corporal, U.S. Marine Corps, 7th Marine Combat Engineers, Da Nang, 1966–67*

As a matter of fact, I never really drank much. Before I went to Nam I used to go to clubs and drink some beers, but over there most of the stuff was warm because I was in the field most of the time. I never really could get accustomed to drinking warm beer. Every now and then I'd have a few. As far as drugs and that stuff, I saw too many guys get smoked on drugs, so I didn't get involved in it.

Dick Turner enjoys a cold beer outside his tent. (Courtesy of Dick Turner)

Michael Toner Farrell, *Specialist Five, U.S. Army, 544th Replacement Company, Cam Ranh Bay, 1969–70*

I used to do the maid run each morning in the deuce-and-a-half. What this meant was, I had the assignment of picking up the local females in the village and bringing them back to the compound so they could do all the housewife duties. On these runs, either coming or going, I picked up pot.

I guess the word spread because I used to have notes left under my door by new guys coming into my company, which basically said something like, "The CO and the first sergeant told me to stay away from you and your roommate, so when can we get together?"

We all had our own rooms with air-conditioning, Hollywood beds and box springs, and all the comforts of home. I had this expensive stereo and a TV, although I couldn't get many stations. I mean, I had it made.

We use to hide our pot by placing it in a false hole in the hanging ceiling in our room. There remained about a foot of space between the false one and the real one. We used to always wear thin plastic gloves so there wouldn't be any fingerprints, and more than once, it paid off.

One day, our commanding officer, first sergeant, and supply sergeant came in and told my roommate and me to get out of bed. This was about seven A.M.

He said, "I've been informed that there is a cache of marijuana in this room." Even till this day, that word "cache" hits me funny.

Anyway, my response was, "I don't know what you're talking about."

So he pulls over a chair, goes right to the exact spot in the ceiling, stands on the chair, and slides the panel open and proceeds to pull down the pot.

I said, "Gee, I don't know where the hell that came from. Somebody must be trying to set us up."

That evening, I did the maid run again and purchased more pot from the locals. The next morning, they came back. I never, ever imagined they would come back two days in a row. This time, he was livid and threw the stuff down on the bed. Because we didn't have it on our person and the bags had no fingerprints, they couldn't prove it was ours. The only thing we lost was our pot. Several days later, I went out and bought some more.

Thomas Finn, *Specialist Four, U.S. Army, Company A, 519th Military Intelligence Battalion, 525th Military Intelligence Group, MACV-J2, Saigon, 1966–67*

It was still early in the war when I was there, and I personally did not smoke any marijuana or do any drugs. I'm not a beer drinker, although I enjoyed the hard stuff considerably.

My unit wasn't made up of Rambos, and we certainly weren't like the combat soldiers in the movie *Platoon*. It was, in fact, a unit that lived to party and drink a lot of booze. I was there at a time before the drug scene took hold, although there were a few guys trying marijuana and who got into trouble for using it. I really can't attest to the drug scene in '66 and '67, but I sure can attest to the booze. Thank God, I met my wife when I did.

We all got pretty loaded one time in downtown Saigon, and it was past the curfew. We couldn't find any taxis to take us back to our compound. There were only the Honda mopeds. So there I was, feeling no pain whatsoever, and I flagged down this Vietnamese civilian for a ride.* Now, I had entrusted my life to this individual. The other three guys I was with also got moped rides. However, we all took different routes back. The guy driving my moped decided he wanted to make a pit stop to see his girlfriend in the middle of the boonies.

I said to myself, "This is it, this is really it! I'm a goner!" I was thinking, "I've got no recourse; I can't get off the bike; I'm simply stuck." Even if I could have gotten off the bike, I had no idea where I was.

I guess he detected my nervousness, and instead he changed his mind and took me all the way back to my compound. As we got closer to the gate, he was laughing and I was saying to myself, "I'm gonna live!" I don't know what I paid him in Vietnamese currency, but it had to be the equivalent of ten dollars, which was a considerable sum of money for a Vietnamese civilian in those days. During that ten-mile stretch, I didn't have a friggin' clue where we were.

When we got to the gate, he looked at me and said, "No need to worry, I'm armed!" He had what appeared to be a .45 pistol stuck in his belt. Had I known that from the start, I would have been even more nervous.

Most times we wore civilian clothes so as not to intimidate the prisoners. In our unit we worked early in the morning and through the day, sometimes six or seven days a week, but we always got off pretty early in the evening, usually by six. Then the drinking would start. We'd party all night long, every friggin' night. Thank God, I met my wife a few years after Vietnam, because I could have easily become an alcoholic. I loved the booze, the real hard stuff, and it would have got me if I hadn't met her.

At the clubs, they drank Saigon Tea. It was this extremely mild alcoholic drink mixed with Coca-Cola, but the price was outrageous—somewhere around a buck and a half a pop. Usually it was just tea, literally tea. And we're talking over thirty years ago. It was a huge rip-off by any standard.

---

* These moped drivers were called cowboys by American soldiers, and they would do just about anything for a buck.

David Rossi, *Specialist Four, U.S. Army, 1st Infantry Division and 25th Infantry Division, Di An, Tay Ninh, and Cu Chi, 1969–70*

I did my fair share of drinking beer. Once we got in the field, I did a little bit of marijuana, but not much. The Vietnamese women used to take American cigarettes that they received for favors, strip the tobacco, and re-pack them with marijuana, only to sell them back later to perhaps the same GIs. You'd get nineteen back in the pack, and boy, they were strong.

Bill McCollum, *Sergeant, U.S. Army, 173rd Airborne Brigade, Charlie Company, 4th Battalion, 503rd Infantry, LZ-English, 1969–71*

In my tour-and-a-half (eighteen months all together), I bet I didn't get back to base camp more than four times. The rest of the time I was in the field.

I smoked marijuana before I went to Vietnam, so when I got there, it was no big deal. You just had to be careful with whom and where you smoked. When I first got there, everybody was kind of unsure about me, and they had to be certain I wasn't a plant. Eventually, I was accepted. You know, we'd go out on patrol just so we could smoke!

We each knew who smoked in the company. My best friend, Ralph, didn't smoke. A lot of times, Ralph didn't go with me on patrol, yet we were still very close. The rest of us would do our jobs and go set up an ambush, but we'd smoke, too.

When we went into the village, we'd run into what we called the Coke Kids. These kids would run out to us and sell us Cokes, bring us blocks of ice and joints, which we called Com Si Bombers. We'd say to the kids, "Bring me some Com Si," and they would come out with these joints, ten to a pack for a dollar, and they were as big as cigars.

Marijuana was extremely plentiful. Matter of fact, I had a platoon sergeant ask me one time, "How come you send so many clothes back home to the States?" Well, it wasn't clothes; it was packages of marijuana.

One of our big concerns was if you made contact and someone got hit, especially if he were unconscious, we'd check to make sure no marijuana was found on him. A wounded guy never went back to the rear without somebody first frisking his clothes.

When it came to cigarettes, we guys in the field were the lucky ones. The choppers dropped us Pall Malls, Chesterfields, and chewing tobacco. The supply sergeants would get the Coca-Cola and the Budweisers, you know, all the good stuff, and they probably sold it on the black market, because we never saw it. We got all the garbage that was left over, but we made do. We didn't get much beer because we were out in the field so much.

Howard North, *Lieutenant j.g., U.S. Coast Guard, Coast Guard Squadron One, USCGC* **Point** Clear *(WPB 82315), An Thoi and Cat Lo, 1967–68*

For six months, we were at sea and never touched land. During this time, we occasionally tied up to the mother ship. We'd come in for ammunition, fuel, food, cigarettes, and other supplies. Per boat, we were supposed to get two cases of beer for every patrol. A patrol usually lasted four to five days, sometimes longer. There were times when we didn't get our full ration.

ENLISTED, NCO, AND OFFICERS' CLUBS

Everyone needed time to relax, to be entertained, or to find a place to gather for a few beers and conversation with friends, away from work assignments or when coming out of the field. The enlisted, NCO, and officers' clubs were set up for this purpose. All major bases had these facilities, and they always appeared to be well attended by the troops. Because fraternization between enlisted personnel, NCOs, and officers was not allowed in any of the services, an individual's military rank dictated which club he was allowed to attend.

The clubs opened around noontime and remained in business until late in the evening. In some of the larger establishments, you could even order food. For nightly entertainment, Asian rock 'n' roll bands were employed, the vast majority of which came from Thailand or Taiwan. The female performers (dancers and singers) were scantily clad, often in miniskirts. Whether the band had any talent or the girls could really sing made no difference to those attending the show. The beer was cold, and more importantly, the band had female performers, so everyone had a good time.

Salvatore T. Raffa, *Airman Second Class, U.S. Air Force, 377th Security Police Squadron, Tan Son Nhut Air Base, Saigon, 1967–68*

Before I got to Vietnam, having known guys who had died there or who became drug addicts or alcoholics, I told my wife that I wasn't going to fall into that trap. When I got over there, I went to the library every night and wrote letters to my wife and relatives back home. I'd also go to the chapel, which had a nice little sitting area in the courtyard. It was beautiful. You've got to understand, this was a sprawling air base, and it rivaled some of the big air bases back home for comforts.

One night, I heard this horrendous explosion. The Viet Cong had put a rocket right in the library and just blew it down to the foundation.

So I said to myself, "Well, I'm not gonna let this upset me; I've got to stay focused. I'll go to that chapel every night, sit in that courtyard, and write letters home," which I did for a while.

Not long after, I made the chapel courtyard my personal hideaway. Early one evening while I was still in my barracks, I heard this tremendous explosion. You guessed it! The chapel was blown right off the foundation. Thank God, no one was killed in either of the explosions.

That's when I started going to the airman's club. That took care of any ideas I had about not taking part in the festivities.

Bill McCollum, *Sergeant, U.S. Army, 173rd Airborne Brigade, Charlie Company, 4th Battalion, 503rd Infantry, LZ-English, 1969–71*

I went into an air force NCO Club once and thought I was in Las Vegas. I think this club was in Cam Ranh Bay. I said to myself, "Boy, these guys know how to live."

The night I was there they had a battle of the bands; there were two bands from the States. For a club that far away from civilization, I hadn't seen anything like it in the States; you wouldn't even know you were in a war zone. It was all first-class material.

I met a Newporter there in Cam Ranh Bay. He was driving a Jeep. I couldn't think of his name for a long time, but he looked just like Mick Jagger of the Rolling Stones. It turns out it was Michael Toner Farrell. I met him twice. He got into the army after having had open-heart surgery.

Thomas Finn, *Specialist Four, U.S. Army, Company A, 519th Military Intelligence Battalion, 525th Military Intelligence Group, MACV-J2, Saigon, 1966–67*

We'd go to happy hour at the enlisted club, and the mixed drinks would only cost twenty-five cents each. For a couple of bucks, you were . . . phew!

Because of the extra subsistence pay, we were making a lot of money in comparison to other soldiers in-country with the same rank; however, we spent every penny we made.

Dick Turner, *Boatswain's Mate Third Class, U.S. Navy, River Assault Squadron 15, River Division 152, Task Force 117, Dong Tam and My Tho, 1968–69*

We were a tight crew, and we knew how to fight and play. We'd take a boat over to this great big enlisted club at Dong Tam. They had pool tables, and we'd spend the night shooting pool and getting drunk.

One night we got so drunk we couldn't get the boat back. We called back to the ship and said, "We're too drunk, and we can't get the boat back until morning." We got ourselves into some deep shit over that one. I mean the old man was pissed.

William Sullivan, *Lieutenant Commander, U.S. Navy, Fighter Squadron 213, U.S.S.* Intrepid, *Air Wing, U.S.S.* Kitty Hawk *(CVA-63), U.S.S.* Intrepid *(CVA-11), U.S.S.* Paul Revere, *and U.S.S.* Blue Ridge, *1965–68 and 1971–72*

On a carrier, each squadron had its own ready room, and that's where you tended to congregate when not flying or performing your other squadron functions. It's the room where you had all your briefings before your mission. During the off hours, you used it to watch movies or as a place to socialize.

Peggy R. Zarek, *Lieutenant Commander, U.S. Navy, U.S.S.* Sanctuary *(AH-17), Coastal Waters off South Vietnam, Military Region 1, 1969–70*

When I first got to the ship, it was the day before New Year's Eve. I saw a flyer posted on a bulletin board that said they were going to have a party up in Phu Bai; and if you wanted to go, you could sign up for it. I said to myself, "You've got to be kidding. This is a war zone. What are they talking about?" Only so many people could go, and I got lucky. The helicopters came and we flew out to Phu Bai. We had this great party.

I also went to the mainland, just to get off the ship. It wasn't every day. The Third Marine Battalion was stationed in and around Da Nang harbor, and we used to go to a cocktail hour around four P.M. at a captain's party.

Howard North, *Lieutenant j.g., U.S. Coast Guard, Coast Guard Squadron One, USCGC* Point Clear *(WPB 82315), An Thoi and Cat Lo, 1967–68*

The only club I ever got to go to was in An Thoi. It wasn't much of a club. It had four seats at the bar, and it was really small.

A strange thing happened there one night. I was sitting in the club, and this officer looked at my name tag and I looked at his. He recognized me first. He was a guy I was in the sixth grade with. He was a navy brat and traveled all over with his military family. He graduated from the Naval Academy. I hadn't seen him since the sixth grade. Turns out he was a naval advisor in the area working with the Vietnamese. We spent the rest of the evening drinking together and just reminiscing.

Doug Johnson, *Specialist Four, U.S. Army, 25th Infantry Division, 2nd Battalion, 12th Infantry, 1968*

When I was in the base camp, I would occasionally go to the NCO club. I didn't go that often because drinking with a bunch of sweaty guys was not my idea of a good time. The NCO club did occasionally offer some comic relief, especially when the Korean guys would show up from God knows where with their assorted—or should I say sordid—collection of stag films. These films, as I recall, offered every depravity known to mankind, including bestiality. Most guys, myself included, were not expecting to see anything that was likely to win an Academy Award—we were easily entertained. The best part of the show, however, was not what was being projected onto the dirty sheet that served as a screen, but rather the comments from the peanut gallery. It would not take long after the film began and the first unspeakable and often indescribable actions began to take place that someone would be sharing loudly with the group that the person on the screen was the girlfriend, fiancée, wife or other relation of another soldier in the room. Fortunately, the uproarious laughter and welcome relief it provided from the day-to-day reality of Vietnam resulted in few people taking any offense, and most guys could give the verbal assault back as well as they took it.

SOME REALLY FOWL STORIES

Foraging for food and having some fun at the same time was a way of diverting one's attention from the rigors, or boredom, of war. After reading the following accounts of impromptu hunting escapades, you might no longer wonder why we lost the war. At a minimum, some additional marksmanship training certainly was in order.

Stephen Butler, *Lance Corporal, U.S. Marine Corps, 7th Marine Combat Engineers, Da Nang, 1966–67*

Being bored one day, two other marines and I decided to go hunting for wild chickens. Clearly the chickens knew more of this process than we. After unloading what seemed like a couple of hundred rounds of ammunition and missing every chicken in sight, we returned to our field area with no game. We were immediately disciplined by the man in charge—not for hunting, but for pinning down an entire company of marines, who thought the bullets were coming from enemy sniper fire. This story is a lot funnier now than it was at the time.

David Rossi, *Specialist Four, U.S. Army, 1st Infantry Division and 25th Infantry Division, Di An, Tay Ninh, and Cu Chi, 1969–70*

One day we found a big cache of rice. So we called for a helicopter to come in and take it away. Eventually, the rice would be disposed of, and most likely it was set on fire. Anyway, a few of the ARVN soldiers decided to cook some of it up. All of a sudden, my friend and I saw some wild chickens running around, and we figured they'd go well with the rice. Picking up some sticks on the run, we followed them down this path when, all of a sudden, we came upon a Viet Cong soldier dressed in black silk pajamas. He looked to be no more than a boy of thirteen or fourteen years old. He was holding a bag of pineapples and an AK-47 rifle. Here we are, just standing there with a couple of sticks. We were no more than twenty to thirty feet away from him. The guy I was with, a corporal, thought fast and yelled to the kid in Vietnamese, "*dee dee,*" which roughly translated means "get out of here." The kid took off and ran away. If he had been older or realized we were unarmed, I have no doubt he would have taken us out.

We never did catch the chickens, nor did we resume the chase.

Howard North, *Lieutenant j.g., U.S. Coast Guard, Coast Guard Squadron One, USCGC* Point Clear *(WPB 82315), An Thoi and Cat Lo, 1967–68*

We used to travel in and out of the mouth of the Mekong. I guess I really never appreciated just how big that bloody river was. There were seven mouths fed by the river, and because of it the Vietnamese named it *The Seven Dragons.*

One day, we went up the Bassac mouth, cruising up to a small navy harbor where they had their river patrol boats. They were neat little boats, kind of like the boats in the movie *Apocalypse Now*. That movie destroyed the reputation of these guys and did them a real injustice, as they were topnotch professionals in every sense of the word.

Our main purpose for going up the river was to get water from the mother ship of the PBRs. Anyway, we were going back down the river, and there were millions of ducks in the water; every duck in Asia must have been sitting on this river. I guess you could call them sitting ducks—no pun intended.

Now, we decided we were going to have some duck for dinner. The cook came up with his shotgun and blew off an incredible number of rounds. He didn't touch one duck, not one duck. It was almost a mathematical probability that he couldn't miss, yet he did. He was so frustrated that he wanted to use the .50 caliber machine gun on them. If we let him and he hit a duck, there wouldn't have been anything left to cook.

There was no duck on the table that night.

A POTPOURRI OF OTHER TALES

Some of the following unique stories are humorous, while a few, although funny, could have ended in a disaster.

Betsy Wylie, *Lieutenant, U.S. Navy, Management Information Center, Headquarters, Naval Forces Vietnam (NAVFORV), Saigon, 1967–68*

My roommate and I had flown up to Da Nang because she needed to see the individual in charge of Marine Corps personnel, and I wanted to go out to the hospital ship, the U.S.S. *Sanctuary,* in Da Nang Harbor to take some pictures for our command brief. So Vera and I went out to the ship in a boat. It was sort of a cloudy, overcast day; and as long as we were inside the harbor, the passage on this sixteen-foot Boston Whaler was relatively easy. But as soon as we got beyond the breakwater, we got into very choppy water. Of course, we were in the front of the boat and the water just came over the bow. We were soaked by the time we got to the hospital ship, and we looked like drowned rats.

We pulled up alongside the accommodation ladder, and we got off and climbed up to the deck. When we came on deck, the executive officer of the ship was there to greet us. He took one look at us and said, "Are you visitors or patients?" He was kidding, of course.

Howard North, *Lieutenant j.g., U.S. Coast Guard, Coast Guard Squadron One, USCGC* Point Clear *(WPB 82315), An Thoi and Cat Lo, 1967–68*

In bad seas, we used to go up and down swells because if you took them sideways, you just rocked and got the crap beat out of you. One of our first-class mates could never figure out that when you went with the swell, you went further than trying to go against it. He just never could grasp the concept and because of that used to get us hung up all the time near shore.

One day, he wasn't paying attention, and he ran into this nylon fish net which got caught in our propellers. Because we were too close to shore, we were also in muddy water. So there we were, about a mile off the beach, almost stranded. Fortunately, we were able to crawl out far enough to get into cleaner water.

We realized we'd have to dive down and cut the net by hand in order to untangle it, so we got out the diving gear (a mask, a pair of fins, and a snorkel). We decided to take turns jumping into the water and working on cutting away the net.

It started to get dark, so we had to use our boarding lights to illuminate the water where we were working, but the lights attracted sea snakes. These suckers were big, black, and ugly and grew to about three feet long. They were also really poisonous, almost as bad as a cobra. You could see them coming on top of the water. Because of this, we stationed a few guys with weapons in strategic locations on each side of the boat to blow them away if they got near the diver.

Our Vietnamese officer refused to go into the water; he absolutely refused. I guess he knew better.

Before it came time for my turn to go down, the net was removed and we were on our way. Thank God!

Dick Turner, *Boatswain's Mate Third Class, U.S. Navy, River Assault Squadron 15, River Division 152, Task Force 117, Dong Tam and My Tho, 1968–69*

Once we lost our book of radio transmission codes overboard when it blew off the top of the pilot house. That meant that every boat in the squadron had to have a whole new book issued because, had the enemy found it, our intelligence could have been compromised. Naturally, that didn't make the higher-ups very happy.

We had a lot of funny things happen to us. Once we pulled what they called base defense duty, which was simply three boats circling the ships anchored in the river all the time. Occasionally, you'd get a call from one of the ships to drop an offensive grenade in the water to prevent any enemy swimmers from attaching charges to the hull of the ship. Also, if any mines floated down the river, the grenades would detonate them. These grenades were filled with gunpowder wrapped up in cardboard, and when they exploded, they made an incredibly loud noise but caused no damage. They were kind of like big firecrackers, or glorified cherry bombs, to be more exact. Underwater, I guess, these things make a real loud bang, and the blast concussion would kill some fish, which could be seen floating to the surface. Anyway, one night, the guys had the offensive grenades stacked up near the well deck. One of the guys pulled the pin, but it slipped out of his hand and fell into the well deck, where a number of us were sleeping. The thing went off. God, what a noise! It didn't do anything or hurt anyone, it just made an incredible noise. I tell you, our ears were ringing for a week after that.

Mike Pinksaw, Specialist Four, U.S. Army, 60th Land Clearing Company, 62nd Engineering Battalion, 20th Engineering Brigade, Long Binh, Bien Hoa, Lai Khe, 1968–69

We had this really old staff sergeant in our unit, and he used to come up with some incredibly obvious conclusions. Remember, during this period of time, we were getting the shit kicked out of us, day in and day out.

One night, at a platoon briefing for the next day, he said to us, "Intelligence shows, and the CO knows, there's VC in the area."

Now, we're getting rocketed every morning, rocketed every night, we're getting the shit kicked out of us in the field, and he's telling us this. He had to have been operating in a different time warp than the rest of us, like in the Civil War or something. I mean, he had no clue. This guy was old. I would guess he was in his sixties.

I remember one time we got hit by a few mortar rounds. By the time he was able to get in the bunker to protect himself, the attack was over.

Ken Garthee, Private First Class, U.S. Marine Corps, 3rd Battalion, 3rd Marines, 3rd Marine Division, Da Nang, Rock Pile, 1966–67

In June 1966, our company was assigned to guard several relay communications dishes atop the highest mountain outside of Da Nang, called Monkey Mountain. It was named appropriately, as monkeys lived all over the mountain. Several times they tried to get into our relay station or our tents in order to steal food. Occasionally, they would get caught in the barbed wire that surrounded the complex and either freed themselves or waited until we freed them. I can also remember them sitting along the roadside begging for food.

This turned out to be good duty because no one was shooting at us. As an added benefit, the communication station was operated by the air force, and that meant good food and a tent to sleep in.

While still on Monkey Mountain, the sergeant was looking for anyone who wanted to become a reconnaissance scout. I volunteered and was accepted. As a scout, we worked in teams of two, gathering intelligence, which was used to develop strategies for future operations. I learned to use night vision detection devices and motion sensors and even had an opportunity to use my Boy Scout skills—map and compass reading and knot tying.

Stephen Butler, *Lance Corporal, U.S. Marine Corps, 7th Marine Combat Engineers, Da Nang, 1966–67*

I was hooking a ride from Da Nang to—well, I can't remember where—with some Seabees to pick up a drill rig. It was one of the first helicopters I ever rode in. I'd always thought they were built solidly, out of metal, but the one I rode in—I don't know where the hell it came from—it had some kind of cloth or fabric sides. I jumped in and I had all my combat gear on and as I pushed against the side of the chopper, the whole side bellied out about eight inches. I thought I was going to fall right out.

THE JOHN WAYNE STORIES

In his review of Samuel Hynes's book, *The Soldier's Tale: Bearing Witness to Modern War,* Joseph L. Galloway made the following observation:

> The truth of war is not found in John Wayne movies, or the mouths of politicians, or the memoirs of general officers who operate at too great a distance from the mud and blood, or even in great sweeping histories filled with strategy, tactics and numbers so great they submerge mere humans.*

* Joseph L. Galloway, "The Truth of War," *Washington Post,* April 14, 1997, p. 34.

Doug Johnson, *Specialist Four, U.S. Army, 25th Infantry Division, 2nd Battalion, 12th Infantry, 1968*

I recall seeing a movie titled *The Green Berets* starring John Wayne, and the movie actually made me vomit. The reason for this violent reaction was my realization of how unrealistically the Vietnam War was depicted in this movie. I was angry at this blatant, unrealistic propaganda and glorification of war. It made me sick because I was certain that some young men would watch the film and run down to the local recruiting office to sign up for a real-life war, which could bring them death, mutilation, or a lifetime of painful memories. To this day it galls me that Hollywood stars have made incredible sums of money capitalizing on the public's fascination with war without ever setting foot on foreign soil to fight for their country.

Rob Roche, *Sergeant, U.S. Army, 101st Airborne Division, Da Nang, 1967–69*

When I was recuperating from my leg wound in Cam Ranh Bay, one of the few times I got to have beer, I went to the movies. It was like being at a drive-in movie, with the screen outside and all the stars overhead. You just lay in the sand, relaxed, and watched the movie. The only thing missing was the cars. The movie playing that night was John Wayne's *The Green Berets.* What a f—in' joke. Oh man, it was corny. I'm smoking grass, sitting on the sand, and I've got my crutches next to me. It was so ridiculous that the guys started throwing beer cans at the screen because he's like this big invulnerable hero and all that kind of stuff. It was ridiculous. War just wasn't that way. Yeah, that was funny.

REST AND RECREATION (R & R)

After serving in Vietnam for more than six months, all military personnel were entitled to one R & R outside the country. R & R was the military term for what could best be described as a vacation. Places to visit varied as the war went on, but the usual list of destinations included Hawaii, Australia, Thailand, Taiwan, Singapore, and the Philippines. Centralized R & R departure points were out of Da Nang in the north; Cam Ranh Bay, which was centrally located on the east coast; and Saigon, further south.

A soldier's money went further in the Asian countries, as the standard of living was considerably less than say, Hawaii. Many went to these locations because of that. There was also another consideration. If an individual was single, Hawaii was difficult to book. As a destination, it always appeared to be reserved far in advance by married military personnel who were to meet their wives there, who flew in from the mainland.

Bangkok, Thailand, and Sydney, Australia, were the more popular R & R destinations for the single guys because of the favorable ratio of females to males. It would be an exaggeration to believe that all who departed on R & R went there to chase women. In fact, many military personnel led the typical life of a tourist, visiting zoos, museums, parks, and taking part in recreational activities. Of course, others simply chased skirts and made no bones about it.

Those who served in the infantry and others with stressful and risky military assignments were also entitled to in-country R & Rs. These were well-deserved and always taken full advantage of by the troops who qualified. Two of the more well known in-country R & R locations were Saigon in the south and Qui Nhon, which was situated a considerable distance to the northeast.

These in-country R & Rs weren't always a bed of roses. Take, for example, the city of Qui Nhon, located off the coast of the South China Sea in the central highlands. Qui Nhon's Red Beach, as it was called by the troops, could have been a beautiful vacation resort, if not for several drawbacks. First, U.S. soldiers burned out most of the foliage on the hillsides surrounding the beach to prevent the Viet Cong from establishing sanctuaries. The hills were always barren and black. Second, the South Vietnamese civilians used the beach as a toilet. When the tide shifted, the beach had to be put off-limits to avoid hepatitis outbreaks. Third, the Viet Cong were still in the area, and remote sections of the beach were mined.

Thomas Finn, *Specialist Four, U.S. Army, Company A, 519th Military Intelligence Battalion, 525th Military Intelligence Group, MACV-J2, Saigon, 1966–67*

R & R was kind of uneventful. I went to Hong Kong for a week. I hung around with a guy named Benny from another unit, and we went shopping, sightseeing, and ate at a lot of restaurants. It was basically a drying out time for me.

My in-country R & R was a little different. My friend Ron and I were given a three-day pass, and we decided to go to Vung Tau. Why we were ever given that privilege, I still don't understand. It was a resort area where the French military used to hang out; but when we got to the beaches, they were completely devoid of people.

From the day we arrived, it was wine, woman, and song. Well, the women were more like *Ba Muoi Ba,* the local bar girls, but who cared at the time? In a short period of time, we were both two sheets to the wind as we attempted to hit every bar on our way back to the hotel. Just about the same time, Ron got his hands on a lovely young lady, so Ron and I parted ways.

Later in the evening, I arrived back at the hotel. It was sparsely furnished with a dresser, two beds, and maybe a window. I'm not really sure. Anyway, I jumped into bed, perhaps it was more like collapsing, and I fell asleep immediately.

It was kind of a half-sleep. In a short while, I woke up to hear really heavy breathing coming from the next bed. I tried to turn over and go back to sleep, but the breathing got heavier and louder. I tried to ignore it, but I couldn't.

I started to think about the Polaroid camera I had brought along to capture the scenery. Grabbing the camera, I rolled out of bed and did a low crawl to the foot of Ron's bed. I could still hear the heavy breathing. Just when it seemed to be the loudest, I jumped up and clicked off a shot with the camera.

All pandemonium broke out. The girl yelled and screamed, probably from being thrown on the floor by Ron. Apparently he thought he was under attack, especially because of the bright flash of the camera. Neither one had expected me there, and I really caught them by total surprise.

When all quieted down, I showed the young lady the camera and the picture I had taken. She had never seen an instant camera before and thought we were from Hollywood. Thinking quickly, we told her we were Hollywood producers that got drafted. We asked her if she wanted to go to Hollywood, and she said yes, so we told her, as producers, she would have to audition for us in front of the camera. It didn't take much prodding. She said yes. I got out all my film and I explained to her we needed all the pictures we could get of her to send them off to the big boss in Hollywood. Ron and I really got into the act, taking turns with the camera.

Finally we ran out of film and we all went to bed. When we woke up in the morning, she was gone, and so were some of the pictures. She must have wanted to show them to her family or something. Ron and I split up the ones that were left. I guess she never wanted to go to Hollywood, as we never saw her again after that.

As for the pictures, I'm not one hundred percent sure what I did with them; I hope that I destroyed them so my mother wouldn't find them. I don't think she would have believed me if I told her they were educational.

Looking back, I guess you could say that taking any kind of R & R over there was a way of keeping our sanity.

David Rossi, *Specialist Four, U.S. Army, 1st Infantry Division and 25th Infantry Division, Di An, Tay Ninh, and Cu Chi, 1969–70*

I went to Bangkok, Thailand, twice for my R & R. Both times, I went by myself and both times, I met some interesting company. A taxi driver stayed with us for most of the time and took us all around the city of Bangkok.

Bill McCollum, *Sergeant, U.S. Army, 173rd Airborne Brigade, Charlie Company, 4th Battalion, 503rd Infantry, LZ-English, 1969–71*

I went to Bangkok. I was supposed to meet my brother there, but for some reason, I got bumped from the flight, and I ended up going there much later. I was never able to locate him. It wasn't so bad, as I went with another guy from my unit. We had a blast, but the only problem was, I didn't have enough money.

While there, I had some of the funniest experiences of my life. We walked into this place and the owner sat down next to us and gave us each a drink. I looked around and I saw in the center there was this big square area enclosed in glass with all these girls in there; one was knitting, one was reading, another was making faces at me, and they were all wearing numbers.

The owner said, "Any girl you want, and I'll bring her out to talk to you."

The name of the place was the Happy-Happy Turkish Bath.

So I said, "Okay, let me speak to number 56," and a girl wearing a tag with the number 56 came out and I talked to her. Of course, the first thing to come out of my mouth was, "Do you smoke Com Si? You don't! Get out of here! Let me speak to 34," and 34 came out. The same conversation took place. "Do you smoke Com Si?"

"Yes," she responded.

"Can you roll joints?"

When she said she could, she was the one I picked.

It cost around fifty dollars for the girl for the week and another twenty dollars for the cab; and anytime you wanted the cabdriver, he was at your beck and call, day or night. The only restrictions at your hotel was if the girl you picked up was from somewhere other than from the one you were staying, they couldn't swim in the hotel pool. I guess this was because they weren't medically certified to be disease free, and the hotel didn't want to ruin its reputation. It was quite the experience.

William Sullivan, *Lieutenant Commander, U.S. Navy, Fighter Squadron 213, U.S.S.* Intrepid, *Air Wing, U.S.S.* Kitty Hawk *(CVA-63), U.S.S.* Intrepid *(CVA-11), U.S.S.* Paul Revere, *and U.S.S.* Blue Ridge, *1965–68 and 1971–72*

When you're aboard a ship, particularly on a carrier, the R & R you get is when you pull into port for a period of three to seven days. In approximately a year, you'd get perhaps four R & Rs in ports located in Asian countries like Hong Kong, Japan, and the Philippines.

Peggy R. Zarek, *Lieutenant Commander, U.S. Navy, U.S.S.* Sanctuary *(AH-17), Coastal Waters off South Vietnam, Military Region 1, 1969–70*

I went with another nurse to Bangkok and Hong Kong. It was great just to be away! When we got to Hong Kong, there was heavy flooding like they hadn't experienced in years. Because of it, our movement was somewhat restricted. But the food was great. Just being in Hong Kong was exciting.

Howard North, *Lieutenant j.g., U.S. Coast Guard, Coast Guard Squadron One, USCGC* Point Clear *(WPB 82315), An Thoi and Cat Lo, 1967–68*

I took all the required inoculations to go on R & R, and as luck would have it, I had a reaction to one of the shots the night before I was supposed to leave. I had a fever of 102 or 103 degrees. Whatever, I was not to be denied. I flew from Vung Tau to Saigon and arrived at a personnel transition base, which I think was called Camp Alpha. In a few days, I felt better. From there, I flew via Pan Am to Sydney.

As I remember, landing in Darwin for refueling, I saw this Australian guy getting on an airplane with a ball and chain secured to his leg. He was holding the ball in his hands as he climbed the stairs into the cabin. We're all looking at him wondering what that was all about. Someone got the lowdown before we took off. It turns out the guy was getting married and his friends threw him a bachelor's party the night before. Everyone got bombed at the party, and someone got the bright idea to tie this ball and chain on him. Either they lost the key or didn't give him the key, I don't know. He had to go back to where the hell he was going and apparently had to get married with this ball and chain still secured to his leg.

In Sydney, I lived in the real world for a change. I went out at night and ate at some really good restaurants. I also had a chance to catch up on some sleep. Some of the guys back in Vietnam who had gone to Sydney gave me names of some locals, whom I looked up when I got there. They treated me swell. I went all over the place: the zoo, the opera house, the pubs, all the places a typical tourist would go. The Australians were very nice and very friendly. It was great!

Michael Toner Farrell, *Specialist Five, U.S. Army, 544th Replacement Company, Cam Ranh Bay, 1969–70*

When we first got off the plane, we walked into the reception area and there was this guy giving an orientation about Australia. When he concluded he said, "Orson Bean, the movie star, wants to invite three soldiers to his rented home to have Thanksgiving dinner with him and his wife."

Apparently, he was filming a movie on location in Australia and was renting a bungalow in the vicinity of the airport. The way I remember it today, the first three guys who made it to the exit door of the reception area got the invitation. Guess who made it first? So I spent my Thanksgiving Day eating turkey with a movie star.

When I got to Sydney, I went to my room and dressed as a hippie. I had bought a long-haired wig and wore it for most of the time I was on R & R. I had blue jeans that were all embroidered and everything. The local girls loved me. I had an incredible time.

Dick Turner, *Boatswain's Mate Third Class, U.S. Navy, River Assault Squadron 15, River Division 152, Task Force 117, Dong Tam and My Tho, 1968–69*

I went to Japan and visited my cousin, who was an officer in the navy at a base there. During the day he had to work, so I stayed on the base and swam, met some girls, did some screwing around. Later, the girls and I went downtown and got messing around.

When it was getting close to the end, I knew I had to go back to that god-awful place. After seven days of fun, I didn't want to go back. I almost went AWOL.

When I got back, I stayed in Saigon for three days before I went back to the squadron. So actually, it was a ten-day R & R, but I didn't get to see Saigon because I was restricted to the hotel, the same place where I stayed when I first came in-country several months earlier.

Ken Garthee, *Private First Class, U.S. Marine Corps, 3rd Battalion, 3rd Marines, 3rd Marine Division, Da Nang, Rock Pile, 1966–67*

I had been in-country for about ten months before I was finally asked if I wanted to go on R & R for seven days. I thought, "You've got to be kidding me—no one shooting at me, a real bed, real hot food, and a call home. You bet I want to go!"

I was given several choices—Bangkok, Singapore, or the Philippines. I chose Singapore. Since I hadn't spent any money the whole time I was in-country, I had more than a few American dollars in my pocket by the time I was ready to leave.

Singapore was beautiful—aqua, blue, and green water, plush green foliage. The streets were clean and the people very friendly and helpful, although it was usually to obtain one of my American greenbacks.

After checking in at the hotel, I immediately called home and spoke to my mom and dad. I had forgotten that I was calling ten thousand miles away and fourteen hours behind the time in Singapore. No one complained, though. The bill for the phone call was over one hundred dollars, but it was worth every penny.

The next thing I did was go to the hotel restaurant to get some real food. I ordered a pitcher of cow's milk. That's right, I ordered a gallon of cold fresh cow's milk. Everyone at the table thought I was crazy not to order a beer; but as I didn't like alcohol and I hadn't had any milk in a long time, I took the milk. I just plain liked milk.

Every day I did something different. I visited the downtown shopping areas one day. There, I bought a bronzeware service for my mom and dad. Another day, I went to the zoo. Later in the week, a taxi driver drove me to the countryside, and I went to other local points of interest. I also spent some time by the hotel swimming pool, just relaxing.

During the week, I was asked by a local man who worked for the hotel if I would like to have dinner with him and his family. I accepted. We ate Malaysian cuisine: rice and fish with vegetables. It wasn't my favorite dish, but I ate it to be polite.

I had an opportunity to go to the Singapore Country Club to play golf. I had never played golf before in my life. I figured, what the heck; I even got a caddie. It rained the whole round, and my caddie and I were the only ones on the course. When I finished, I tipped the caddie well for putting up with me and the weather. The country club president and course superintendent were waiting for me in the club house. They were not pleased that they had had to hang around waiting for me to finish my game. Who cared? I was on R & R.

Salvatore T. Raffa, Airman Second Class, U.S. Air Force, 377th Security Police Squadron, Tan Son Nhut Air Base, Saigon, 1967–68

I traveled to Hawaii with my buddy Gary. When I arrived, I met my wife. It was paradise.

I can remember it was the first time I ever used a four-letter word around my wife because I was so used to being around guys. It just kept slipping out. Back in Vietnam, we used them constantly without even thinking about what we were saying.

It was a wonderful stay, but all good things must come to an end. When it got time to go to the airport to catch our flights, hers to Rhode Island, mine to Vietnam, she couldn't find me. Of all places, I was in the bathroom throwing up. I had made myself so sick because I knew I had to go back. My wife was hysterical because I just couldn't get myself straightened out to go back on that plane.

I always said that if I had to do it all over again, I would have never met my wife in Hawaii. It was like leaving home all over again. I should have gone somewhere with the guys or something. It was very hard . . .

Stephen Butler, Lance Corporal, U.S. Marine Corps, 7th Marine Combat Engineers, Da Nang, 1966–67

I never took an R & R. I tried to stay away from all that stuff. Why didn't I take an R & R? Because so many guys I knew who went on R & R would come back and a few days later would be killed because they had their heads up their butts. They'd still be thinking about home instead of doing their jobs. This was a lesson I learned from the guy I worked for when I was a kid—to just go, do the job, focus on it, and get out of there.

Betsy Wylie, Lieutenant, U.S. Navy, Management Information Center, Headquarters, Naval Forces Vietnam (NAVFORV), Saigon, 1967–68

I decided, because I'm part Australian on my mother's side, that I would go to Sydney. Sydney was a very popular choice, so you had to sign up for it way ahead of time.

My week came. Now, I was very healthy in Vietnam. However, two days before I was supposed to get on the plane to go to Sydney, I came down with the most awful stomach flu that I had in years. I could not have crawled onto that airplane. I was in bad shape, and the thought of spending six hours on that airplane was not a fun thought. So, of course, I had to call up the R & R people and say, "Hey, I'm not coming. Please give my spot to somebody else." So I never saw Sydney.

I never went on R & R after that, although I did get to go to Honolulu periodically.

Mike Pinksaw, Specialist Four, U.S. Army, 60th Land Clearing Company, 62nd Engineering Battalion, 20th Engineering Brigade, Long Binh, Bien Hoa, Lai Khe 1968–69

I never got the chance to go on R & R because I was seriously wounded two days before my R & R was scheduled to begin. I was supposed to go to Bangkok.

Doug Johnson, Specialist Four, U.S. Army, 25th Infantry Division, 2nd Battalion, 12th Infantry, 1968

The highlight of my R & R was planning for it, because it never came to pass. I decided that I wanted to wait until I had completed nine months in-country so that I could go on R & R and come back with less than three months to go before climbing on the freedom bird for the good old U.S. of A.

Almost from the time I arrived in-country, I can remember being entertained and intrigued by the variety of stories brought back by the guys returning from R & R. As I reached about six months in-country, I can remember harboring the illusion that maybe I could meet my fiancée in Hawaii for a marvelous fantasy trip. Any thought of that magical mystery tour was quickly dispelled when my fiancée ran the idea by her parents and got a quick thumbs down. I guess I wasn't really surprised that a couple of conservative good old-fashioned Catholic parents with a healthy concern for their daughter's welfare could see the perils of that proposed rendezvous.

At any rate, I decided to go to Australia because I had heard that the women genuinely liked the American GIs and didn't go out with them just for money or other considerations. I also think that I liked the distance between Australia and Vietnam, the fact that they spoke English (or something similar to it), and I knew that I probably would never have the opportunity to travel there again in my lifetime. Armed with this fabulous game plan, I put in for Sydney for R & R and got an allocation for exactly when I would have completed nine months in-country. Unfortunately, after eight and one-half months, I had an argument with a Vietnamese mortar shell and lost. Even today, almost twenty-eight years later, I still get depressed when I see pictures of the famous opera house in Sydney, and I get as depressed as the Qantas koala when I think of what could have been.

SEVEN

NOWHERE TO HIDE

THE MAN HE KILLED

Had he and I but met
By some old ancient inn,
We should have sat us down to wet
Right many a nipperkin!

But ranged as infantry,
And staring face to face,
I shot at him as he at me,
And killed him in his place.

I shot him dead because—
Because he was my foe,
Just so: my foe of course he was;
That's clear enough; although

He thought he'd 'list, perhaps,
Off-hand like—just as I—
Was out of work—had sold his traps—
No other reason why.

Yes; quaint and curious war is!
You shoot a fellow down
You'd treat, if met where any bar is,
Or help to half-a-crown.—Thomas Hardy

PULLING GUARD DUTY

EVERY night, a contingent of soldiers were stationed in the middle of nowhere, looking out into an area which was pitch black, guarding a location they knew little, if anything, about. It was called guard duty, and just about everyone who stepped foot in-country had to do it. Those who experienced it for the first time quickly learned it wasn't fun.

Guard duty was normally performed in increments of two-hour shifts —two hours on and two hours off. Those who were relieved had a chance to rest until their shift came around again. It became a real problem, however, when the individual assigned to the next guard shift would also fall asleep. This happened all too frequently.

Fatigue and sleep deprivation were the soldier's worst nemesis, and the darkness of the night and chirping of the insects had a tendency to lull even the most hardened individual to sleep. This was when a soldier was at his most vulnerable. Viet Cong sappers had a virtual field day in cutting through concertina wire and setting off satchel charges of explosives they carried on their backs without being detected until it was too late. Many a soldier lost his life because someone had fallen asleep during guard duty.

Surprisingly, there were some soldiers who relished the assignment. It gave them the opportunity to smoke joints without fear of disciplinary action and just to be away from petty details associated with life back at base camp.

Thomas Finn, *Specialist Four, U.S. Army, Company A, 519th Military Intelligence Battalion, 525th Military Intelligence Group, MACV-J2, Saigon, 1966–67*

In our unit, the Plum Farm, where our S-4 (supply area) was, was the most feared place to pull guard. It was relatively small and situated out in the middle of nowhere, and a number of shootings and killings had taken place in that vicinity. Out there, you were basically on your own— you could kiss your ass good-bye. But other than a few stray rounds, I survived that scare.

David Rossi, *Specialist Four, U.S. Army, 1st Infantry Division and 25th Infantry Division, Di An, Tay Ninh, and Cu Chi, 1969–70*

I pulled guard duty in the field and at my base camp in Di An. Di An was located about fifteen miles outside of Saigon, right off Highway 1. Not much happened in Di An, but in the field we did take rounds from time to time. The real hard part about pulling guard duty was staying awake. When I was in the CP with the lieutenant, one of my duties was to telephone each of the fox holes every fifteen minutes or so, just to make sure the guys on duty were awake. It also helped me stay awake. Normally, we stayed in the field for about five days and returned to the base camp for three.

Doug Johnson, *Specialist Four, U.S. Army, 25th Infantry Division, 2nd Battalion, 12th Infantry, 1968*

The thing I remember most about pulling guard duty is how scared I was that *Charlie* was going to cut all the claymore wires and barbed wire, crawl right up to my position, and slit my throat while I drifted off into dreamland. I don't think that I ever slept when I had guard duty, even when it was not my watch, because I never had full confidence in whomever I was with on guard. It was an eerie feeling straining your eyes and ears into the Vietnamese night trying to pick up any signs of movement or sounds of danger. Some nights as I strained to listen, it seemed that every dog in Vietnam was barking—but when they got quiet, then I got really scared. It never ceased to amaze me how many tricks your eyes and your imagination play on you when you are scared.

One night at Pershing, I was out on the perimeter with one of the radar guys. We were having a relaxed and peaceful conversation because he was not picking up any movement on the radar screen. All of a sudden, we came under some rather intense sniper fire, which ended quickly, and all was quiet again for the rest of the night. No one was hit, but never again did I put a lot of confidence or stock in the benefit of radar as an early-detection system.

Mike Pinksaw, *Specialist Four, U.S. Army, 60th Land Clearing Company, 62nd Engineering Battalion, 20th Engineering Brigade, Long Binh, Bien Hoa, Lai Khe, 1968–69*

When I was with the construction battalion in Bien Hoa, I pulled guard duty once a week. It was always a long, boring night. We used to get strong coffee brought out to us around four o'clock in the morning, to keep us from falling asleep. Occasionally, we'd take some harassing mortar fire around the air base, but nothing bad.

Salvatore T. Raffa, *Airman Second Class, U.S. Air Force, 377th Security Police Squadron, Tan Son Nhut Air Base, Saigon, 1967–68*

It was horrible. It could get very lonely out there. The sergeant of the guard puts you in a bunker by yourself, or so you thought, when next thing you know you'd hear voices, and in a short time you'd be joined by an ARVN soldier who had come to assist you, only he brought his entire family with him, including his wife and children. I swear, these guys made the place into their home away from home.

Bill McCollum, *Sergeant, U.S. Army, 173rd Airborne Brigade, Charlie Company, 4th Battalion, 503rd Infantry, LZ-English, 1969–71*

I found this diet medicine called Obesitol on the Vietnamese black market. It had a hell of a taste. I mean, it was horrible; but if you took it with some Coca-Cola, it wasn't so bad. It acted like speed, and it kept me awake on guard duty.

After I hurt my ankle, I was sent back to the outpost. There, I was put on night guard, and I remember living off the starlight scope, which enabled us to see at night. There were five of us up there. I'd catch these bastards coming through the valley, and we'd call in for gunfire. We'd have a field day out there. Most of the time, we took small-arms fire, which didn't bother us; but when you heard the *thump, thump, thump,* it was time to protect yourself, 'cause the mortars were coming in.

I loved guard duty. I just wanted to be there, but I really don't know why. I guess that's kind of strange, huh?

GOING ON PATROL IN THE BUSH

In a land of such incredibly diverse terrain—muddy rice paddies, raging streams and rivers, steep mountain ridges, and triple-canopy jungles—patrolling required a nearly superhuman effort. Many remote areas were virtually impenetrable. The effort of humping the bush, as the grunts called it, especially in the intense heat and stifling humidity, was an almost insurmountable task—a dehumanizing effort—requiring an individual to use all of his basic survival skills.

Obstacles included elephant grass—tall, razor-sharp strands of grass that had to be hacked away with a machete—neck-deep streams that had to be forded, and triple-canopy jungles, which made the surrounding area musty, cold, and dark, a potential sanctuary for the enemy. If that wasn't bad enough, everything and everyone seemed to be contending for a soldier's blood—insects such as mosquitoes, leeches, and above all, VC guerrillas and NVA soldiers.

The enemy was as cunning as they were stealthy, and they planted booby traps in the jungle just about anywhere an American soldier would traverse. Because of this, the infantryman had to be on constant alert for any signs of danger.

In his widely acclaimed book, *Vietnam: A History*, Stanley Karnow mentioned a memoir by Tim O'Brien, *If I Die in a Combat Zone*, in which the author discussed his recollections of humping the bush. His paranoia was evident in the following:

> Should you put your foot to that flat rock or the clump of weeds to its rear? . . . You try to trace the footprints of the man to your front. You give it up when he curses you for following too closely; better one man dead than two. The moment-to-moment, step-by-step decision-making preys on your mind. The effect is sometimes paralysis.*

Rob Roche, Sergeant, U.S. Army, 101st Airborne Division, Da Nang, 1967–69

There were a lot of places when the lead man in the platoon, the one who was walking point, had to cut his way through the jungle with a machete. Fatigue became a real factor. When I came back home, I think I weighed only one hundred and twenty pounds. Oh, the sweat! I think I sweat it all off in the jungle.

And the friggin' leeches, man, they were bad, too. I just pulled or popped them off.

One day, we were dropped off in a mountain area near a place called the Ashau Valley. It had been reported by intelligence that the valley was a sanctuary for over ten thousand NVA regulars. Those guys didn't screw around. They stood their ground and fought you. Now, we were up in the mountains that surround this valley for two to three weeks, and we just watched the planes and jets flying in and bombing the shit out of the valley to kind of make it safe for us to walk down there. Around the area, we had set up a number of recoilless rifles and other weapons to fire into the valley, supposedly to help soften the position, to make it safer for the infantry.

While waiting for our unit to be called into action, a friend of mine from Montana, Randy, had just received a letter from his wife announcing that he was the proud parent of a baby boy. He was a great guy!

---

* Stanley Karnow, *Vietnam: A History* (New York: Viking Press, 1983), p. 472.

Randy had recently made buck sergeant and had been in-country for a while. He only had a short time left on his tour before he would rotate back home. We were smoking grass, enjoying a hot chocolate together, and having as good of a time as you could have under the circumstances.* It was kind of like a great thing, him being a new father and all. We were all really happy for him.

Then we got word it was time to move out. We suited up and started moving down the mountainside. I was walking point, and we got down

to where we were supposed to be, when all of a sudden we hit a bunch of shit. Randy was our platoon sergeant at the time. He started to wave us forward when he was killed instantly. After the fight, it was a real bad thing. I had to put him in the friggin' poncho and, with three others to help me, throw his body on the helicopter. Oh man, that really sucked!

As for the battle itself, it was a terrible waste. The entire episode seemed pointless. Oh man, that was a tough one! We went down there, and we got our asses kicked. The NVA were dug in deep and actually baited us into a fight. We took the bait hook, line, and sinker. After we made a number of

Rob Roche at the Birmingham Tactical Compound, two days before he was wounded in the Ashau Valley. (Courtesy of Rob Roche)

assaults, the area was finally taken at much too great a cost. The irony of the whole thing was we evacuated the area a short time later, and it was retaken by the NVA.

Don't kid yourself. The NVA were good. In all the time we fought them, we rarely got the best of them. I mean rarely! Of course, this is not how the newspapers reported it at the time.

---

* Surprisingly, even in hot and humid conditions, a hot chocolate drink was enjoyable. The chocolate powder came in a packet as part of a C-ration box. As it was made with canteen water, "hot chocolate" may have been a misnomer. More appropriately, it should have been called "lukewarm chocolate."

David Rossi, *Specialist Four, U.S. Army, 1st Infantry Division and 25th Infantry Division, Di An, Tay Ninh, and Cu Chi, 1969–70*

It was early May when we went into Cambodia. On our helicopter that day were reporters from *Life* magazine and *Stars and Stripes.*

You could tell that you were seeing another country other than Vietnam. On one side of the river, there were all these bomb craters, but on the other side it was nice and green. I mean, it was beautiful! That was Cambodia as I first saw it from the air.

Remember, at the time, I had just barely arrived in-country. I mean, I had never seen any real combat action to speak of.

We were told we were going there, and I remember a lot of guys saying, "I'm not going to Cambodia," and, "I don't get paid to fight there," and things like that. Eventually, after all the griping was over, everybody went.

We were dropped off in this rice paddy, and there were snipers in the trees. The reporters had helmets and uniforms, but no weapons—only pens and paper. Anyway, they got trapped behind a big anthill. Some of those anthills went over ten feet high and twenty feet across. As there were several reporters, we had to go out there twice to bring them in. The snipers continued to fire, and we had to jump behind one side of a rice paddy dike while the bullets landed just behind us. Because we were virtually pinned down, air support had to be called in. Fighter jets came in not long afterwards, perhaps fifteen to twenty minutes, and I was surprised at just how low they were flying. They couldn't have been more than forty feet over the treetops. They did their thing and helped soften the area.

The next thing I remember, the sergeants threw smoke grenades to give us cover from the snipers. Fortunately, everyone got out without being injured.

Ken Garthee, *Private First Class, U.S. Marine Corps, 3rd Battalion, 3rd Marines, 3rd Marine Division, Da Nang, Rock Pile, 1966–67*

I had just turned twenty years old when I started making these patrols of hunt and search encounters. It went on day after day, week after week. It seemed like we were always making contact with the VC on patrols during the day or patrols and ambushes during the night.

Sometimes I would walk point, and other times I'd bring up the rear in the *Tail-end Charlie* position. Most of the times, however, I was somewhere in the middle—it was safer in the middle. There were actually guys who loved being in the lead or at the end of the patrol. As far as I was concerned, they could have it.

At night when it was my turn to stay awake to watch for movement, I would focus on the tree line and listen. Sometimes during my watch, I'd look into the night sky and see millions of stars, and I'd watch for shooting stars.

There was an incident one night while we were on an ambush. We were deployed in an ambush formation among the trees and high grass in the shape of an L. After completing my turn at watch, I woke the marine beside me, who was scheduled to have the watch for the next two hours. Sometime later, I was awakened by sounds of someone walking through our position. The guy next to me, who was supposed to be on watch, had fallen asleep, and a patrol of Viet Cong was walking through. Every marine lay motionless with his eyes wide open, fully aware of every step the VC made. We were ready to shoot if the VC discovered us. Fortunately, the VC patrol walked through our position without realizing we were there. None of us ever told anyone about this incident.

One thing I seemed to always notice while walking through the different villages and hamlets was the lack of children running around. There wasn't a family unit to be seen. The younger ones were clinging to their mothers, while the older kids, who should have been in school, were trying to hustle us for candy and cigarettes. There were also a lot of older men and women—faces without expression—with their eyes just following us, making sure that we didn't take anything or disturb their homes.

Of course, the most noticeable absence was the men above the age of sixteen in any of these villages or hamlets. I learned that they had all been recruited or taken to support the VC effort. It appeared there was not a single family unit intact. It was during these times that I realized the importance of family and the family unit.

Later, when I worked as a reconnaissance scout, we were dropped in the middle of the jungle, north of Da Nang. Our mission was to lead several marine companies into the jungle and make contact with the VC or NVA. We were now on our way north to the demilitarized zone.

I remember it being hot, with temperatures over ninety degrees, high humidity, and very little breeze. It was the start of the rainy season. It rained every day, sometimes all day long, and we got soaked. I mean, everything got wet. We walked and sometimes rode trucks. The further north we went, the thicker the jungle became. More than once, we had to walk through triple canopy rain forests, and about every fifteen minutes we had to stop to do a leech check. I hated the rain!

On one leg of the operation, we were given supplies and rations for seven days. It rained all day long, day after day, night after night. We had to do everything in the rain, including eating and sleeping, and it was hard to find a spot on any of us that was not soaked. By the eighth or ninth day, we were looking for helicopters to bring us more food and supplies. Unfortunately for us, the helicopters couldn't fly in the rain and heavy overcast skies. We were getting real hungry.

One of us took off his helmet, filled it with water and rice we had acquired in a village, and began to cook it. We put in anything we could find, including leftover beef from one of our ration meals and a package of lime Kool-Aid someone had received with a letter from home, just to sweeten the mixture. As it was cooking, the clouds suddenly broke, and we heard the helicopters flying overhead. They dropped the rations and supplies, and we ate as if we had never been fed before. As for the concoction we were cooking, we didn't eat the green beef and rice. We weren't that hungry anymore.

On the next leg, we went through Hue, Quang Tri, and Cam Lo until we reached our northernmost position near the DMZ. When we arrived, we learned that the NVA were moving south from North Vietnam along the Ho Chi Minh Trail. It was still raining.

We continued to conduct patrols every day, rain or shine, but still made no contact with the enemy. At night, well, that was different. The NVA would launch mortars on our position. When we completed our patrol and returned to our position, we filled what seemed like a million sandbags to build bunkers on top of our mountain, which overlooked a mountain range called the Rock Pile.

Bill McCollum, *Sergeant, U.S. Army, 173rd Airborne Brigade, Charlie Company, 4th Battalion, 503rd Infantry, LZ-English, 1969–71*

I see this all the time—it's like an instant replay through my head. It happened during the Tet. We went out on patrol and were ordered not to make contact. All we were ordered to do was recon the area, but how do you tell the VC in the mountains that you're on a cease-fire? You can't do it.

We were standing at the gate of this village, and Ralph said, "I'll walk point today."

I said, "No you're not. I'll walk point."

We had kind of a friendly argument, which lasted less than a minute. I loved walking point. This was about six months into my tour, and I was just aggressive—I liked being up front.

I said, "Look Ralph, if I get it today, you can have this; if you get it, I'm gonna have your dogs and your girlfriend."

He always talked about his dogs. What a stupid thing to say, even though I just said it jokingly. Two hours later, he would be dead.

I can see it like yesterday. We were at the base of the high ground. I was walking point; Ralph, the next guy, was ten feet behind me. Ralph was considerably taller than I, and he could see over the top of my head. That's why I liked walking point with him behind me. I was walking point, looking for booby traps, and he was scanning the area. The rest of the guys were about twenty-five meters behind us. Now, the platoon was in an open rice paddy. It just so happened we had some ARVN soldiers with us. I looked over, and out of the corner of my eye, I saw two VC running right at the base of the mountain, and as I turned to let Ralph know that we had two *dinks* there, he was already shaking his head.

He said, "Yeah, I see them!"

So we ran up into this graveyard, and I dropped down behind a gravestone. Ralph was on the side of one when these guys opened up. They just sprayed us with bullets right in front of our position. In slow motion, I could see his body fly through the air, even though he was lying down at the time.

I felt the dirt hit me in the face, and I was saying to myself, "Oh shit," and at the same time, I saw Ralph's body, in slow motion, going through the air. He ended up on his back. I was still trying to fire at these guys as I was shouting for a medic. They couldn't get to him because of the intense fire, so I went right back to my training. I rolled, and when I got to him, I just knew that he was gone. He had been shot through the head.

So, now another guy dropped up beside me and told me, "Get over there, get over there, and put down a base of fire!"

So I started running, and I didn't even know where I was going. And as I was running, I was just firing.

Then it was over. There was a helicopter flying over us, and I wanted to shoot him down because they hadn't given us any air support. The sad part about it was, I had to make a litter and carry the body back to the CP.

Shortly thereafter, I ran into a *papa-san* in the area, and I called him over to me in Vietnamese.

I said to him, "Did the VC come here?"

I knew he was going to say no. As soon as he said no, I coldcocked him with my closed fist, and he fell face first into the rice paddy. I think

I left the indentation of my Rogers High School ring in his forehead. I know that *papa-san* was out there, and he could have warned us about the VC in the area, but he didn't. In fact, he could have been a VC himself.

One of the guys in the platoon said to me, "Mac, aren't you going to pick him up?"

I said, "No!"

Whether anyone ever picked him up or not, I don't know.

GOING ON A BOMBING RUN

Early in the war, there were several reasons for bombing both North and South Vietnam, but as the fighting escalated, two primary reasons prevailed. The first objective was to protect American ground soldiers from the enemy. The second aim was to cut off enemy supply lines along the Ho Chi Minh Trail.

Bombing missions were flown by both F-4s and B-52s. F-4 Phantom fighter-bomber jets were flown by two men. The plane was capable of carrying 14,000 pounds of explosives, all of which had to be jettisoned on the intended targets during a single mission. In 1968 and 1969 alone, over one million tons of ordnance—one megaton—per year was dropped on South Vietnam. These two years were recognized as the peak of the most fierce fighting of the war, for both ground and in-air fighting.*

William Sullivan, *Lieutenant Commander, U.S. Navy, Fighter Squadron 213, U.S.S.* Intrepid, *Air Wing, U.S.S.* Kitty Hawk *(CVA-63), U.S.S.* Intrepid *(CVA-11), U.S.S.* Paul Revere, *and U.S.S.* Blue Ridge, *1965–68 and 1971–72*

When at sea we would fly one or two missions per day, but not more than two. On a carrier, we would awaken and get dressed for our mission by putting on our flight suits and helmets and our lifesaving gear and proceed to the ready room. In this room, we would be given a briefing about our mission for that day. We'd usually get our assigned targets for the mission from the flight operations targeting officer. Then we would take the escalator to the flight deck, man our planes, check

* Raphael Littauer and Norman Upshoff, *The Airwar in Vietnam* (Boston: Beacon Press, 1972), p. 10.

them all out, and then get catapulted off the carrier deck at 0–150 knots in just about two seconds. It was a pretty good jolt.

Usually, there'd be no fewer than two aircraft in formation at any given time. The missions were mostly direct bombing missions, where we'd carry heavy bomb loads or air-to-ground rockets. In some cases, the mission would be either escorting reconnaissance aircraft or acting as combat air patrol, watching for enemy fighters that might try to attack the carrier.

In the air over South Vietnam, we'd look for a prominent landmark that we could pick up on radar and then take a bearing and distance from that landmark. In some cases, there would be Vietnamese ground spotters in the area, who would radio us of suspected enemy positions. Also assisting us to locate the enemy were American personnel known as the Airborne Close Air Support, who would be flying low in that area.

In North Vietnam one of the ways to find the target was by inertial navigation instruments, which we had and used in conjunction with radar. The other way was by visual location, using road layouts.

After completion of the mission, the pilot (I was the flight officer in the back seat) had the difficult task of landing the aircraft on the carrier flight deck, one which became even more challenging when landing in the dark. Landings in bad weather were an incredible challenge. A strange phenomenon existed in the Western Pacific in the Tonkin Gulf off the coast of North Vietnam. There'd be rainstorms, particularly in the summertime, and the wind would shift around. The carrier below would be turning, trying to find the wind, and you'd try to line up the aircraft to land, and the carrier would turn again to try to find the wind again, weaving and turning, as you're in the aircraft getting closer and closer, attempting to follow the carrier's path. It was extremely difficult in those conditions for the pilot to land safely, and it took all of your powers to do so.

THE CRAZINESS OF IT ALL

War by its very nature is chaotic, and rarely do events in combat follow systematically planned and predetermined courses of action. Coupled with the lack of a clearly defined mission and an overall strategic war objective—that is, a vision—all too frequently circumstances proved confusing and, at times, disastrous to the lower-ranking soldiers in combat zones.

Over the years, negative reports about the Vietnam War suggest that this conflict led all others in terms of absurdities. From the standpoint of poor leadership skills, ineffective or illogical tactics, questionable policy decisions, and incongruous command strategies, high-ranking Vietnam War policy advisors and decision makers certainly contributed to this belief. Undoubtedly, because Vietnam was the first war this country would lose, critics were in a better position to spread the blame. Yet to assume that these erroneous actions could only be attributed to this war is incorrect. There hasn't been a war fought by Americans where significant blunders did not occur. During the Civil War, both World Wars, Korea, and the Persian Gulf Conflict, disheartened troops suffered from sometimes comical and, at other times, painfully disastrous leadership decisions.

American military personnel saw firsthand the preposterousness of restrictive policies and questionable leadership judgments and the consequences it had on them. It is appropriate that some of these examples be mentioned here.

At other times, unfortunate circumstances that had nothing to do with war strategies took an unlucky toll on military personnel. In yet other cases, the average soldier created his own asininity.

Thomas Finn, Specialist Four, U.S. Army, Company A, 519th Military Intelligence Battalion, 525th Military Intelligence Group, MACV-J2, Saigon, 1966–67

The VC floated down the river one night, camouflaged with shrubs. They floated past our compound, perhaps by a hundred yards or so, and set off charges that destroyed a bridge. The sky was lit up like it was noontime, and the concussion from the blast blew me out of my bunk. I put on my steel pot helmet and jungle boots while still in my skivvies and picked up my M14 and tried to look for the ammo. All the ammunition was locked up at that time in a Connex container. So for the longest time, we're looking for someone who's got a key to unlock it. The only guys who had ammo were the guards in the towers. It seemed that the higher-ups were more concerned with misappropriation of rounds than protecting against a quick and potentially devastating attack. If you can, visualize a hundred guys running around the compound in various stages of dress with their M14s, looking for a magazine. It was crazy.

Doug Johnson, Specialist Four, U.S. Army, 25th Infantry Division, 2nd Battalion, 12th Infantry, 1968

One of the things that I found particularly troublesome about guard duty at Pershing was the requirement to call for permission before you could fire off the perimeter. The reasons given were that there was usually one of our ambush squads in one direction and that there were villages in other directions. I had no problem with avoiding fire in the direction of our ambush squad, but as far as I was concerned, the villages that were off our perimeter in the other directions were not friendly. Somehow I didn't picture that they were holding Kiwanis, Rotary, or Optimist Club meetings in the dead of night or pro-USA rallies. This was one of the many ways that we were fighting a war against an enemy with our own rules and regulations stacked against us. In my mind, I determined that if the shit hit the fan, I would shoot first and ask questions later.

Howard North, *Lieutenant j.g., U.S. Coast Guard, Coast Guard Squadron One, USCGC* Point Clear *(WPB 82315), An Thoi and Cat Lo, 1967–68*

We'd go as far out as ten miles from the coast, all day and all night long, boarding *sampans* and fishing boats, looking for contraband weapons and drugs. Our boardings averaged between sixty and seventy boats a day.

The only guy I ever saw that I think was a VC was this native standing on the shoreline in a very conspicuous area, an area in which he wasn't supposed to be. A pilot flying a Piper Cub as a forward observer was flying along the coast, and for a number of days he was taking small-arms fire from this area of the village. He was pissed! Four days in a row he got shot at. So he made arrangements for us to meet him at a particular location at noontime.

Here's the incredible thing, though. Unless someone was being directly attacked by the enemy, for us to provide artillery support, it nearly took an act of war to fire back. We had to radio our headquarters, they had to radio Saigon, the Vietnamese district chief had to approve the request, then it had to go in reverse through the same channels before we were granted the authority to fire back. Luckily, in this instance, the pilot obtained clearance for us to fire without all the formality normally associated with our providing the necessary assistance.

Anyway, there was this break in the mangrove swamp, and all of the sampans saw us coming and went right in to shore. They sensed what was going to happen. Everyone jumped out of the sampans, and, I mean, they did a *dee dee* and quickly retreated for cover. Now, the pilot was so pissed, he came out of the clouds and fired these two smoke bombs at the supposed VC. Next, I see the guy running through the mangrove swamp with the smoke bombs going after him. As close as it was, I think the guy managed to dodge the rounds and get away. He may have been the luckiest man in South Vietnam that day.

We shot perhaps fifty to sixty mortar rounds at the village during the engagement and sank a few sampans. For a war trophy, we confiscated two undamaged sampans as contraband, and they eventually ended up in Hawaii in front of the Coast Guard Headquarters.

In all the time we were patrolling the waters, all we found was one set of crummy radio plans. It was nothing more than a schematic for a radio. Why the hell they ever had a schematic for a radio, we never found out. In addition, we had one Vietnamese that had a bad ID. All those times, and that's all we ever found. And we were boarding boats constantly.

On another night we were ordered to pursue a radar contact. At best, all we could do was maybe fourteen knots. This sucker was doing about twenty-six. Come to find out, it was an American freighter we were chasing.

William Sullivan, *Lieutenant Commander, U.S. Navy, Fighter Squadron 213, U.S.S.* Intrepid, *Air Wing, U.S.S.* Kitty Hawk *(CVA-63), U.S.S.* Intrepid *(CVA-11), U.S.S.* Paul Revere, *and U.S.S.* Blue Ridge, *1965–68 and 1971–72*

As I stated earlier, when we flew over large cities like Haiphong and Hanoi, we'd find targets there by street layout. These cities were large enough to visually allow us to follow the streets from the air.

In some cases, there were an awful lot of targets that were excluded from attacks. Let me give you an example. One day, we broke out of the clouds and penetrated land over Haiphong, a major port in North Vietnam, and right below us was a Polish freighter. It had a cargo of ammunition and military vehicles which were in the process of being unloaded. The Russians and Polish, under communist rule at the time, were supplying North Vietnam with these goods. Now, we knew what the cargo was and that it was used against the Americans, but we couldn't touch it.

Mike Pinksaw, *Specialist Four, U.S. Army, 60th Land Clearing Company, 62nd Engineering Battalion, 20th Engineering Brigade, Long Binh, Bien Hoa, Lai Khe, 1968–69*

These North Vietnamese regulars infiltrated our perimeter one night and were shot and killed. I happened to have a regular bull blade on my 'dozer, so a sergeant from the 1st Infantry Division came over to our area and said, "We need somebody who operates that 'dozer to go out and bury the two dead North Vietnamese soldiers."

Reluctantly, I said, "That's my 'dozer." So I was elected.

Two other guys on an armored personnel carrier, and I on the 'dozer, drove over to the area where the bodies were left. These were the first dead bodies I had ever seen in-country, and they weren't pretty. One of the bodies showed signs of being hit by a .50 caliber. I remember briefly looking at them; one had a gaping hole in his stomach, and the other had had his throat blown away. The bodies were already black and decomposing from lying in the hot sun all day.

I said to myself, "Oh, no!"

I immediately started to dig a four-foot-deep trench.

When I completed digging the hole, one of the other guys said, "Come on, we'll throw them in."

"No, wait a minute." I backed my tractor around, and with the bull blade, I just pushed them in and covered them up. Then I said, "Let's go!"

It wasn't a fitting burial for any human being, but I wasn't going to touch those bodies for anything. I don't think the other guys wanted to either.

Salvatore T. Raffa, *Airman Second Class, U.S. Air Force, 377th Security Police Squadron, Tan Son Nhut Air Base, Saigon, 1967–68*

Saigon used to serve as an in-country R & R for the marines and infantry guys coming in from the field. These guys were right out of the jungle. They would come in and see the security police force with spit-polished shoes, starched fatigues, and helmets that reflected the sun, and then be given orders by these guys like "Button your shirt," or "Blouse those boots," and things like that. Those kinds of commands didn't go over too well with the grunts.

I remember this one guy, a tech sergeant, whom I saw on TV on the *Ed Sullivan Show* after I got home. He was in charge of the Air Force Drill Team. He was a tall, thin, black guy and I can remember him looking so sharp in his uniform. He had sewn all of his pockets shut so they wouldn't bulge. I mean, this was his job, to look sharp as part of the elite guard.

Michael Toner Farrell, *Specialist Five, U.S. Army, 544th Replacement Company, Cam Ranh Bay, 1969–70*

I was stationed in a replacement company. Soldiers arrived and left Nam from there every day. Being in Nam was dangerous even when your tour was over.

An infantry soldier that I knew was going home, and he had survived a year in the jungles. He called his parents and told them that he was out of the jungle, was safe, in a secure environment, and that he would be coming home in three days. Later that same day, he lost his life in a drowning accident. This must have been devastating for his parents.

Ken Garthee, *Private First Class, U.S. Marine Corps, 3rd Battalion, 3rd Marines, 3rd Marine Division, Da Nang, Rock Pile, 1966–67*

Back at a place we called The Hill, there would be an opportunity to shoot all the ammo we had. It was called a mad minute. When we would make contact with the VC, in less than a minute we would fire, throw, and detonate every bullet, shell, hand grenade, or piece of ammo we had had to carry in the last week. Parachute flares would light up the night sky. Streams of tracer rounds would connect from one end of the horizon to the other. With our automatic rifles, clips of ammo would be emptied in seconds. It was like the Fourth of July!

The VC wouldn't dare return a shot; not even a tree would be spared. The mad minute was fun, but the end result was usually a lot of cleanup for us. All the brass from the spent cartridges had to be collected for recycling; however, it was all worth it.

I recall this particular moonlit night when one of the guys shouted that he saw two VCs running inside the tree line. He called for everyone to fire on that spot, which we did. It was another mad minute. Afterward, the sergeant sent out a patrol to look for bodies (the marines were big on body counts). When we checked the area out, we found a blood trail, but no bodies. We continued to follow the blood trail until it disappeared. The VC never took bodies with them, as they had no time or any place to put them. The following morning we continued to search.

Later that morning, we were assigned to patrol through a village near our base camp. As we passed by the marketplace, where the Vietnamese sold produce and meat, we saw a cleaned and quartered water buffalo with a million holes in the carcass. Was this the two VC we thought we saw the night before? We all looked at each other and laughed.

Betsy Wylie, *Lieutenant, U.S. Navy, Management Information Center, Headquarters, Naval Forces Vietnam (NAVFORV), Saigon, 1967–68*

After the Tet Offensive, we were required to wear our weapons all the time, but the army didn't allow weapons to be worn or carried in the mess hall, by either officers or enlisted men. Now, there was a rack outside the mess for holding hats, but none of us were willing to give up our weapons because we knew what would happen if we lost a weapon. We'd just about signed our lives away for our weapons. So we had a hell of a time trying to figure out how we were supposed to eat. I don't remember that problem ever being resolved. I put my .45 in my briefcase and carried it into lunch with me, but the guys were really upset because many were issued carbines. After two to three weeks of trying to figure out what to do, those that went to lunch with me felt that because I had the weapon, they could go without one. It was one of those cases where one order was not thoroughly researched, and nobody had a solution for the problem it created. It's called the Law of Unintended Consequences.

Bill McCollum, *Sergeant, U.S. Army, 173rd Airborne Brigade, Charlie Company, 4th Battalion, 503rd Infantry, LZ-English, 1969–71*

I had been in-country only a short time, and our platoon was going to be dropped off in a field for a mission. Sure enough, the goddamned dog was already on the chopper again. We took off and we flew in our formation towards the mountains. The Cobra helicopter gunships had gone in before us to clear out the area; however, when we came in, there was red smoke on the ground, which signified a hot landing zone.

Of course, everyone in the chopper was yelling, "Red smoke, red smoke!"

I asked, "What's red smoke?"

Well, it simply meant there were enemy in the area, and the drop zone was most likely under fire.

I was thinking the pilot was going to land it there and let us off. But he never did. It hovered about ten feet off the ground and the dog, who had more brains than I, jumped out first. When I jumped, I hit the ground and sprained my ankle and fell down. When I rolled over, the chopper started to descend, and I thought it was curtains.

I really thought he was going to land on top of me, and I was trying to tell the guy, "Get away, get away!"

Luckily he never did touch down.

A few hours later, my ankle was worse. They had to take me out of there because I couldn't walk. In the clearing, a chopper came in; I got on it, and I was taken out. It was a beautiful ride back. There were no doors, and the scenery was beautiful to look at from the air, as long as no one was firing at you.

On another occasion, we were on patrol, and as we were coming down the side of this hill, I found a skull. You could tell it was Vietnamese.

So I said to the lieutenant, "What do you want to do with it?"

He said, "Why don't you just leave it there?"

"Okay," I said, but then I had second thoughts, so I took it and put it in my rucksack.

I guess about three or four days went by; we were out on patrol again. When we stopped to eat, I pulled out the skull, which I had named Charlie; and I'd sit it down and make believe I was feeding it diced peaches, pineapple slices, and cocoa from my rations.

Finally the lieutenant came to me and said, "Mac, you're starting to worry the guys. The skull's got to go."

I said, "He doesn't bother anybody," but he made me get rid of it. I think he was getting nervous about it, not the guys."

NEAR MISSES

Whether soldiers served as support personnel or in a combat unit, close calls were an inevitable reality in a war zone, and nearly everyone lived through at least one harrowing experience. Infantry soldiers suffered a preponderance of near misses due to their military designation and its inherent risks. These men were frequently exposed to the guerrilla tactics of the enemy.

Close calls came in many forms, from bullets passing by to misfired rockets. While humping the bush, some members of a patrol might pass a hidden booby trap, such as a tripwire tied to explosives. The trap might not be discovered until several men had already traversed the area. An unlucky soldier walking just a few feet to the left or right could set off the explosives and be wounded or killed.

Luck played a significant role in determining who would live and who would die. However, there was no substitute for a soldier's preparation for battle, remembering lessons he learned from prior skirmishes, using effective teamwork, his physical conditioning, and his own mental alertness.

Thomas Finn, *Specialist Four, U.S. Army, Company A, 519th Military Intelligence Battalion, 525th Military Intelligence Group, MACV-J2, Saigon, 1966–67*

The times I pulled guard duty in the towers was perhaps the closest I came to being killed. On occasion a sniper would fire a few rounds at us, and you didn't know whether to fire a few rounds down-range or restrain yourself so you wouldn't piss 'em off more.

I remember at least one time asking the officer of the guard at the bottom of the tower, "Should I send a few rounds down?"

His response was, "No, hold on, hold on, hold on."

You just seemed to play it by the seat of your pants. No one really wanted to start anything.

Betsy Wylie, *Lieutenant, U.S. Navy, Management Information Center, Headquarters, Naval Forces Vietnam (NAVFORV), Saigon, 1967–68*

For some reason, I was flying in a helicopter down to Can Tho in the Delta. When we landed, the pilot said, "Somebody shot at us on the way down." There were holes in the helicopter.

We didn't know we were being shot at, which was probably just as well.

Stephen Butler, *Lance Corporal, U.S. Marine Corps, 7th Marine Combat Engineers, Da Nang, 1966–67*

I remember sitting on a tire in the back of a six-by [truck] with a flak jacket on. I heard this explosion, and the next thing I remember is seeing a guy about three tires down from me sail right over the tailgate. It must have been a small personnel mine, because it didn't lift the truck up. The guy thrown out of the truck had a busted shoulder and some other stuff.

Then, another time, the driver got whacked. We were coming back down the side of Monkey Mountain, and they shot the driver and the whole truck. It was weird, because I was sitting in the back with a friend, and we were just shooting the breeze back and forth. And we started to go around a hard curve—sometimes you just get those feelings—and I looked again, and when I looked, I could see the curve on Monkey Mountain, and I knew the truck wasn't going to make it around the curve. Through absolutely no motivation of my own, or planning, the next thing I knew I was outside the vehicle, with my weapon, rolling on the ground. My friend was beside me. The truck went over the side of the mountain, and six or seven guys who were still in the truck got really screwed up. The driver had been killed—whether instantly or not, I don't know—he had been shot right through the neck. The whole thing was a bloody mess.

Afterward, I asked my friend, "Did you yell *jump,* or did I yell *jump?*"
Neither one of us remembers how the hell we got out of the truck. So
obviously, sometimes it's just luck.

Salvatore T. Raffa, *Airman Second Class, U.S. Air Force, 377th Security
Police Squadron, Tan Son Nhut Air Base, Saigon, 1967–68*

I had only been in-country a short time when I had this near miss. I was
shaving in this big long bathroom with about eighteen other guys in the
building with me. I thought a bug whizzed by me—actually, I couldn't tell
what the hell it was—but it turned out to be no bug. I looked to my left and
then to my right, and the guys I was shaving next to weren't there anymore.

I said to myself, "What's going on?"

All of a sudden, a hand reached up and grabbed me and pulled me
down to the concrete floor. We were getting sniper fire, and I had no idea
what was going on. That's when I realized that these guys were actually
trying to kill me!

I used to say, "They don't even know me, why do they want to kill
me?" I had a hard time coming to grips with all of this.

Mike Pinksaw, *Specialist Four, U.S. Army, 60th Land Clearing Company, 62nd Engineering Battalion, 20th Engineering Brigade, Long
Binh, Bien Hoa, Lai Khe, 1968–69*

We were in the jungle one day, clearing out an area, when I hit a mine with
my bulldozer. I remember the operation like it was yesterday.

We were working in a big square area, just like you would when mow-
ing grass at home. The tractor in front of me was called the lead plow.
The guy driving this thing wore headphones and was taking orders from
a guy on an armored personnel carrier, as we had the armored infantry
with us that day. This guy was getting his orders from a chopper flying
overhead.

I replaced the lead plow after the driver hit a land mine, and the vehicle became disabled. The rest of us all went around the square in basically
the same area as before, and this time I hit a mine in almost the exact same
place. I remember a bright flash and the concussion of the blast knocking
the wind out of me. My squad leader in the armored personnel carrier saw
the whole thing, and he anxiously called me on the headphones. I had the
microphone in front of my face, but nothing would come out of my mouth.

He was asking me, "Are you all right?"

I was moving my mouth trying to answer him, but nothing would come out. Finally, I managed to say that I was okay.

In normal conditions, the blades of this bulldozer looked like a big snowplow with an attachment we called a stinger, which was used for pulling out trees. After gaining my composure, I got off the tractor and looked at the blade. It was peeled back like a banana, and the stinger was completely turned around in the opposite direction. I think my eardrums were probably spared because I had the headphones on.

William Sullivan, *Lieutenant Commander, U.S. Navy, Fighter Squadron 213, U.S.S.* Intrepid, *Air Wing, U.S.S.* Kitty Hawk *(CVA-63), U.S.S.* Intrepid *(CVA-11), U.S.S.* Paul Revere, *and U.S.S.* Blue Ridge, *1965–68 and 1971–72*

There was an American seaplane that had been shot at and disabled, and the crew had to make an emergency landing in the waters of North Vietnam. We were called in to render some assistance.

After we made a couple of passes over the aircraft, an enemy shell hit near the opening of the door and blew the seaplane up just as we were flying overhead. Fortunately for us, we were not hit by any of the flak from the exploding aircraft.

In Vietnam, of the over three hundred missions I was involved in, I'd say the pilot and I took fire on approximately one hundred of them.

Dick Turner, *Boatswain's Mate Third Class, U.S. Navy, River Assault Squadron 15, River Division 152, Task Force 117, Dong Tam and My Tho, 1968–69*

Our boat was modified from a regular landing craft. The manufacturer had put quarter-inch steel plate on the outside of it, using reinforcing rods, and stuffed it with blocks of Styrofoam. One day our boat got hit by a rocket on our starboard side in the ammo room. The rocket came right in over the top of the 20mm ammunition boxes and never hit them. Most of your B-40 rockets are point-detonated, so if they hit something, they're going to go off. Luckily for us, this round went clear through the starboard side, about a foot over the ammo boxes, through the steel plate on the other side, and detonated on the other bulkhead near the water tank. It made a hole in the boat which you could look right out of.

We had another close call. We had this hand-held M79 grenade launcher which had to be cranked in order to be fired; we called it a hurdy-gurdy. A guy was doing maintenance on it and had it pointed up without realizing that he had a grenade chambered in the weapon. When he cranked it over, the grenade fired and went up and hit the flight deck; but it didn't travel far enough to arm itself. So we just picked it up and threw it over the side.

Doug Johnson, *Specialist Four, U.S. Army, 25th Infantry Division, 2nd Battalion, 12th Infantry, 1968*

I was in many rocket and mortar attacks at Cu Chi, Fire Support Base Stuart, and Fire Support Base Pershing. Because of the unenviable position that the 25th Infantry Division occupied near the Cambodian border, we were often targeted by both the Viet Cong and the NVA. About the only thing I can tell you for sure is that I soon learned to be less concerned about rockets and mortars if I could hear them and have time to find some type of cover. I always figured that you had to be a pretty unlucky bastard to be hit by a mortar or rocket, although, in retrospect, I'm not sure what the basis for that misguided confidence was. I measured some pretty close calls when I compared the hole left by a shell from where I was hanging out when it hit. I never felt completely comfortable in the solitude of our luxurious outhouses, as I could picture no more ignominious a death than literally having your shit blown away while answering the call of nature.

Too Close for Comfort

One time we had a rather extensive rocket attack in Cu Chi while we were replacing and refilling some of the sandbags on one of the bunkers outside our shack. A bunch of us jumped to safety into the bunker and rode out the barrage. When we emerged from the bunker, seemingly unharmed, we began to relax and return to the task at hand. All of a sudden, we were all yelling and tearing off clothes—we were under a fierce attack by an enemy I had not encountered until that day, the famous monster red ants of Vietnam. I swear that they stood on their heads when they bit you so that they could extract large quantities of skin from your body. As with so many other of life's little pleasures and discoveries in Vietnam, I kept my eyes open from that day forward for the friendly fire ants.

Bill McCollum, Sergeant, U.S. Army, 173rd Airborne Brigade, Charlie Company, 4th Battalion, 503rd Infantry, LZ-English, 1969–71

It was during the days of the pacification program when this incident happened. The company commander selected me to walk point on this particular patrol in the mountains. We were going up the side of a hill. I had a guy directly behind me, and the guy who was the RTO was near him. We were called on the radio and ordered to hold up.

I looked back down the hill and said, "What the hell is going on?" Apparently, someone had fallen and had a back injury, and we had to wait for a chopper to get him out.

We were just sitting there waiting when all of a sudden I thought I heard a radio playing; so I said to one of my guys, "Who the hell is playing the radio?"

"No one's playing a radio."

"Like hell, I hear a goddamned radio," and it was American music I heard.

So I started looking around, and I saw this big boulder to the left of us. I figured it should be investigated, so I called my platoon sergeant and told him what was up, and that I was going to check this out.

"Take a couple of guys with you," he said.

I got about twenty-five meters from it, and I said, "What the hell?"

I walked around the boulder, and there was shit everywhere. This area was being used as a latrine, and the droppings were fresh. So I called back and told them what I saw, and the fact that someone had been there recently. Again, I was ordered to take my squad and check it out.

Shortly thereafter, I found an opening to a cave. I called back and told them that I found a cave complex, and that I was going to check it out. I took off my rucksack and got down on my hands and knees and started to go down. It was a tight fit. All I went down with was a penlight flashlight. It was a slight drop down, and I immediately found medical supplies and two full rucksacks (NVA type). I yelled the news back up to my squad at the top of the opening. I expected to find some more souvenirs, but I really didn't expect to find anyone in there. I mean, I had forty guys behind me while we were walking up that hill; what nut's going to stick around?

It was deep and dark down there, and I heard water. I walked forward a little, and I found an underground stream.

I still could see the rays of the sun coming down through the opening, so I yelled up to the guys, "Send me a weapon."

With only the flashlight, I walked a little further and saw a hammock strung up and bolted in the rocks on each side. The hammock was covered with a simple black plastic garbage can liner, so I said to myself, "I'm going to pull it off and see what supplies are under it." As soon as I grabbed it, I felt a roundness. My hand was on this guy's head, and he immediately popped up. I thought, "Oh f—, I don't belong here." Then I pissed on myself!

Everything was happening really fast. I had to get out of there, but I was worried he was going to shoot me in the back. I had to do something. I really didn't want to do anything to him, I just wanted to get out of there with my life. So I hit him with my fist and knocked him out of the hammock.

I got back to the opening, and the guys were yelling, "Here, Mac, take the pistol."

I yelled back, "F— you, I've got a gook down here." So they dropped the pistol down to me, anyway.

I went back, and now my eyes were somewhat adjusted to the dim light, and I saw him getting up off the ground, so I told him to "*den-den,*" which I thought meant "lie down" in Vietnamese but actually means "come." What I should have said was "*dung lai,*" which means "halt."

I kept saying, "*Lai dang, lai dang, lai dang,*" or something like that, and he just kept walking toward me. I didn't know what I was saying; I was so confused and scared.

I realized I had to do something, and I no longer wanted to be in there with him, so I fired the pistol. The echo in that little hole in the ground was unreal from the blast of my .45. I saw him fly to the side, and later, I saw I caught him in the side of his neck. He wasn't dead, though. So I wanted to fire again. But the pistol wouldn't fire. I threw it down and pulled out a knife. I went at him, and I heard a noise behind me. I glanced backward and saw my lieutenant, who had just dropped down to the floor from the opening. Quickly, I jumped on the gook and hit him once with the knife. The second time I went at him, he tried to block it. I put it through his hand and into his forehead. Now I had to put my knee on him to get it out.

The lieutenant behind me, seeing the whole thing, screamed out, "Okay, okay!"

"One more!" I yelled back. I gave him one more. I just couldn't leave there knowing he wasn't dead.

Now I turned to the lieutenant, and I was all over him like stink on shit. "You stupid f—," I said, "you gave me a pistol that didn't work!"

The lieutenant picked up the pistol and tried to let the hammer go. It went off, and for whatever reason, he had his other hand over the barrel. He blew a hole clear through the middle of his hand. The expended round went right past my leg, nearly giving me a sex change.

Needless to say, the pistol was fine. I guess that in my crazed state I had had my hand on the safety.

I got out of the tunnel first, and they were trying to interview me for a report, but I said, "Wait a minute, I need a medic for the lieutenant, and I need a dry pair of pants because I pissed all over myself." I never saw the lieutenant again. He really did a job on his hand. He must have been sent back to the States after that accident.

The Tunnel Rat—Bill McCollum excavating a cave entrance. (Courtesy of Bill McCollum)

When things calmed down a little, I wanted to go back down to see the dead guy, but they wouldn't let me. Why that guy was down in the tunnel in the first place was beyond me. He looked to be about eighteen or nineteen years old, and he had to be sick, wounded, asleep, or just plain stupid when I caught him. You know, he just shouldn't have been there. I think he was trying to hide under the plastic garbage bag.

Later, when the guys retrieved the body, they said to me, "Mac, you're damned lucky."

"What do you mean?" I said.

The gook was wearing a pistol belt with a grenade attached to it, they told me.

It was the scariest moment in my life!

EIGHT

MY GOD, WHY ME?

THE UNITED STATES OF AMERICA
To all who see these presents, greeting:
This is to certify that the
President of the United States of America
has awarded the PURPLE HEART
established by General George Washington
at Newburgh, New York, August 7, 1782
to an American soldier
for wounds received in action.

BEING WOUNDED

MINOR wounds were treated in the field, and if follow-up treatment was required, the individual was transported to a local field hospital. Those who suffered more serious or life-threatening injuries experienced something entirely different. Those who remained conscious during the ordeal most certainly went through a feeling of overwhelming helplessness. Close proximity to a mortar or rocket explosion usually resulted in horrendous shrapnel wounds. The blast peppered the entire body with both small and large pieces of jagged-edged steel. In many cases, the wounds proved fatal.

If a soldier was hit by small-arms fire, the entry wound was merely a small circular laceration, while the exit wound left a gaping hole with large chunks of muscle and tissue torn away. Internal and external bleeding was profuse, and if it was not checked by the immediate application of pressure to the impacted area, the patient had little chance of survival. The exit wound was usually packed with surgical gauze by an experienced medic.

After receiving first aid in the field, the soldier was taken by helicopter to the nearest aid station or hospital for initial treatment. The main purpose of this step was for patient stabilization. If the wounded soldier made it through this checkpoint, his chances of survival increased significantly.

Unfortunately, that hospital stay was only the first in a long series of hospitals and rehabilitation centers to come. Depending upon the extent of the injuries and what portion of the body was affected, the patient could spend as much as the next few years in and out of military hospitals.

Dick Turner, *Boatswain's Mate Third Class, U.S. Navy, River Assault Squadron 15, River Division 152, Task Force 117, Dong Tam and My Tho, 1968–69*

I was wounded in the U Minh Forest. It was extremely well fortified by VC. It was like walking through a door. However, once you got in, the door closed behind you.

We got in there and got into a firefight that lasted seventeen hours. I mean, we took a beating. Our boat took a hit right near where I was, and I took a piece of shrapnel in my knee. That's how I got my Purple Heart. A piece of metal is still in there.

Our boat captain lost the use of his right arm. 'Til this day, I don't know if it was because of enemy fire or friendly fire. The boat behind us was firing what they call beehive rounds, 20mm shells that are filled with nails. He got hit with something, maybe with one of those, and he was screaming in pain. We had to get him the hell out of there and get him some medical attention.

Glen never came back to us. He probably was sent back to the States for an operation, and 'til this day I don't think he has the use of his right arm. It really did a job on him. I saved him by putting a tourniquet on him. If I hadn't have done it, he probably would have bled to death. I mean, his arm was gone; it was just gone.

Doug Johnson, *Specialist Four, U.S. Army, 25th Infantry Division, 2nd Battalion, 12th Infantry, 1968*

On October 7, 1969, I was assigned to pull guard duty on the perimeter at Fire Support Base Pershing. For most of my life up to that fateful evening, I had a well-deserved reputation for being late. The only thing that had really changed with age, and hopefully a little maturity, was that I was not ridiculously late, as I had been in my younger days. On that evening, right around dusk, I did something uncharacteristic and started over toward the perimeter early. As I got closer to the perimeter, I remember hearing a loud explosion, and my attention was immediately diverted to a distant shower point, where I saw naked bodies running in panic from the area. I don't know how long it took my mind to register, but at some point I realized that a rocket or mortar had landed by the shower point. In all my army training before Vietnam, and in the experience and training I had received since I had been in-country, one of the cardinal rules was to get down and get cover whenever there is any kind of incoming fire. The only thing I can say for sure is, on that evening my legs began moving before my brain came up with a wiser choice. I could see a bunker within sprinting distance from my position and almost immediately started to run to the safety of the bunker. I soon proved a theory that I had deduced even without any personal experience before that evening: No human being is faster than a speeding bullet.

Shortly after I began my sprint, I remember a blinding flash and literally being picked up and hurtled through the air like a rag doll and propelled for some distance. When I landed on the ground, I began to experience a pain unlike any I had ever experienced previously and which, fortunately, I have not since experienced. Somehow, and I don't know how, I managed to stand up briefly before I exclaimed to myself in disbelief that I had been hit and collapsed in a heap. There was an unbelievable ringing in my ears and a pain beyond description as I lay helplessly on the ground. Strange as it may sound, my religious beliefs and Catholic training briefly took over, and I began reciting an Act of Contrition. It seems to me now, in retrospect, that I recognized the severity of my wounds from the beginning. About halfway through my Act of Contrition, the pain became so intense that I started yelling for a medic. One of the first guys to arrive on the scene was a guy from my unit named Burbank, and I could discern from the horrified look on his face that I was in deep shit. It wasn't long before the battalion doctor was attending to me and beginning to cut my jungle fatigues off of me.

At some time during this odyssey, I remember reaching down, in probably one of the most instinctive moves known to man, and checking to see if the family jewels were still intact. The doctor, obviously sensing my concern, assured me that everything was intact.

Pain is a curious thing, and soon it began playing tricks on my mind. As I said, I had briefly stood up after I had been hit. Despite my knowledge of that fact, the pain emanating from my left lower extremity, especially the area of my left leg, had me convinced that my entire left leg had been blown off.

Soon thereafter, another interesting phenomenon began to take place—I was slowly slipping into shock. Shock is a very fickle friend to a man in excruciating pain. The temporary relief from pain provided by the shock eventually results in certain death from the very same shock, if left untreated.

I don't know how long it took for the medevac chopper to arrive, but it seemed like an eternity. Unfortunately, because the external shrapnel wounds in my back and my buttocks did not accurately reflect the internal damage, there was some discussion about whether I would be flown out on the first medevac. Soon, however, the shock gripped me to such a degree that my vital signs dipped drastically, and the medics realized I was fading fast.

I remember being loaded onto the chopper and shaking uncontrollably, as all my clothes had been cut away, and I was naked except for a blanket covering me and probably some crude field bandages. I sat up frequently on the helicopter ride to Cu Chi, and I remember one crew member gently telling me to lie down, and that we would be there soon, and everything would be all right. I distinctly recall that I resolved not to close my eyes for fear that I would never open them again. After a flight that seemed to last a lifetime, we arrived at the Evac Hospital at Cu Chi.

I don't recall how quickly I was taken to the operating room, but a priest later told me that they would not hold up my litter long enough for him to give me the last rites of the church.

I remember lying naked on what seemed to be some type of stainless steel table and still shivering uncontrollably—probably a combination of being cold, in shock, and probably terrified. This condition was not aided by the next words that I heard, which were uttered by the medic who had presumably just taken my vital signs—"No pulse and no blood pressure." I would have liked to have pretended that he was talking about someone else, but soon realized that I was the only casualty in the room. I have often wondered whether that was only a bad dream, but then I had the opportunity, years later, to review my medical records and see the same fateful words I heard that day written in black and white. At any rate, my body began to stiffen up shortly after the words were spoken, probably the result of massive shock. The only way I can describe what was happening is that it felt like rigor mortis was setting in even though I was still alive. I only knew that I was in deep, deep trouble. After I began experiencing the stiffness, I apparently lost consciousness and would not wake up again until I had undergone some extensive surgery.

I really couldn't tell you how long I was out of it, as I only recall living from one morphine injection to another. When I was able to grasp what had taken place, I realized that I was one big mass of stitches, both internally and externally. The shrapnel from what was apparently an 81 millimeter mortar shell had entered from behind me through my buttocks and lower back and had pretty well scrambled my insides. In the surgery, I had been cut from the end of my rib cage to my abdominal area in some type of major exploratory surgery. A section of my small intestine, which I believe is called the jejunum, was perforated by the shrapnel and had to be taken out, and the intestine had to be resected. I was later told by my surgeon that there was a considerable amount of shrapnel around my spine, but they decided to leave it intact because it might do more harm than good to go after it on any aggressive basis. I swear that I set off the metal detectors at airports for years afterward due to my sizable metal deposits. I had further extensive surgery on my buttocks and lower back to remove the shrapnel and to explore my sciatic nerve. It left extensive scarring in that area such that my days of mooning anyone were over, unless you wanted to see what the moon truly looked like, close up with all its craters.

A large piece of shrapnel had badly bruised my sciatic nerve, which resulted in horrific shooting pains down my left leg, indescribable stiffening of my leg like the worst charlie horse you could imagine, and a feeling on the bottom of my left foot like I was walking on broken glass any time I would put any weight on my foot. I realized that I was extremely fortunate when the doctor told me that if the sciatic nerve had been severed, I would have lost the use of my left leg. I had trouble sleeping, since the only area of my body that was not occupied by large, pointed metal stitches was on my right side, and for weeks I endured soaking sweats to such a degree that I was tested for malaria.

Immediately after the surgery, they had placed a tube through my nose into my stomach, which was crudely performing the functions of expelling wastes that had previously been performed admirably by other portions of my anatomy. One day, the tube become irreparably clogged, and they had to insert a new stomach tube while I was conscious. There is something indescribable about someone telling you to swallow while you are choking on a plastic tube being inserted down your nose and into your throat.

In short, I was a mess and remained that way for some time. The surgeons had only been able to stop the massive internal bleeding during my initial surgery by packing me internally. Three or four days later, they had to bring me back to the operating room, after I had somewhat stabilized, to remove the packing and stop the remaining bleeding. The doctors and nurses in the Evac Hospital were terrific, and I can't say enough about their dedication and miraculous work putting together the badly broken and mangled bodies that were sent to them every day. I remember how proud the doctor was when he talked about my recovery, and I knew instinctively that he probably had some severe reservations about whether I was going to make it when I was first presented to him on the operating table.

After three weeks in the Evac Hospital in Cu Chi, I was flown to Japan, where I was to receive continuing treatment on the long road to recuperation. I was still unable to walk and made my rounds terrorizing the other wards in a wheelchair.

Two incidents that I will never forget involved two doctors whom I hope to never run into again in this lifetime. Shortly after arriving in Japan, one of these doctors came to my bedside to examine me. At this time, the various wounds in my lower back and buttocks were still healing. This doctor stuck his fingers in the open wounds while I was lying on my stomach, and the next thing I knew it seemed that I was reaching for the ceiling. The other guys in nearby beds looked on in disbelief and later told me that he was gritting his teeth while he was pushing down on my wounds. Needless to say, that doctor never saw me again the remaining time that I spent in Japan, as I would hide from him when he made his rounds. The other incident involved a doctor who was attempting to inject intravenous dye in my veins for various tests. Anyone who has ever observed the size of the needle used for this testing knows why you want the doctor to find your vein on the first attempt. Unfortunately, most of my veins had collapsed from multiple IVs and blood transfusions, and I lost count of how many attempts my hapless doctor made before he finally found pay dirt. I was so pissed off at him that were it not for my extremely weakened state, I would have gotten up and kicked the shit out of him.

The ward I was on in Japan provided me with a minor degree in medical training, as many procedures were performed right on the ward at bedside. One guy had sustained a sucking chest wound—that's a massive trauma wound from a projectile—and had developed a lot of blood in his chest cavity. The doctor gave him a local anesthetic in the back and proceeded to poke a hole in his upper back area with scalpel and forceps to drain the blood from the cavity. It was truly amazing. It enabled me to develop some diagnostic skills of my own that weren't always appreciated by the medical staff, especially the nurses.

One day when I was extremely constipated, I suggested to the nurse on duty that the reason I couldn't evacuate was because there were so many holes in my ass that the feces were having trouble deciding which exit to use. Although it would be some time before I would be in decent physical shape again, it was good to see the glimmers of my sense of humor emerging from the shadows.

Rob Roche, *Sergeant, U.S. Army, 101st Airborne Division, Da Nang, 1967–69*

We were pinned down by a sniper one day. You couldn't tell where the rounds were coming from, and this guy was effectively picking us off left and right. The bullets were hitting all around us. I got shot in the calf. For whatever reason, the bullet never exited my leg. Perhaps it was nearly spent when it hit me. I don't know. Besides the obvious pain, I still can remember it burning like hell. Not long after I was shot, somebody finally spotted the sniper's shadowy figure in the tree and fired a number of rounds there. He fell from the tree, dead.

When calm finally prevailed, a helicopter was called in to remove me from the field. It seemed like it took forever to get there. It hovered over me and would not or could not land. Supposedly, there was a risk that the enemy was still in the area. The crew dropped a small platform down, which was secured to a cable. I took my rifle, strapped it over my arm, and hobbled onto the platform. As we took off, I was still being pulled into the helicopter, and that's how I got out of there.

I was brought to a field hospital, which was nothing more than a number of tents. A bunch of us were lined up waiting our turn to be operated on. There were a lot of people who got hit, and they took the more seriously injured first; you know, the ones with life-threatening wounds. I had a big gauze bandage wrapped around my leg, and they had given me crutches at the hospital, so I could hobble around while waiting in line.

They called me in and helped me to lie on my stomach on the operating table. There were lights overhead. The nurses gave me a rag to place in my mouth and bite on. 'Til this day, I swear I was not given any anesthesia, even though the pain was unbearable. I really don't think they had any. The surgeon cut where the bullet went in. I'm not certain about the rest, but I think he cut up about an inch and made another incision on the side. Then he just dug in. I could feel his fingers or instruments inside my leg. All the while, I felt this incredible pain. Eventually, he found the bullet and removed it and showed it to me. He put it in a jar. For years, I kept the bullet as a souvenir; but somewhere along the line, I either lost or misplaced it. For whatever reason, he stitched it back up with wire, not like what regular stitches are made of, but wire, real wire! It was very painful. Then the wound was dressed with gauze.

I hobbled around for a while; the wound healed, and in a few weeks, the stitches were removed. The doctors considered me fully recovered— no limp, no pain, no nothing. Within a few weeks, I was back with my unit in the field.

The second time I got wounded . . . that sucked! I thought that was it, I really did. I had seen guys get shot in the neck before. It was on one of the hills, 327 I think, or one close by, and I couldn't believe it. I really thought I had bought it.

It was the second day after the battle started. A round from an AK-47 rifle hit me in the back of the neck and exited fairly close to the entry wound. Oh man! Later at the field hospital, I was told if it had been a half-inch closer to my spine, that could have been it for me. It was a clean wound. All it did was cut the muscles. Fortunately for me, my head was turned sideways in the mud. Otherwise, I could have drowned there. I tried to lift my head, but I had no muscles, and I couldn't lift or turn it. Someone screamed for a medic, and a Polish American guy we called Doc came running to me. I was screaming for him also. He stayed with me the entire time. He was a great guy. Grabbing my head, he turned it toward him. He had this big round face, and I was looking straight at him.

I said, "Come on, Doc, am I gonna make it?" I guess anyone who was hit bad and remained conscious said basically the same thing.

Of course he said, "Yeah, you'll be all right!" He was saying I would be okay, but believe me, I had my doubts.

I don't know how they got me out of there; by stretcher, I guess. I don't know if I lost consciousness or not. There are blank spots in my memory about it. When you're like that, you're at the total mercy of someone else. I was placed on the helicopter and remember being conscious at that time. I was taken back to Da Nang. In the hospital there, they did some kind of operation. They wrapped my neck up, and I stayed that way for a long time. I was also given painkillers, which doped me up quite a bit.

From Da Nang I was taken to Cam Ranh Bay, and there I was operated on again. A short time later I was manifested on a medevac flight to Tokyo. If my memory serves me right, in Japan I was operated on for a third time. Eventually, I was put on another plane for transport back to a stateside hospital. The entire time on the plane, I was prone on a stretcher.

Mike Pinksaw, *Specialist Four, U.S. Army, 60th Land Clearing Company, 62nd Engineering Battalion, 20th Engineering Brigade, Long Binh, Bien Hoa, Lai Khe, 1968–69*

It was a typical day. We went out to clear more jungle, came back in after we finished the job, and I did my normal preventive maintenance on the tractor. I remember replacing something on the tractor, but I forget what it was.

Not long after, I managed to take a hot shower. That's right, a hot shower. The way we managed to do that was easy. We'd carry two five-gallon cans of water inside the cab of the tractor, and the natural heat of the sun and the confined area would raise the water temperature to the perfect heat for a shower. I swear, it must have gotten up to 125 degrees in that tractor by day's end. When we got back from the field, we used a five-gallon bag with a shower head attachment and hung it by a tripod over our heads. It was beautiful, man!

So I completed my hot shower and went back to my tent and sat on my cot. Suddenly, I heard an explosion outside the perimeter, and I immediately yelled, "Incoming!" and everyone started running for the bunkers. I mean, the VC aimed rounds right down the row of tents. They knew where everything was.

As quickly as it had started, the first attack stopped. By now I had my steel pot and flak jacket on. It was between eleven and twelve o'clock at night.

I was with my squad leader, and he told me to find the CO and see what he wanted us to do. So I ran to the CO's tent, but nobody was there. I ran back and told my squad leader I couldn't find him, then the VC started the second volley of rounds. The first round landed smack-dab in front of me on a sandbag. My squad leader was directly behind me. (Just this past summer I found out there was a guy beside me who remembered the round blowing apart, the one that got me. I don't remember it.) I heard myself scream, and after that, things were very vague and confusing. The next thing I remember, my squad leader was holding me in his arms. A piece of shrapnel had torn the nerves in my arm, and it felt like it was gone.

I yelled to Dave, "I can't feel my arm."

"Don't worry about it, it's still there," he told me.

Also, I couldn't see because one of my eyes was blown out. To make matters worse, I was choking on my own blood from a piece of shrapnel that went through my lower lip. In fact, I received shrapnel all over my body—in both my arms, my right knee, my head, my face, my eyes, my chest, my stomach, and my lips. I mean, I was a mess.

A medic ran over and was bandaging me up the best he could. My squad leader, whom the guys used to tease because he always wore first-aid packs with the other supplies on his combat web gear, started to bandage me. By the time the medic arrived, he had used every first-aid pack he had.

I was told, years later, that the wounds were so severe that they didn't expect me to survive. Because of this they wanted to evacuate me last, only after those with lesser wounds had gone first.

But my squad leader wouldn't hear of it.

Carrying a wounded soldier to a helicopter "dust-off" pad.

Amazingly, and for whatever reason, probably because I was in shock, I could feel no pain. I mean, there was absolutely no pain whatsoever. I don't remember getting any morphine injections, although I probably did.

In the distance, I could hear a medevac chopper flying in. As the chopper reached the perimeter of the compound, the VC opened up, and we took a full-scale ground attack.

I remember praying to myself, "Please God, don't let them shoot the chopper down."

The next thing I remember, I was being loaded onto the chopper. There was a guy on it who took my hand and held it while he comforted me. It really helped. Shortly thereafter, I lost consciousness.

Years later, my squad leader told me that after he came back from putting me on the helicopter, he was covered in blood, and the medics tackled him, thinking he was seriously injured. But it was my blood, not his. Later I found out that during the same attack about fifty guys were wounded; three were killed by a direct hit on an APC.

They flew me to a first-aid station in Vhoc Vinh. From there, I was transferred to an evacuation hospital in Long

Dog tags, regulation P38 (can opener), and crucifix worn by Mike Pinksaw on the day he was wounded. The crucifix was split in two by a piece of shrapnel. (Courtesy of Mike Pinksaw)

Bien. Most of the initial operations, performed on me over a period of two weeks, were done there. At the time, I was pretty heavily medicated.

While there, I was being taken care of by an army nurse from Warwick. I don't know what she looked like, and I didn't get her name. My squad leader from Warwick did find out the area of Warwick she lived in. I remember she was trying to get an IV started on my left arm, just where I was experiencing considerable pain.

Finally I got fed up and said, "Leave my goddamned f—in' arm alone."

She said, "I'm going home next week, and I'm going to Newport to tell everyone there that Mike Pinksaw swore at me."

"I don't give a f— what you do," I told her, "just leave my arm alone."

After a while I felt bad about saying that to her, but, unfortunately, I never did get the opportunity to apologize. She had departed, and I never saw her again.

I was shipped from Bien Hoa to Yokohama and spent two weeks at the hospital there. That's where they stitched up all my wounds and performed some skin grafts. From there, I flew to the States on a jet and arrived at Fort Devens Army Hospital. Ironically, I arrived there on Memorial Day, 1969.

The hospital at Fort Devens was unable to deal with the shrapnel in my eyes, so I was transferred to the Chelsea Naval Hospital for surgery. I had three operations performed on my eyes. One was to remove the shrapnel, one to repair the retina, and, unfortunately for me, the final time was to reverse the surgery performed on the retina during the second operation because it was unsuccessful. Remember, at that time, they didn't have laser surgery to perform such operations. It was all done with scalpels.

After the eye operation, I was transferred to the VA Hospital in Boston and had a plastic surgical plate permanently embedded in my forehead. I'm not sure exactly why that operation had to be performed. I've got all the papers at home, and someday I've got to take them out and find out why.

God only knows how many operations I had on my entire body during that period of time. I know I had over twenty large shrapnel wounds from that one round, not to mention all of the smaller ones. One thing's for certain. I'd never want to go through something like that again.

Ken Garthee, *Private First Class, U.S. Marine Corps, 3rd Battalion, 3rd Marines, 3rd Marine Division, Da Nang, Rock Pile, 1966–67*

After several days of routine patrols, the lieutenant asked me to lead the company on one last reconnaissance mission, along with a new scout. His name was Jack, and he was from Cleveland, Ohio. He was newly married and a quiet sort of guy, yet eager to be a scout. This was our first recon mission together. Our destination was to be the Rock Pile.

There were reports of NVA movement near the mountain range. The Rock Pile was about a half day's walk from our present location through triple-canopy jungle, a river, and some open areas at the base of the mountain.

We didn't know what we were going to encounter, so we took an ample supply of ammunition and supplies, along with forward observers. The FOs were marines who, if needed, radioed for air support or, if necessary, heavy-duty gun fire, like naval guns from ships offshore or cannon fire from a nearby artillery base.

At sunrise on December 9, 1966, Jack and I led the way with about fifty marines not far behind. We stopped often for leech checks and rest breaks through the jungle. Until that point, fording the river was the riskiest and the hardest effort we had to make. There was an open area on the other side of the river, so we had to move quickly, fording the river and making sure everything remained dry. Being in the river and in the open like that made all of us extremely vulnerable. So while crossing, cover was provided—should we be fired upon—from those who had already crossed and those who were about to.

After some time we all made it across safely and gathered in a well-protected area in the overgrowth at the base of the mountain. Jack and I moved up the ridge a short way to get a better view of any enemy movement.

I took off all my gear, grabbed the binoculars, and climbed up a tree to check our location. When I looked out over the trees and towards the Rock Pile, I saw movement—a lot of movement, to be specific. It was the NVA, and someone was looking back at me through his binoculars. I couldn't get down from the tree fast enough. I told Jack that I had seen NVA regulars, and we should get the word back to the lieutenant.

Before I could do anything else, I heard three bullets crack past my head. Jack and I were being fired on. I tried to dive for cover behind a nearby tree when all of a sudden, I felt something strike me in the left side of my chest. I was hit! Later, I found out it was a bullet from an AK-47, fired by attacking NVA regulars who were holed up in the Rock Pile.

It seemed like it all happened in slow motion. My arms were outstretched as I turned, twisted, and rolled over. My body then arched on the ground. After an instant, at normal speed and without warning, I felt as if a 50-pound sledgehammer were being slammed into the middle of my back. It was the most painful feeling I had ever experienced.

Jack immediately ran up to my side and shielded me with his body. He returned fire the best he could, while the rest of the company came running up the side of the mountain. They were returning fire the best they could.

It immediately became chaotic; rifle and machine-gun bullets were whizzing, cracking, and flying all over the place. People were yelling and screaming, and the lieutenant was shouting orders. Those who were hit were calling for the corpsman, and those who ran out of ammo were yelling for more. During the firefight the FOs called for air support, and helicopters were requested to get us out of there.

A navy medical corpsman came to my side. I had been the first combat casualty during this encounter. Like Jack, he, too, had just arrived in-country. Quickly, he administered first aid for a gunshot wound by placing a cellophane wrapper from a pack of cigarettes onto the entrance of my chest wound and packed the exit wound in my back with several large gauze bandages.

My veins had collapsed, so the corpsman couldn't give me an intravenous to stabilize me, nor could he inject any pain medication. Because of a collapsed lung, I needed to breathe as fast and as much as I could.

Suddenly, I felt no pain. I saw myself beginning to get up from where I was lying, although my body was still on the ground. I happened to glance at a hand resting on my left shoulder; and although I didn't look up to see who was there, there was no need. I no longer felt frightened or afraid of what had just happened to me. I was at peace. No words were spoken; just a sense of calm and relief prevailed.

Together, we rose to the top of the Rock Pile, overlooking the fighting. We watched the planes fly under us, while helicopters were being shot down beneath us as well. I still had no need to look, as I was being reassured by a calm feeling from within me that everything was going to be okay.

After the battle subsided, I was given a gentle nudge from the hand that rested on my left shoulder. I slowly went down and back into my body. During all this time, I felt no pain, anxiety, or hesitation in doing what I was being directed to do. I felt total contentment.

Then it became dark. I was being placed in a body bag.

Jack, the two forward observers, and another marine carried me for quite a distance to where the helicopter could land and proceeded to drop me near the stump of a tree. I let out a groan.

"Hey, Garthee's not dead!" shouted Jack.

I heard an unzipping sound and saw light come through the opening of the body bag. Jack gave me a sip of water and wiped blood from my face. I still felt no pain.

The helicopter arrived.

"Hurry!" Jack yelled. There was no time to take me out of the body bag. In fact, the killed-in-action tag was still attached to the zipper.

The helicopter took all those who were injured to a nearby field hospital, where we were given medical treatment for our wounds. The doctors made every effort to stabilize my condition. I was told that a tube would have to be inserted into my chest to drain the fluid that had collected in my lung in order for it to inflate again. The corpsman apologized before driving the chest tube between my ribs. Now I began to feel pain, as that really hurt a lot.

While there I received excellent treatment and care. Several days later I was able to write to my family and tell them that I was going to be okay. Little did I know the seriousness of my wounds. After all, I could see my two hands, legs, and feet; that's all I needed to see to know that I was going to be fine.

A few days later I learned that shortly after I was put on the helicopter, the FOs called in another air strike on the Rock Pile. A Phantom jet dropped six bombs, of which five landed on the Rock Pile and blew off the top of the mountain. Unfortunately, one bomb ricocheted off the side of the mountain and landed in the middle of the marines who had been left behind. Sixteen marines, including Jack, the two forward observers, and the other marine who carried me to the helicopter and saved my life, were killed instantly.* I was devastated.

While in the hospital, I don't remember talking to anyone about that tragedy. Anyone who knew that I had been involved in the Rock Pile bombing just let me be by myself.

I thought, "My God, why me? Why was I saved and given another chance?"†

TREATING THE WOUNDED

Other than engaging in combat, serving as a nurse in a combat zone had to be one of the most trying and stressful duties an individual could be assigned. Not only were these nurses required to provide medical care and reasonable comfort to their patients, but they also served as surrogate

---

* It was called amicide, friendly fire, or blue-on-blue. Even as far back as the ancient Greeks, battlefields have been strewn with such casualties. In his book *Blue on Blue: A History of Friendly Fire,* Geoffrey Regan gave this assessment of why air warfare, with ground troops below, was so dangerous: "Friendly and enemy troops could and frequently did occupy almost exactly the same grid references, requiring pinpoint accuracy in bombing runs, something that was often beyond the capability of the pilots. Both planes and pilots were being asked to perform beyond their technological—and their human—limitations" (p. 181).

† Ken Garthee's story is printed here for the first time, and it's one that I and a few others always felt needed to be told. Previously, Ken had been reluctant to release it in deference to his wife and family. That's the way Ken was and still is today.

mothers, sisters, wives, psychologists, and clergy. Unquestionably, to those who required their services, the nurses were extremely effective performing all of their duties; assigned or assumed.

The exact number of women who served in Vietnam is uncertain, and perhaps this fact will forever remain obscure. Depending on what account you read, there were as few as 12,000 or as many as 30,000. Several sources claim 15,000, but how that number was determined is anyone's guess.

What is known is that over 250,000 women performed military service during the war years.

From 1966 until 1975, eight nurses (all officers) lost their lives in the war; seven were army nurses, and one was an air force flight nurse. Two died in helicopter mishaps, three in plane crashes, one succumbed to shrapnel wounds, while pneumonia and stroke claimed the other two. Several were in their twenties, while one was fifty-six years old.

Second Lieutenant Carol Ann Drazba from Dunmore, Pennsylvania, was the first to be killed, on February 18, 1966.

On April 4, 1975, a C-5A Galaxy plane crashed just outside Tan Son Nhut Air Base in Saigon. The flight was to be a mission of mercy, manifested to evacuate orphans destined for adoption in the United States. Captain Mary T. Klinker of Lafayette, Indiana, was killed in this unfortunate accident along with 155 others. Sadly, most were Vietnamese infants and children. Captain Klinker was the last nurse to lose her life in Vietnam, nearly two years after American combat troops had already departed.

Considering all the inherent risks involved in serving as a nurse in Vietnam, it should come as no surprise that many suffered war-related stresses to the same extent as combat soldiers. In actuality, both were exposed to frequent traumatic experiences. One early study revealed that 50 percent of the nurses that served in Vietnam suffered from symptoms similar to PTSD. Of that total, 20 percent felt that the stress they served under caused a significant disruption in their daily lives.*

The nurses were, in truth, angels in disguise—ask any veteran who was treated by a combat nurse during the war.

On November 11, 1993, the long-deserved Vietnam Women's Memorial was dedicated to the women who served in Vietnam as members of the United States Armed Forces. Their time of honor had finally arrived.

---

* Diane C. Evans, et al., *Celebration of Patriotism and Courage* (Washington, D.C.: Vietnam Women's Memorial Project, 1993), p. 33.

Peggy R. Zarek, *Lieutenant Commander, U.S. Navy, U.S.S. Sanctuary (AH-17), Coastal Waters off South Vietnam, Military Region 1, 1969–70*

I remember one fellow who had a bilateral amputation. That means both legs were amputated. And he had a tracheotomy. His arm was also amputated. I was reading a letter to him from his wife. Naturally she had not known he was wounded. I was reading this letter to him, and she was describing how she had moved into this new house, and everything was so wonderful, and how she couldn't wait until he came home. That's the one time it almost got to me, with him right there. I said to myself, "I don't believe this." But I didn't let it out.

Peggy Zarek (center), wearing jungle fatigues, with two of her fellow nurses. (Courtesy of Peggy Zarek)

I remember another man, who was only nineteen. He got hit right between the eyes. The wound was from a bullet, and he was totally blind because of it. There was not a scratch anywhere else on his body. Fortunately, he still had all of his mental faculties. For some reason, that case really bothered me.

There was an army sergeant who had been blown up by a mine—I don't know if you want to put this in your book—from his neck down to below his knees was practically blown away. It was just horrible to see. I don't know how, but he survived.

In the ICU there were what we called circular-electric beds. They continuously moved in a circular fashion and were used for patients who had horrible burns, like when helos blew up. The continuous movement was to prevent them from lying in the same position all the time. These beds were forever in motion.

The patients were dressed in special wrappings, which seemed to take all day to put on; and no sooner was it done, when we had to start all over again. That really sticks out in my mind; also, because they were mostly nineteen years old.

Those marines were wonderful guys. Their morale was great; it was unbelievable to see them react so well to adversity. They just wouldn't quit; they never quit.

EVADING THE ENEMY

While flying a combat mission in his F-4 Phantom jet, Flight Officer William Sullivan and his pilot were shot down by the enemy. Although the entire episode lasted a little more than three hours, it probably felt like a lifetime to both of them. Sullivan's story is a harrowing one.

William Sullivan, *Lieutenant Commander, U.S. Navy, Fighter Squadron 213, U.S.S.* Intrepid, *Air Wing, U.S.S.* Kitty Hawk *(CVA-63), U.S.S.* Intrepid *(CVA-11), U.S.S.* Paul Revere, *and U.S.S.* Blue Ridge, *1965–68 and 1971–72*

It was to be a very routine mission; in fact, it was to be my last mission on that particular cruise, since the carrier was due to begin the long thirty-day trip back to San Diego the next day. We were to conduct a bombing mission in the southern part of North Vietnam. The day was overcast, and we had to work around the weather. About twenty minutes after we got airborne, we were called to provide cover for the pickup of an air force forward air controller who had been shot down. So we navigated to that position and saw enemy soldiers approaching the downed aircraft; we started making bombing runs in order to keep the enemy back so the helicopters could move in and try to make a rescue. It was mid-morning.

The enemy ground fire was very intense, and on our fourth pass, we got hit. The shells hit the back of the aircraft behind where I was sitting, and one shell came into the cockpit right behind me and exploded. A few seconds after that, the aircraft caught fire and the pilot was losing control. We figured we'd have to punch out.

The pilot yelled, "Eject, eject!"

I pulled the handle, although I had second thoughts about ejecting because I was afraid that the ejection seat had probably been damaged with the shell exploding in the cockpit behind me. Sure enough, after the ejection I looked up and the chute had deployed, but it had a large hole in it. I was accelerating toward the ground much faster than normal. The other predicament was that I was suspended upside down with my feet entangled in the lines, looking up at the sky while the ejection seat had not fully separated.

We had ejected at 2,000 feet, so it was a very short descent. I just barely righted myself when I saw the trees coming up at me. The limbs from the trees had partially broken my fall, but they also knocked me out. I was unconscious for perhaps fifteen minutes. The pilot had ejected also, and he was picked up safely by an air force helicopter about fifteen minutes after he ejected. In my particular case, the crew of the rescue helicopter didn't think I had survived because I had been unable to communicate with them while unconscious.

By the time I woke up, I was bleeding from both ears, had a severe concussion, singed hands and forearms, and a very sore back (later to be determined as three broken vertebrae, all caused from hitting the trees). Then it was a question of getting out of the chute and looking for a place to hide while waiting for the rescue attempt. That didn't seem to be coming, so I finally got on my small radio and made a call giving them my proper call sign. That was the first time they knew I was still alive, but at the same time, I heard voices in the distance and assumed the enemy was probably searching for me. I was able to unstrap the chute without cutting it off and fell about ten feet to the ground. Again, I heard voices speaking Vietnamese, so I started taking evasive action in order not to make contact. I evaded for about three hours before I was rescued.

In the area I had parachuted into, there were no open fields, so I knew my pick-up was going to be difficult. Using the radio, I had to steer the helicopter in visually from my position. The paramedic in the helicopter had been wounded earlier, when they had taken shots from the ground while searching for me. Normally, the paramedic would have come down with the line, but in this case I had to grasp the line and secure it myself. Then I was winched back into the chopper. When I was pulled in, I was happy to see the pilot of my aircraft, who had been rescued earlier.

We were taken to Khe Sanh, and from there we were evacuated to the hospital in Da Nang. That night, in Da Nang, they experienced attacks against the compound. So they took us out of the beds and put us underneath them just in case the building was hit.

I guess I said to myself, "Hey, this has not been a good day."

After the alert, we were placed back into our beds. One of the guys in the bed next to me had lost his arm in some battle, and he died during the night. I felt really bad about that and less sorry about my own situation.

The next morning, while recuperating, I sent a communiqué to the commanding officer of the U.S.S. *Kitty Hawk* that basically said, "Rather than being medically evacuated by air to a hospital in the U.S., I'd prefer to complete my recuperation period in the infirmary on the U.S.S. *Kitty Hawk* during the thirty-day transit back to San Diego so I can meet my wife standing up rather than on my back."

The captain replied: "Bill, I'll have a helicopter in there and pick you up in about an hour."

I was brought back to the ship, and that's where I stayed until I was ready to go home. In the meantime, a telegram was sent to my wife following my rescue. It said, "Feeling better. Walking around ship. In Goof shape. All my love, Bill. U.S.S. *Kitty Hawk.*" It should have said, "in good shape." The message was garbled from the *Kitty Hawk* to Western Union, which was then relayed via telegram to my wife in California.*

MISINFORMATION REACHES HOME

It had to be every parent's worst nightmare—the unwanted knock on the front door by military personnel in uniform, sometimes accompanied by a priest or minister. Their arrival always signaled bad news about a son's or daughter's fate in Vietnam. Either he or she was listed as missing, seriously wounded, or killed in action. In most cases, it was the latter.

But what about those whose status or condition was mistaken or misrepresented? It happened, and it happened to families from Newport County.

Mike Pinksaw, Specialist Four, U.S. Army, 60th Land Clearing Company, 62nd Engineering Battalion, 20th Engineering Brigade, Long Binh, Bien Hoa, Lai Khe, 1968–69

My mother saved all the telegrams she received from the army from the time I was hit until the day I was to be sent to Fort Devens in Massachusetts. The first two are of particular interest. The initial telegram sent home two days after I was wounded said that I only had an eye injury. The second one, received two days later, was a lot more accurate about my condition, but still lacked detail about the number of wounds I had received.

This telegram really scared the hell out of Mom and Dad. In part, it simply stated, "In the judgment of the attending physician, his condition is of such severity that there is cause for concern."

---

* After I interviewed Bill, he sent me a letter describing an incredible coincidence: "Regarding that rescue, I forgot to mention, it was sort of mystical in the sense that several years later I found out that the time of my birth, thirty-three years earlier, was 2352 hours on 17 May. This coincided to the minute with the time of my rescue at 1252 hours on 16 May, Vietnam time. When you consider the day (they are a day ahead of us) and difference in Greenwich Mean Time, it was nearly exact."

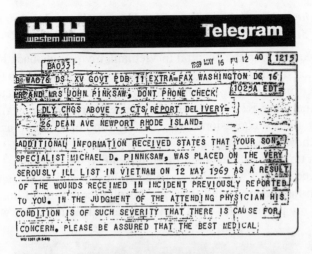

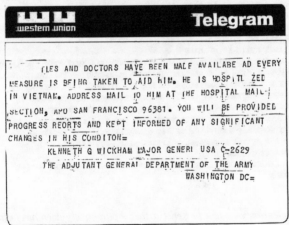

The second, more accurate telegram sent to Mike Pinksaw's parents, reporting his condition after he sustained major injuries. (Courtesy of Mike Pinksaw)

Doug Johnson, *Specialist Four, U.S. Army, 25th Infantry Division, 2nd Battalion, 12th Infantry, 1968*

When my parents were originally informed that I had been wounded, they were told that I had been slightly wounded and it was expected that I would return to the field in a couple of weeks. I don't know which Specialist Four Doug Johnson they were talking about, but it sure as hell didn't describe my condition or my prognosis. Imagine their shock when they saw the real condition instead of the one portrayed in the telegram.

Ken Garthee, Private First Class, U.S. Marine Corps, 3rd Battalion, 3rd Marines, 3rd Marine Division, Da Nang, Rock Pile, 1966–67

While I was lying in the hospital in Vietnam, my parents back home had been visited by the marine corps recruiter, who informed them that I had been killed in action. Somehow, the KIA tag had been collected along with all the other KIA tags from that December afternoon. You know, there was a lot of confusion during the fighting, evacuation, and bombing, and these things happen.

Like a typical mother, she refused to believe the recruiter. Truly, she felt and knew that I was going to be all right. Several days later my letter, which had been written from my hospital bed, arrived home. It revealed to my parents that I had survived the ordeal and that I was okay.

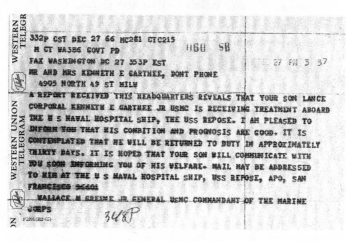

This telegram was sent to Ken Garthee's parents eighteen days after he was shot, on December 9, 1966. Contrary to the telegram, Ken never returned to full duty. He was ultimately discharged from the hospital in May 1968, over a year and a half after he had been wounded. (Courtesy of Ken Garthee)

FATIGUE AND ILLNESS

There is only so much a human being can be expected to do. On top of the environmental factors a soldier had to deal with, such as the heat and humidity, and emotional factors, such as fear, fatigue became a constant nemesis. An infantry soldier trudged through elephant grass day after day, facing relentless rain and winds; a naval boatsman rode the waves in a patrol boat for weeks at a time; a support soldier back in base camp pulled guard duty all too frequently at night. Dealing with sleep deprivation became a way of life.

Vietnam was a very underdeveloped country with significant public-health problems almost anywhere that military personnel were required to travel. Major cities lacked proper sanitation. In the rural areas, sanitation was virtually non-existent, and disease was always a significant concern.

The possibility of contracting malaria was a constant danger. Six days a week troops ingested a small orange tablet; a large white one was substituted on Sunday. In fact, taking the white one was usually the only reminder that it was Sunday. In base camp, troops slept under mesh netting to prevent mosquito bites. In the bush, however, no such luxury existed. Those in the field spread liberal amounts of mosquito repellent over their uncovered faces, necks, and arms to ward off the numerous little, yet dangerous, insects.

Salvatore T. Raffa, *Airman Second Class, U.S. Air Force, 377th Security Police Squadron, Tan Son Nhut Air Base, Saigon, 1967–68*

I can remember going days without sleep. It was not only during Tet but another time when intelligence said the 377th Military Police Squadron was being targeted by the Viet Cong. They were going to get rid of us. The rumor was they were going to use some type of gas on us, and during the alert, we actually had to live underground when not performing our duties aboveground. We lived in a tunnel complex originally built by the French during their occupation in the early '50s. The alert lasted about four days. Nothing ever came of it except we lost a lot of sleep.

David Rossi, *Specialist Four, U.S. Army, 1st Infantry Division and 25th Infantry Division, Di An, Tay Ninh, and Cu Chi, 1969–70*

I was out in the field during the dry season, and water had to be transported to us. It came in ammo-like cans. To make a long story short, I think the water was contaminated, as I became extremely ill after drinking some. Most likely it was dysentery. It lasted about five days or so. I never did leave the field though.

At night, I'd get wicked diarrhea, gas, stomach cramps, the whole bit. The guys I was with were not happy campers. They were getting upset, as I was keeping them up for most of the night. We had no tents; the ground was our bunk, and there I was sleeping next to them, passing gas.

Bill McCollum, *Sergeant, U.S. Army, 173rd Airborne Brigade, Charlie Company, 4th Battalion, 503rd Infantry, LZ-English, 1969–71*

Because of the heat, you got tired. I mean, there were days that you just didn't want to do anything. During the monsoons you'd hump through rice paddies in the mud, and then more mud, and you'd get nowhere fast.

One day I got food poisoning. We had just gotten back from a patrol, and it was a hot-chow day. The cooks had brought hamburgers out to us in the field, and we ate them all up. About an hour later I had to take a dump, and then I got wicked stomach cramps. Eventually, all of us were afflicted with the same symptoms. I guess the food had been left out uncovered in the hot sun and spoiled, but not long enough for us to notice any smell. We were all sick for about twenty-four hours.

Doug Johnson, *Specialist Four, U.S. Army, 25th Infantry Division, 2nd Battalion, 12th Infantry, 1968*

I can't say that I experienced any physical fatigue while in-country because I was young and in pretty good shape. There were days that I was exhausted from physical exertion, coupled with the mental fatigue associated with the fear that something catastrophic was about to happen.

The most consistent form of fatigue for me probably resulted from emotional strain. It was that constant tug on my emotions that resulted from knowing I was in a situation that was often totally out of my control and wishing I could be anywhere else doing just about anything else. I managed to keep my spirits up pretty well for the first weeks that I was in-country. Gradually, however, the letters and tapes from home, the drudgery, and constant uncertainty of day-to-day existence led to a certain sense of hopelessness and despair. I never totally gave up hope that I would return home safe and sound and in one piece, but that belief was periodically challenged by snipers, mortar and rocket barrages, and the constant realization that *Charlie* and his buddies from North Vietnam had plans to send us home in metal caskets if they had the opportunity.

One of the ways that we would cope with this constant uncertainty was with a sick sense of humor, the type of humor that I have since heard referred to as gallows humor. An example of this was the joke circulated among the troops that a lot of guys were leaving Vietnam with a CMH—no, not the Congressional Medal of Honor, but rather a casket with metal handles!

Dick Turner, *Boatswain's Mate Third Class, U.S. Navy, River Assault Squadron 15, River Division 152, Task Force 117, Dong Tam and My Tho, 1968–69*

I was tired all the time. We rarely got a chance to rest, as we worked long hours into the night getting these boats ready to be used again. It was a constant go, go, go. When you came back from an operation, you got on the ship, took a shower, and cleaned up; by then you had to go back to the boat. You had to fuel it, fill out your boat report, reload your ammo, and make sure all the guns were up to snuff. If you weren't doing those things, you were doing something else. There wasn't much time to relax.

Peggy R. Zarek, *Lieutenant Commander, U.S. Navy, U.S.S.* Sanctuary *(AH-17), Coastal Waters off South Vietnam, Military Region 1, 1969–70*

Depending on the extent of the fighting, you could gauge your day. Sometimes I'd go down to the ICU at 7 A.M. and probably not get out of there until 10 P.M. at night. That wasn't all the time, but it happened enough times to make you really tired. The fact is, you just did it.

Howard North, *Lieutenant j.g., U.S. Coast Guard, Coast Guard Squadron One, USCGC* Point Clear *(WPB 82315), An Thoi and Cat Lo, 1967–68*

We were exhausted the entire time we were there. I'd get up around quarter after seven, eat breakfast, go on watch from quarter of eight to just before noontime, eat lunch, work in the afternoon, eat supper, go on watch at quarter to eight at night; and every two or three nights, we'd end up firing mortars. Finally, we'd get off watch at midnight. During all this time, we'd be getting beat to death because of the winds from the monsoons.

I remember one night in particular; in fact, it was the first night that I was back from R & R, and I got sick and caught all kinds of shit. We came out of Vung Tau and headed up toward Cam Ranh Bay. The wind was blowing out of the northeast, and we were doing about 12 to 15 knots into a four- to five-foot sea, and we were getting pounded. I got sicker than a dog. It was sea sickness. Fortunately, it only lasted a night.

When we finally went to bed, we used to tuck the sheets so that they were tied around the wire springs of the mattress. That way we wouldn't get thrown around while trying to sleep in our bunks.

Mike Pinksaw, Specialist Four, U.S. Army, 60th Land Clearing Company, 62nd Engineering Battalion, 20th Engineering Brigade, Long Binh, Bien Hoa, Lai Khe, 1968–69

The only thing I got one time was this bright red rash. The doctors there didn't know what it was. It was all over my hands and arms. I surmised years later that it could have been caused by exposure to Agent Orange while in the field, but who really knows?

HOMESICKNESS, LETTERS, AND "DEAR JOHNS"

The following letter, and variations thereof, made the circuit in Vietnam. The one printed below was received by Thomas M. Finn and was sent to him courtesy of his friends at Sully's Publik House in Newport. These letters were not meant as cruel jokes from the people back home. On the contrary, they were intended to pick up the spirits of the troops by injecting some fun into a subject which normally would not be humorous at all. In Vietnam one had to maintain a sense of humor.

On the other hand, receiving a real *Dear John* letter could be devastating, and two such stories are recounted at the end of this section.

> Dear Buddy:
> Nothing much doing back here. I sure do envy you in Saigon right in the thick of things. Bet you never have a dull moment.
> I was over to see your wife last night and I read all of your letters. They were a bit mushy, but I don't blame you. Frances is a swell girl, wonderful figure, good looks and personality. The guys still whistle at her when she walks down the street.
> Your brother-in-law Smedley dropped in. He was wearing the brown suit you bought just before you left. Fran gave it to him, as she thought it would be out of style when you get back. Several other couples came in and we killed two cases of beer. We wanted to chip in for it, but Fran wouldn't let us. She said you sent her ten dollars extra for her to spend as she wishes. One of the guys is buying your golf clubs too, and he paid $25 for

them and will pick them up tomorrow. That is more than she got for your movie camera and projector.

Frances is the life of the party. I thought she would be a little shaken up after the accident last week with your new Chevy, but you'd never know she had been in a head-on collision and smashed your car to bits. The other driver is still in the hospital and threatens to sue. Too bad Fran forgot to pay the insurance, but the funny thing is she isn't a bit worried. We all admire her courage and nonchalance and especially her willingness to mortgage the house to pay the bill. Good thing you gave her power of attorney before you left.

Well, to get back to the party, you should have seen Fran do an imitation of Gypsy Rose Lee. She was still going strong when we said good night to her and Clarke. Guess you know Clarke is still rooming at the house. It is close to his work, and he saves a lot on gas and lunch.

Nothing much new with me except my wife got another raise. $110 a week now. So we do okay with the $95 I get at the office. It is getting late, so I will stop. I can see through my window across the street to your front porch. Frances and Clarke are having a nightcap. He is wearing the smoking jacket you wore so often.

Well buddy, I sure wish I could be over there with you. LUCKY GUY! Give those Viet Cong hell.

> Your Pal,
> Joe

P.S. Pay no attention to the rumor that Frances is pregnant.

Dick Turner, *Boatswain's Mate Third Class, U.S. Navy, River Assault Squadron 15, River Division 152, Task Force 117, Dong Tam and My Tho, 1968–69*

I wrote my folks back home. I guess I got homesick a bit, but no more so than anyone else did. I didn't have a steady girlfriend at the time, so I wrote my folks a lot. The squadron would send newsletters back home, and I think my folks were getting worried because the newsletters would say that we were getting closer and closer to Cambodia. That's when they really got nervous.

Across the street from my parents' house, there was a retired captain who used to be a supply clerk in the service. He talked quite a bit to my parents and tried to comfort them the best he could.

I couldn't say it in the letters, but we were actually performing night operations in Cambodia with the Navy Seals, but we just couldn't tell anyone. In one case, we were watching this one particular area where Charlie were sending signals with lights attached to fishnets, hoisted up in the air. We watched this for three straight nights.

Finally, the officer in charge said, "Tonight's the night, we're going to blow the village away," and that's exactly what we did. It was later confirmed that the village was a VC stronghold.

Doug Johnson, *Specialist Four, U.S. Army, 25th Infantry Division, 2nd Battalion, 12th Infantry, 1968*

I've never really done too well in the correspondence department, and being in Vietnam didn't really help matters all that much. When I first arrived in-country, I did manage to send a few letters to my mom and dad back in good old Newport to try to catch up on what was going on in the big city, especially the Fifth Ward. We had decided before I departed to purchase tape recorders so that we could exchange cassette tapes with the latest news in our respective lives. I enjoyed receiving tapes from home because it would be interesting and funny to hear the big news from my three brothers and two sisters, who were still at home. My oldest brother was in the coast guard, and my next-youngest brother was in college, and the three of us never really corresponded. I found that my letters and tapes home began to diminish as my time in-country increased. I couldn't really make up any good stories to tell Mom and Dad and the kids about my fabulous exchange program in Southeast Asia. The longer I stayed, the less it seemed that I had to tell them because my reality and their reality had become so different. Somehow it didn't seem right to share with them the experiences to which I had become accustomed, which ran the gamut from the drudgery of burning shit in gallon drums to the excitement of just trying to stay alive one more day. Besides, it was also hard to find the time to correspond on tape when there wasn't some interesting background noise competing with my attention.

For all of the above reasons, I rarely corresponded with my fiancée. She represented a world from which I was far removed, and her news about the weddings of my friends and the world that kept moving on its axis without my presence was often more disturbing than welcome.

Stephen Butler, *Lance Corporal, U.S. Marine Corps, 7th Marine Combat Engineers, Da Nang, 1966–67*

I wrote home, but I hated it. I found that the more I distanced myself from corresponding and communicating with people back home, the easier my job was over there. I just didn't want to be encumbered.

Michael Toner Farrell, *Specialist Five, U.S. Army, 544th Replacement Company, Cam Ranh Bay, 1969–70*

Karen was my first love, and we had been dating for a year when I received my orders to go overseas. She wanted to get married; I didn't want to leave a widow. We wrote each other every day for three months. One day, I received a letter and in it it said, "Dear Michael, Blah, blah, blah." I was devastated and hurt. Going to the beach at Cam Ranh Bay eventually snapped me out of it.

Salvatore T. Raffa, *Airman Second Class, U.S. Air Force, 377th Security Police Squadron, Tan Son Nhut Air Base, Saigon, 1967–68*

I had seen guys over there who were destroyed not by bullets, mortars, or rockets, but simply by Dear John letters. When I first got to Tan Son Nhut Air Base, a tech sergeant (I can't remember how many stripes a tech sergeant had; all I know is he had a ton of them), came to pick me up in a Jeep. He had just gotten to Vietnam a little bit before me. He received a Dear John letter from his girlfriend a couple of months later. In a short period of time, I watched this man virtually destroy himself with alcohol, drugs, and depression.

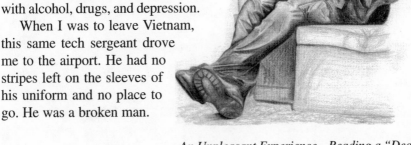

When I was to leave Vietnam, this same tech sergeant drove me to the airport. He had no stripes left on the sleeves of his uniform and no place to go. He was a broken man.

An Unpleasant Experience—Reading a "Dear John" Letter

NINE

BEING SHORT

He who pretends to look on death without fear lies. All men are afraid of dying, this is the great law of sentient beings, without which the entire human species would soon be destroyed.—Jean-Jacques Rousseau, *Julie, or the New Eloise*

THE SHORT-TIMER'S ATTITUDE

IN a way, Vietnam was an individual soldier's war. Each had his own DEROS, an acronym which stood for date of expected return from overseas. A one-year tour of duty normally had to be served before one could return to the States (marines had to serve thirteen months). Each day served was one less day to live in hell. For many, especially the infantry and others in the field, it became a simple ordeal of survival. Being "short" or a "short-timer"—one who had relatively few days left to serve in Vietnam—was a status symbol.

Troops drew calendars on the canvas cover of their steel pot helmets, crossing out another day, or another month, in their DEROS countdown. They wanted everyone to know their status. With less than a hundred days left to serve in-country, they called themselves "double-digit midgets"; less than ten days, they were "single-digit midgets."

Along with short-timer status came the attitude. The attitude could sometimes be seen in the expression on the individual's face—a combination of a smirk and a weary look of experience.

The short-timer was also vocal. When in base camp, he'd yell the word "SHORT," loud enough for all to hear throughout the compound. In some ways it was almost comical, while in other ways other soldiers (not short-timers) had to feel envious. A soldier's reaction to the yell depended on his individual state of mind and, even more importantly, on the time remaining to reach his DEROS.

After serving in Vietnam for eight to nine months, which seemed like an eternity, qualifying as a short-timer allowed the troops time to regain their sense of humor, some of which they may have gradually lost during their tour of duty. About a month prior to their departure from Vietnam, some GIs sent humorous form letters to their parents back home. It was intended as a joke; but the real irony was that some of it was true, at least for a few. The following letter was used by the marines:

HEADQUARTERS

FROM: Rehabilitation Office

TO: Mr. and Mrs. John Doe

SUBJECT: Vietnam veteran attempted; rehabilitation of

Having completed his tour of duty in the Far East, John Doe, Jr. is being permitted to return to the land of the big PX for attempted rehabilitation. Please keep in mind that your Marine has, in all probability, been subjected to severe psychological trauma, Asiatoons fenations, rice paddy fever, Viet Congitis, and too much Kool-Aid. In making joyous preparations to welcome him back home, you must allow for the crude environment in which he has existed for the last year.

For both your convenience and safety, the following set of guidelines has been prepared. Strict compliance with them is highly recommended for your peace of mind and well-being.

A. Show no alarm if he is not housebroken for the first ten days.

B. If he complains of sleeping in a room without a mosquito net, humor him with a net and a few mosquitoes to lull him to sleep.

C. Show reverence when he mentions coupon photos or Baby Jane.

D. Be understanding when he insists on building a machine gun bunker in the front yard.

E. Don't attempt to stop him when he walks around fully armed and encourages others to do the same.

F. Don't be surprised when he starts a neighbor-hood (*sic*) Pacification Program and divides the neighbor-hood (*sic*) into groups and has them digging foxholes, filling sandbags, or making night patrols.

TAKE THESE PRECAUTIONS

A. Shock may be caused by the sight of a beautiful woman, people laughing and dancing, television, or the sight of a foamy head of beer.

B. Don't let him associate with mixed groups until his profanity decreases and his English is back to normal.

C. Get your women off the street, hide the corn liquor, and put a lock on the refrigerator.

PAY NO ATTENTION WHEN

A. He mixes snails with his rice or pours catsup on his food to make it taste better.

B. He sits squat-legged on the floor.

C. He drinks milk out of a bowl or uses two forks to cut his meat.

SAY NOTHING WHEN

A. He stares at chairs or a soft mattress.

B. He talks to himself when alone in a room.

C. He mumbles in Vietnamese to anyone he doesn't feel like speaking English to.

DO NOT—I REPEAT, DO NOT—ASK

A. Does it rain in Vietnam?

B. Are the women in Da Nang really flat chested?

C. How was the mail service?

D. How was liberty in Da Nang?

BE TOLERANT WHEN HE

A. Pads around the house, clad only in sandals and a towel.

B. Slyly offers to sell cigarettes to the postman.

C. Picks suspiciously at his food as though you were trying to poison him.

BUT ABOVE ALL

Keep in mind that beneath that tanned and rugged exterior there is a heart of gold (the only thing of value he has left). Treat him with love, kindness, tolerance, and an occasional fifth of good liquor (Boondock Bourbon will not do!). With luck you will soon be able to rehabilitate that which once was (but now is the hollow shell of) the happy-go-lucky guy you once knew and loved.

> by direction,
> Heele B. Homesoon
> Major, USMC[*]

Even though the short-timer tried to lighten the moment during those final months, he was still living in a state of anxiety. Nobody wanted to get blown away so close to going home, so troops used their American ingenuity and looked for ways to avoid going out into the field or performing guard duty at night. Sick call was liberally requested and other tactics were employed—some worked, others didn't. One aspect was certain. Nearly everyone tried to avoid risking his skin when he had so little time remaining in-country. This is how Christian Appy put it:

> Vietnam was, for American soldiers, the perfect training ground for paranoia. To assume that everyone was a potential enemy was, in fact, a reasonable psychological response to the realities of counter guerrilla warfare.[†]

Thomas Finn, *Specialist Four, U.S. Army, Company A, 519th Military Intelligence Battalion, 525th Military Intelligence Group, MACV-J2, Saigon, 1966–67*

I ended up doing thirteen months in Vietnam. By extending that extra month, I was able to qualify for an immediate discharge because I would

---

[*] Charles J. Levy, *Spoils of War* (Boston: Houghton Mifflin Company, 1974), pp. 73–75.
[†] Christian G. Appy, *Working-Class War: American Combat Soldiers and Vietnam* (Chapel Hill: University of North Carolina Press, 1993), p. 317.

have less than ninety days to serve when I arrived back in the States. Oh, it felt good to be a short-timer. That was the best feeling in the world. I counted it down by checking it off, one day at a time, on my wall calendar.

I processed out of Bien Hoa's 90th Replacement Battalion—90th Repo Depo, as it was called. I went from being really excited about being a short-timer to being very scared. Those were some of my most fearful and nervous days. In the three days I was there, I just sat on my bunk. Some of the guys went to the outdoor theater or wherever. I really thought I was going to get it in the last few days because I was there without any of my friends from my unit that I had bonded with over the past thirteen months. It felt like I was alone, although there were hundreds of other GIs there. At least back at my old unit we were all in the shits together, but at the 90th it was just nothing but strange faces.

Stephen Butler, *Lance Corporal, U.S. Marine Corps, 7th Marine Combat Engineers, Da Nang, 1966–67*

I remember just shutting up and keeping a low profile. I felt that the more you focused on something, the less it was likely to happen. I know I wished and dreamed about it on a daily basis, but consciously I made every effort I could to get it out of my head.

Salvatore T. Raffa, *Airman Second Class, U.S. Air Force, 377th Security Police Squadron, Tan Son Nhut Air Base, Saigon, 1967–68*

I was so excited yet scared to death, both at the same time. I was scared because you always heard stories over there about guys near the end of their tours, waiting at a departure point, getting blown away or someone taking a bullet just before boarding the plane.

You'd say to yourself, "I know I'm not going to make it home," hoping what you were saying to yourself wasn't going to happen.

One of my friends from Newport, who had a lot to do with airport security, got me fixed up so that I was issued boarding pass number one. I was the first guy on that plane.

Dick Turner, *Boatswain's Mate Third Class, U.S. Navy, River Assault Squadron 15, River Division 152, Task Force 117, Dong Tam and My Tho, 1968–69*

God, when I got close, it was great. We were up in An Long and we got the word, "Go on back, your boat is being turned in to the Vietnamese navy." We were out of there; we were gone!

When we did turn it in, we had to train the Vietnamese how to run it, and it was hard because none of us spoke Vietnamese. We took them out in the boat each day, teaching them how to operate it, how to land it, and everything else. I tell you, I had to hit the guy over the head because just about everything I told him, he'd do the opposite. Once he smashed into another boat that was tied up at the pontoons. But that's how they learned.

On the final day there was a ceremony, and we hauled down the U.S. flag, and up went the Vietnamese navy flag. We all cheered because that meant we were finally going home. We were taken to Dong Tam, loaded on a truck, and from there we were driven to another location and loaded onto an air force plane for Tan Son Nhut. There we boarded our flight for home.

Howard North, *Lieutenant j.g., U.S. Coast Guard, Coast Guard Squadron One, USCGC* Point Clear *(WPB 82315), An Thoi and Cat Lo, 1967–68*

I was pissed. My boat got shipped out of country to Japan for an overhaul, and I had to go with it. The boat was put on a freighter. The crew was to fly out of Da Nang while we officers were placed on a space-available basis. We waited at the airport for over a day and a half before we were able to depart. Finally, we got seating on a medevac flight. It was a C-141, and it was just loaded to the gills with guys that had been hit. Aft of the plane was nothing but guys on stretchers. They were stacked four to five high.

After seeing these guys, I said to myself, "You're one lucky son of a gun to get out of here in one piece. Jesus, that could be me back there."

I didn't want to go to Japan because I had about a month left on my tour, and I figured I was going to get stuck there. And I did get stuck there for an extra twenty-five days.

Ken Garthee, *Private First Class, U.S. Marine Corps, 3rd Battalion, 3rd Marines, 3rd Marine Division, Da Nang, Rock Pile, 1966–67*

When I got back from R & R, I was refreshed and relaxed and was getting close to the end of my tour. I had about forty days left, and I figured one tour of duty was enough for me. Unfortunately, before I could get to zero day, I was seriously wounded.

Doug Johnson, *Specialist Four, U.S. Army, 25th Infantry Division, 2nd Battalion, 12th Infantry, 1968*

What I remember most about being a short-timer is that I never survived long enough in Vietnam to become one. After listening to all the legions of short-timers before me, I think that it would have been fair play if I could have strutted around with that cocky swagger that only belonged to short-timers and those who had lost their minds. In fact, they may have been one and the same. At any rate, it seemed that not a day passed without hearing the joyful strains of "SHORT" from some lucky soldier who was ready to head back to the world and do all those things that were only the stuff of dreams for the last year.

I had a little calendar when I first came in-country and dutifully scratched out day after day for several months. I soon discovered, however, that this just seemed to make me realize how slowly the

A Short-timer's helmet

hours and days and nights were passing, so I abandoned my short-timer's calendar.

Peggy R. Zarek, *Lieutenant Commander, U.S. Navy, U.S.S.* Sanctuary *(AH-17), Coastal Waters off South Vietnam, Military Region 1, 1969–70*

It's funny. Naturally you do think about going home. There was a group of us that were to leave—about four nurses, a couple of doctors, and some corpsmen—and I thought it was going to be a very happy day, yet we were all very sad. It was sad to leave our friends there still doing the job. I mean, it was sad, really!

LET'S MAKE A DEAL

All branches of the service offered those who had enlisted for a three- or four-year stint the opportunity to stay in Vietnam for a longer duration (usually six months) in exchange for eliminating time left to serve back in the States. It was a crazy war, especially when you think that some soldiers put their lives up for ransom in order to get out of the service earlier. Many took advantage of the deal. It was a decision that an individual had to make on his own. What it really came down to was, did the benefits outweigh the risks?

David Rossi, *Specialist Four, U.S. Army, 1st Infantry Division and 25th Infantry Division, Di An, Tay Ninh, and Cu Chi, 1969–70*

I was given the option of extending sixty days so that when I came back to the States I could have been separated from the service immediately; but I didn't want to extend, especially because I was still in the field. I think I stayed in the field a little longer than I should have. Usually, you were sent back to base camp with less than ten days to serve on your tour. Perhaps they kept me in the field a little longer because I went AWOL for a few days when I visited a friend of mine in Bien Hoa.

Thomas Finn, *Specialist Four, U.S. Army, Company A, 519th Military Intelligence Battalion, 525th Military Intelligence Group, MACV-J2, Saigon, 1966–67*

Prior to my departure from the service, we were given a recruitment speech by a colonel, with the promise of being processed immediately and going home on a thirty-day leave if we would sign up for an additional six months in Vietnam. He had to have been the loneliest colonel in the world, as nobody took him up on the offer. This deal had no advantages for me, as I had already extended in Vietnam to get out early. Whether it had advantages to others I never truly understood. Who would have wanted to go back, anyway, just to get thirty days at home?

Howard North, *Lieutenant j.g., U.S. Coast Guard, Coast Guard Squadron One, USCGC* Point Clear *(WPB 82315), An Thoi and Cat Lo, 1967–68*

When I had three months left to serve on my tour, I was offered the chance to be a CO if I extended for another six months. I didn't take it. I wasn't ready to make that deal.

DECORATED FOR VALOR

The following accounts illustrate that being recognized for valor was the furthest thought from any of these men's minds. Sheer survival was certainly a primary concern. No one was looking for medals, and each one of these men would have gladly returned any medals they earned if it could have brought back to life just one of their friends and fellow soldiers who paid the ultimate sacrifice.

In order to qualify for an award for valor, circumstances dictated an act of heroism or the infliction of a wound (or both).

All major units stationed in Vietnam had award ceremonies, although not all awards were presented at them. Those with serious injuries received their Purple Hearts in hospital beds, while others received their decorations months or even years later because of normal processing time or, in some cases, unfortunate delays. Paperwork glitches in the war zone were a common occurrence.

Mike Pinksaw, Specialist Four, U.S. Army, 60th Land Clearing Company, 62nd Engineering Battalion, 20th Engineering Brigade, Long Binh, Bien Hoa, Lai Khe, 1968–69

I remember that I couldn't use my left hand because of the paralysis, and I spilled applesauce all over my Purple Heart medal and certificate. I'm laughing now, but I wasn't laughing then. I was kind of upset. If you saw my Purple Heart certificate, you'd see it was smudged.

Ken Garthee, Private First Class, U.S. Marine Corps, 3rd Battalion, 3rd Marines, 3rd Marine Division, Da Nang, Rock Pile, 1966–67

Just before Christmas, the commandant of the marine corps, General Greene, pinned a Purple Heart on the blanket that was covering me. I didn't say a word; I just started to cry. It was hard not to think about Jack, the two FOs, and the other marines who saved my life but lost their lives in exchange. Purple Hearts were sent to their families also, but I wondered how the families were feeling about their loss.

Ken Garthee at his base camp. (Courtesy of Ken Garthee)

David Rossi, Specialist Four, U.S. Army, 1st Infantry Division and 25th Infantry Division, Di An, Tay Ninh, and Cu Chi, 1969–70

While in Vietnam I received two Bronze Stars and two Army Commendation Medals. In a way, they didn't mean that much to me. The only one that I was proud of was the Combat Medical Badge, which was presented to all medics after spending twenty days or more in a war zone.

Dick Turner, *Boatswain's Mate Third Class, U.S. Navy, River Assault Squadron 15, River Division 152, Task Force 117, Dong Tam and My Tho, 1968–69*

I received a Purple Heart, a Presidential Unit Citation, a Navy Achievement Medal with a Combat *V*, a Sea Service Ribbon, a Humanitarian Service Ribbon with a Palm Leaf, the Combat Action Ribbon, and a Vietnamese Service Medal. All but two of the medals were given to me at an official award ceremony while I was still stationed in Vietnam. The Purple Heart and the Navy Achievement Medal were presented to me at my next command back in the States at Quincy, Massachusetts. Both of my parents were in attendance. Each medal was presented to me by the CO, and it was a proud moment for my parents and me.

Bill McCollum, *Sergeant, U.S. Army, 173rd Airborne Brigade, Charlie Company, 4th Battalion, 503rd Infantry, LZ-English, 1969–71*

I received the Army Commendation Medal with *V* for valor. It was awarded to me for what I did the day Ralph was killed. You know, they write it up that way, but I didn't look at it that way. I had just lost my best friend.

Doug Johnson, *Specialist Four, U.S. Army, 25th Infantry Division, 2nd Battalion, 12th Infantry, 1968*

I received the Army Commendation Medal for meritorious achievement. The medal was awarded to me at a formation of my company in Cu Chi. I would love to be able to tell you that I achieved this distinction by single-handedly charging and disabling a machine gun emplacement, capturing a squad of VC, or some other act of courage and valor, but such is not the case. In fact, no one ever explained why I was awarded this medal. Since I cannot point to any particular thing that I was doing at the time that was worthy of recognition, maybe someday I will come up with a good story to describe the genesis of this medal.

The other decoration which I received, of which I am extremely proud, is the Purple Heart. All I can remember about receiving this medal is that it was awarded to me at the evacuation hospital in Cu Chi within a matter of days after I was wounded. Some colonel, whom I'd never seen before or since, stood at the foot of my bed and read from a citation. The citation is signed by one Leon M. Dixon, COL, MC, Commanding, and if in my weakened condition I failed to thank him, I take this opportunity to do so some twenty-seven plus years later. At that time, I was in a lot of pain and still fading in and out of consciousness, so he might as well have been reading my last will and testament as a citation for the Purple Heart.

After my interview with Salvatore Raffa concluded, he left me a copy of a newspaper article which appeared to be clipped from an aged *Stars and Stripes* newspaper. It stated in part:

> President Nixon announced the award of the Presidential Unit Citation to the 377th Security Police Squadron at Tan Son Nhut AB [Air Base], Vietnam. The Security Police earned their award for heroism, from January 31, 1968, to February 2, 1968. The award to the 377th Security Police Squadron covered the period Tan Son Nhut AB came under attack from a large, multibattalion hostile force using rockets, mortars, automatic weapons and small arms. Security policemen, armed only with light weapons, established strong defensive positions and held off the attackers until Vietnam and US Army reinforcements responded.

William Sullivan was too modest to discuss his awards during the interview session, but later, upon request, he sent me his certificate of release or discharge from active duty, which documented all of his numerous decorations. Most significant was the Distinguished Flying Cross, which was only awarded to those who exhibited exceptional heroism and/or achievement in flight. The Distinguished Flying Cross is one of our nation's highest military decorations for aerial activities during wartime. Other awards included the Air Medal (eleventh award), the Navy Commendation Medal with Combat *V* and two Gold Stars, the Purple Heart, and several decorations awarded by the South Vietnamese government.

William Sullivan in dress uniform with his wife. (Courtesy of William Sullivan)

GOING HOME (THE FREEDOM BIRD)

Regardless of which commercial airline was scheduled to transport the troops out of Vietnam, that jet was called a Freedom Bird.

The plane ride was different for everyone. For some, it was fun and games; for others, it was a time for reflection and perhaps disbelief and doubt that they had survived the ordeal. Many were tired and emotionally drained and needed to sort out their own individual feelings. Some slept; some tried, but couldn't.

The final destination was the States. To the passengers, it was simply and affectionately known as The World.

Stephen Butler, Lance Corporal, U.S. Marine Corps, 7th Marine Combat Engineers, Da Nang, 1966–67

We flew on a commercial jet from Vietnam through Okinawa. The entire plane was full of marines who were to be discharged when they arrived back in the States. Some officer made a god-awful mistake and arranged for transportation from the airport in Okinawa to a military club and gave us six hours to return. At the club these guys were ordering drinks like Typhoon Fifths—supposedly enough whiskey in a bottle to get you through a typhoon, which lasts nine days or whatever.

So needless to say, the plane ride back to El Toro, California, was an absolute disaster. When we disembarked, this one captain tried to call a formation. We spent more time trying to get into some kind of a formation than it took us to fly from Okinawa!

Betsy Wylie, Lieutenant, U.S. Navy, Management Information Center, Headquarters, Naval Forces Vietnam (NAVFORV), Saigon, 1967–68

I remember when we took off from Tan Son Nhut, everyone on the plane applauded. I was glad to leave and equally excited about going to my new job, which was teaching at Women Officers' School in Newport.* It was something I had wanted to do for some time.

Michael Toner Farrell, Specialist Five, U.S. Army, 544th Replacement Company, Cam Ranh Bay, 1969–70

The night before I was to leave Vietnam for good, for my own protection,

---

* Women Officers' School was integrated into Officer Candidate School. Later the school moved from Newport to Pensacola.

I was given an MP escort to ensure my safety while traveling from my compound to the plane. A few nights earlier, the lifers got good and drunk one night and decided to get me. I heard them coming up the steps, they were so loud.

My door opened and I said, "Oh no!"

The dialogue continued like this: "Farrell, come downstairs with us."

"What do you think, I'm crazy?"

The supply sergeant who was with them said, "Farrell, you're going home in a box!"

There were three of us in the room at the time, and my new roommate, who had been in-country for only a few weeks, jumped off the bed and said, "I heard it, I heard it, I'll be a witness. They just threatened your life."

I proceeded to wake up the entire enlisted barracks. For my protection, they accompanied me to battalion headquarters. If I had to guess, I'd say it was about 3 A.M.

The major was there, and I proceeded to tell him that my life was just threatened by my CO, the first sergeant, and the supply sergeant, and, I said, "You're the next one in the chain of command." Previously, he had never been advised that I had been beaten up by the supply sergeant; it had all been quashed at the company level.

After I arrived back in the States, I received a letter from my friends back in Vietnam, and they told me that all the guys involved in the incident were reassigned three days later to the field. This included not only the lifers but the CO as well.

I was always perceived as the ring leader among the grass users. In fact, no one was any more prominent or responsible than the next. Most of the individual supply each of us possessed was usually self-consumed.

Bill McCollum, *Sergeant, U.S. Army, 173rd Airborne Brigade, Charlie Company, 4th Battalion, 503rd Infantry, LZ-English, 1969–71*

The first time I came home, I had no problems. The second time I came home, after serving my final six months, was a different story. I was at Cam Ranh Bay in a terminal waiting for my name to be called to board the plane. They called six names, of which one was mine. I thought that was odd, only calling six names. I proceeded through the baggage checkpoint with the five other guys, all of whom were E-5 in rank or above.

Then an MP walked in and I said to myself, "What's the deal here?" He called our names out to verify them, and all of us answered in the affirmative. Then he said, "You guys are going to be escorts."

I was thinking, "Jesus Christ, I don't want to escort anybody home!"

All of us ended up escorting drug users and other guys in trouble back to the States. The kid I was escorting wasn't bad. I heard his whole life story on the way home.

We landed in Fort Lewis, Washington. No sooner had we landed than they called all the escorts to the front of the plane. We picked up our baggage first, ate our steak dinner, and we were out of there in a flash. We didn't have to go through the normal debriefing process that everyone else had to go through and which seemed to take forever.

I flew from Washington to Providence, with a stop in between. When I landed in Providence, I took a little shuttle flight to Middletown. One of the guys there gave me a ride to Boulevard Nursery, where my dad worked. My father always used to leave a spare car key under his front floor mat, so rather than take a bus to Newport in my uniform, I just went to the nursery, opened my father's car door, went under the mat, took out the spare key, and drove off.

I had neglected to tell my parents I was coming home, and my father, seeing his car gone, reported it stolen. I was pulled over by the police. I had to explain the whole story to the policeman, who verified it with my father.

Thomas Finn, *Specialist Four, U.S. Army, Company A, 519th Military Intelligence Battalion, 525th Military Intelligence Group, MACV-J2, Saigon, 1966–67*

Ready to go home—Tom Finn completes his Vietnam tour. (Courtesy of Tom Finn)

I was taken by bus to the airport and waited to board a commercial 707 jet. At the time, the 173rd Airborne Brigade guarded the air base. I was dressed in my khakis, a beige short-sleeved uniform, for the trip home. There came a bunch of guys who had been there for a while with the 173rd. They had full packs, were completely armed, and had that real funny stare of an infantry soldier. Then we saw these new guys getting off the 707, the same jet we'd soon be taking back home. Looking up, these new guys caught a glimpse of the infantry soldiers walking by.

You could read the reaction in their minds: "Oh my God, a f—in' year of this!"

The seasoned vets never said anything; they didn't have to.

And I was saying to myself, "Let me get on that plane, please let me get on that plane and get out of here!"

Your baggage was usually checked for contraband prior to your being allowed to board, and weapons, drugs, alcohol, pornography, violent combat pictures, and the like were all confiscated. Total amnesty was granted to all who contributed to the pile. If you were caught with anything, you were given time in Long Bien Jail. But they never did search us.

After all that, we were allowed to board the plane. Shortly thereafter, we took off. After several hours of flying, we landed in Guam for refueling. The next morning we landed in Hawaii, another refueling stop. Here we were allowed to get off the plane. You guessed it! We went to the bar and had a few pops.

After reboarding, we flew for several hours. Then this guy sitting next to me on the plane opened his travel bag to reveal two live hand grenades.

He said to me, "Look what I've got."

I said to myself, "Holy cow, there's one major asshole on this plane, and I have to be sitting next to him."

Finally, we landed in Oakland, California. After getting off the plane and being taken to the main complex, we all went to the mess, which was open twenty-four hours a day. You were allowed to have anything you wanted. Most of the guys had steak and baked potatoes.

The out-processing at Oakland was like an assembly line. You went from one end of a building to another. Finally, all your paperwork was in order, and your uniforms and medals were issued. You were ready to go home.

I diverted my flight through Chicago to visit a friend who, unfortunately, had not yet arrived home from Vietnam. He had gotten hung up in the out-processing somewhere. I spent the evening drinking hard liquor with his father and stayed overnight. During that evening I called home and got my mother. She cried and said she wanted me home immediately. So the next morning I caught a flight home.

My brother was going to pick me up at Logan Airport in Boston. I told him to meet me at the bar in the airport. Unbeknownst to me, there was more than one bar. He finally found me in one of the bars after a while. I was already feeling no pain.

I wasn't home fifteen minutes when I got sick all over the place. Just what my mother wanted to see, right?

Rob Roche, *Sergeant, U.S. Army, 101st Airborne Division, Da Nang, 1967–69*

Due to my neck wounds, I came back home on a stretcher. It was a medevac flight with a number of other seriously wounded soldiers. To this day, I have no clue where we landed in the States, as I was lying down and could only see what was directly above me and a little bit to each side. Most likely, we landed somewhere in California. From there, I was transported to Valley Forge, Pennsylvania, where I was operated on for a fourth time. The other three times were in Vietnam and Japan. During my recovery, I had to wear this huge, extremely cumbersome neck brace.

Ken Garthee, *Private First Class, U.S. Marine Corps, 3rd Battalion, 3rd Marines, 3rd Marine Division, Da Nang, Rock Pile, 1966–67*

I was moved to the hospital ship U.S.S. *Repose,* which was off the coast of Vietnam, and was on it for approximately four months. On the ship, I had three operations, two of which were skin grafts to close the large gaping hole in my back. During this time, I celebrated my twenty-first birthday.

After my skin grafts had progressed to a point where I could travel, I left the *Repose* and stayed at a hospital near the Da Nang Airport. The night before I was to fly back to the United States, the hospital was attacked by VC, who launched a mortar attack against us. Those who could walk helped those who couldn't. Some were put under beds while others were helped to find cover elsewhere. I remember the mortars whistling and exploding all around us. Fortunately, no one was hurt; just a lot of scared and angry marines anxious to get out of Vietnam. Here it was, my last night in-country, and I was still being shot at. I couldn't wait to get out of there.

Before I departed, I called my family to tell them when I might arrive at the Great Lakes Naval Hospital outside of Chicago. The next morning we finally departed. As soon as the plane lifted off, everyone on the plane cheered. I had just survived the most difficult year of my life, while leaving some good friends behind. In less than twenty-four hours, I would be home.

Mike Pinksaw, *Specialist Four, U.S. Army, 60th Land Clearing Company, 62nd Engineering Battalion, 20th Engineering Brigade, Long Binh, Bien Hoa, Lai Khe, 1968–69*

I was placed on a C-141 medevac flight for the ride back to the States. There were a number of guys on the flight lying on stretchers like me or as ambulatory patients.

Doug Johnson, *Specialist Four, U.S. Army, 25th Infantry Division, 2nd Battalion, 12th Infantry, 1968*

After I was wounded, I spent approximately three weeks recuperating at the Evac Hospital at Cu Chi before I was stabilized enough to be airlifted to Japan for further treatment. I don't recall many specifics about the flight from Vietnam to Japan, but I distinctly recall that when we became airborne, I felt overwhelming relief that I had survived and was on the first leg of the journey home. I also remember a helicopter ride from the airport in Japan to the 91st Evacuation Hospital. My first venture out of the States had been to Vietnam, so I was certainly no world traveler. My worldview was so limited that I was surprised to see the huge high-rise buildings that dotted the landscape as we approached the hospital.

I spent another month recuperating in Japan before I was deemed ready to take the last leg of the journey, which I had dreamed about making for so long. I will never forget the flight from Japan to the United States. We were taken out on this huge plane, something like a C-141. I vividly recall that we were stacked up about three litters high as far as the eye could see on the plane, but no one was complaining about the accommodations. It was a surreal sight, and if I hadn't seen it with my own eyes, I probably wouldn't have believed it if someone were to have described the human cargo on this plane.

Before I was placed on the flight, a rather attractive air force nurse asked me if I needed something for pain for the flight home, and I responded in the affirmative. I will never know what she gave me, but I am forever grateful for the most peaceful flight I have ever experienced. I'm not completely sure to this day whether I stayed on the plane or flew home on my own.

David Rossi, *Specialist Four, U.S. Army, 1st Infantry Division and 25th Infantry Division, Di An, Tay Ninh, and Cu Chi, 1969–70*

I left Vietnam from Tan Son Nhut Air Base. On the plane guys were throwing pillows around; it was just a general feeling of joy and relief knowing we were getting out of there. The flight home was pretty active as I remember it. It took us twenty-four hours to get to the States. We landed in Wake Island and Honolulu, and everyone hit the bar. We still had our jungle fatigues on, and, of course, you just couldn't buy a beer for yourself without someone buying you one first. There were a number of friendly civilians there. Kind of a different story from what you normally hear about returning veterans' encounters with civilians.

When I landed at Travis Air Force Base back in the States, it seemed like it took forever to process out of the service. I would guess about twenty hours. The place where I started from to go to Vietnam was in fact where I ended my military career.

Howard North, *Lieutenant j.g., U.S. Coast Guard, Coast Guard Squadron One, USCGC* Point Clear *(WPB 82315), An Thoi and Cat Lo, 1967–68*

I flew out of Tokyo, and it was a major-league disappointment. It was a DC-8, which normally seats three hundred passengers, but all we had was fifteen guys on it. That's right, fifteen guys. I wanted to fly through Hawaii and take a small vacation there, but all I could get was a flight through Anchorage and on to Maguire Air Force Base in New Jersey.

Dick Turner, *Boatswain's Mate Third Class, U.S. Navy, River Assault Squadron 15, River Division 152, Task Force 117, Dong Tam and My Tho, 1968–69*

The trip home was long. It was a drunken time. I mean, everyone on the plane got drunk. Of course, I didn't get that drunk 'cause I knew that I had only an hour between flights, as I had to go through customs in San Francisco before catching a plane for Boston.

When I got off the plane at Logan, my parents were there; and I was in civilian clothes. I had a jacket on which said Vietnam on it.

A guy came up to me in the airport, grabbed me, and said, "You f—in' baby killer." The cops came running, and the incident was over very quickly.

You know, when I stepped off that plane, my mother didn't even know who I was. I was thin as a rail. I had lost thirty-five pounds in Vietnam. The outfit I had on hung on me like a bag. Because of the way I looked, my mother took me to the doctor's the next day. All the doctor said was, "He's fine. Mary, go home and hit the stove. Get him fattened up. All you've got to do is feed him."

THOUGHTS AND REGRETS

During the interviews, I asked the veterans to reflect upon their time in-country, to recall their feelings about the war in general, and elaborate on any regrets that they had about any of their experiences. As to be expected, the jury was split; there were those with regrets and others who had none.

Thomas Finn, *Specialist Four, U.S. Army, Company A, 519th Military Intelligence Battalion, 525th Military Intelligence Group, MACV-J2, Saigon, 1966–67*

We were in a deuce-and-a-half in Saigon. Two guys were in the front seat and maybe six to eight in the back. As I recall, we were going to an armed forces club and swimming pool. We were going there for lunch, and that was to be our treat. American women from the embassy used to frequent the place, and it didn't hurt to ogle the girls a little while there. News correspondents also paid visits to the establishment, and it was an opportunity for us to see some round eyes for a change.

So there we were in the truck when, all of a sudden, our driver ran over a guy on a bicycle. I mean, we literally ran over him. The truck bounced up and down. We just kept on going. I know if we had stopped, we would have been strung up by the civilians. 'Til this day, however, I wish we had gone back to offer some aid. At that time, I didn't care. Now I do.

On another occasion, four of us were returning from a night on the town. The cabdriver of one of these extremely small vehicles took us back to our compound after curfew, and he demanded some god-awful price for the fare. We all got out of the cab and started rocking the sucker back and forth while the driver was still in the cab. The harder we rocked it, the quicker he came down in price. We were close to tipping it over when we decided that his last offer was agreeable. It was about half the fare he originally wanted. I threw the money at him.

Peggy R. Zarek, *Lieutenant Commander, U.S. Navy, U.S.S.* Sanctuary *(AH-17), Coastal Waters off South Vietnam, Military Region 1, 1969–70*

There's nothing I'd change about my Vietnam experience. No, not at all!

Stephen Butler, *Lance Corporal, U.S. Marine Corps, 7th Marine Combat Engineers, Da Nang, 1966–67*

I was about to land in California after returning from Vietnam. It was only then I truly realized some of my fellow marines would never experience my joys, my hopes, or for that matter, life at all! I was happy I was home, yet sad others would never be able to join us.

I was kind of disenchanted with the whole thing. It would have been better if I could have gone home with my friends. By the time I was ready to leave, we were as tight as family. It was good that I was getting out of there, but bad that I may have been letting down some of the guys.

William Sullivan, *Lieutenant Commander, U.S. Navy, Fighter Squadron 213, U.S.S.* Intrepid, *Air Wing, U.S.S.* Kitty Hawk *(CVA-63), U.S.S.* Intrepid *(CVA-11), U.S.S.* Paul Revere, *and U.S.S.* Blue Ridge, *1965–68 and 1971–72*

No, I have no regrets and no shame whatsoever. I think, when you look at it from a historical perspective, that if the United States had not gone to the assistance of Vietnam, there probably would have been repercussions or bad feelings on the part of many people in the States. It was likely that in South Vietnam there probably would have been a big political backlash, particularly among the Catholic population, had we not intervened.

I really gained an awful lot of respect for the foot soldier, especially the marines. Remember, the foot soldiers never had the chance for the regular respite I had access to every night in returning to a ship operating off the coast and out of danger of the enemy.

Howard North, *Lieutenant j.g., U.S. Coast Guard, Coast Guard Squadron One, USCGC* Point Clear *(WPB 82315), An Thoi and Cat Lo, 1967–68*

Other than waking up a couple of times from a sound sleep because I was dreaming about running aground in the waters off the coast of South Vietnam, I haven't given my tour of duty much thought since I left the country. However, every now and then, you start to think about all those rounds you fired, and whom you fired them at. We were fortunate in that we didn't see what we shot. Being on the water, we were a substantial distance from where our artillery shells were exploding.

Bill McCollum, *Sergeant, U.S. Army, 173rd Airborne Brigade, Charlie Company, 4th Battalion, 503rd Infantry, LZ-English, 1969–71*

No, I have no regrets. I have some bad memories and some good memories; no regrets.

Doug Johnson, *Specialist Four, U.S. Army, 25th Infantry Division, 2nd Battalion, 12th Infantry, 1968*

I must admit that I have few regrets about my Vietnam experience. There are some issues that I have reflected on since my return that I may have handled differently given the chance to approach them with knowledge I have gained along the way.

I have thought about my decision to remain a noncommissioned soldier instead of an officer many times since my return to the world in November 1969. I had been offered the opportunity to go to officer candidate school when I was first inducted into the army. At that time, my decision was based solely on one thing: How much more time would I have to spend in the army if I became an officer? When the answer turned out to be one additional year, my decision was based solely on getting out ASAP. I have often wondered since my return whether this was a wise decision. I really believe that I may have had more to offer as a leader of men instead of a follower, especially when I discovered how young and inexperienced many of our officers turned out to be. I believe that I would have learned more about myself and my capabilities at a much earlier age if I had been responsible for the lives and safety of others. I also realize that as an officer, my life would have been more in jeopardy, and that I might not be here today if my decision had been different. So much of life is second guessing and wondering—we shouldn't waste our time wondering about what could have been, but we often do.

Another thing that I regret about my Vietnam experience was the animosity and hatred that was built up and exhibited toward the Vietnamese people, those that I will dub the *innocents,* by many of the U.S. troops. One of the major problems in Vietnam, unlike the other wars in which the United States had been involved, was not knowing exactly who the enemy was and not having any distinctive battle lines. As a result, to many of the GIs the Vietnamese were just *gooks*—some kind of subhuman species all thrown in together and demonized as the enemy.

Many soldiers did not realize that many innocent civilians were caught between a rock and a hard place—if they cooperated with the VC, they would be killed by the Americans, and if they cooperated with the Americans, they were exterminated by the VC and the NVA. The villagers who would have been very happy to go peacefully about their business of tending to their rice paddies and enjoying the peace and security of their villages instead became pawns in a most deadly game of chess.

I remember instances of this animosity and hatred that I personally witnessed which made me ashamed to be associated with our forces. On several occasions when I would ride out to the field by convoy, there would be little children lining the roadway and begging for C-rations. While many of the troops would throw their cans of Cs to the kids, some of the soldiers who had come to hate the gooks would throw their cans at the kids in a sick attempt to hurt them.

Probably the single event I would most like to have changed happened while I was still at Fire Support Base Pershing. While I was outside the perimeter with some other troops, we came across some women and children that had been wounded by a grenade. Medevacs were called in to attempt to save them, but it was pretty clear to me by the severity and location of some of the wounds that some of them were not going to make it. From the information that we could piece together, it appeared that some unknown American soldier, for reasons known only to him, had fired his M-79 grenade launcher at this group with devastating consequences.

This was my encounter with a personal, miniature My Lai, and I considered it to be an inexcusable act of cowardice and malice. I can certainly understand how the heat of battle or the loss of treasured friends can work on minds and emotions, but war does not excuse the slaughter of innocent people. This incident and the more widely known My Lai massacre made me wonder how often these brutal acts may have been repeated during the course of the war. It hurt me to think about it because it detracted from the more widespread bravery, heroism, and selflessness that was being exhibited by our forces day in and day out in the jungles of Vietnam.

I also regret that it took so long for all of us to realize and recognize the many contributions to our efforts in Vietnam by women serving as nurses and USO personnel. I know that I personally benefited from the love and professional care of the army nurses in Cu Chi and in Japan, and they are part of the reason I am still among the living today.

The Nurse's Memorial was recently dedicated close to the site of

the Vietnam Memorial in Washington, D.C. It is a long-overdue monument to the love and sacrifice and compassion of these angels of mercy who made living and dying a journey that did not have to be experienced alone. I brought a picture of myself with an army nurse at the evac hospital in Cu Chi to the dedication of the Nurse's Memorial in hopes

Doug Johnson with an unidentified army nurse, Cu Chi hospital. (Courtesy of Doug Johnson)

of finding her and personally thanking her for her contributions in Vietnam. I don't know her name, so all I can do is keep my eye out for her and thank her and all the other dedicated women in Vietnam who made many contributions to helping to bring us home alive.

Dick Turner, *Boatswain's Mate Third Class, U.S. Navy, River Assault Squadron 15, River Division 152, Task Force 117, Dong Tam and My Tho, 1968–69*

I think the United States never should have gotten involved in Vietnam in the first place. It started off as a policing action, and look what it ended up as. It was a full-scale war.

Michael Toner Farrell, *Specialist Five, U.S. Army, 544th Replacement Company, Cam Ranh Bay, 1969–70*

Regrets? I have none. I loved Vietnam; it was a vacation. I spent every day at the most magnificent beach I have ever seen, and I worked in a mess hall at night. I was fortunate, lucky, and blessed. In all the time I was in Vietnam, I never shot at anyone, and I was never shot at. I look back, and I say, "Thank you, God."

THE GREETINGS

One thing was certain. The Vietnam veterans did not arrive home to brass bands or parades. The reception received was dependent upon a few factors: the city and airport that the veteran was routed through (Los Angeles or San Francisco were among the worst in terms of protesters) and whether the family was present at the airport. If a veteran was wounded and flown back to the United States by medevac jet, the reception was virtually nonexistent—neither good, nor bad, nor indifferent.

Rob Roche, *Sergeant, U.S. Army, 101st Airborne Division, Da Nang, 1967–69*

Just prior to my discharge from the hospital and the service, I was issued a whole new dress green uniform, along with black paratrooper boots, all the medals I had earned during my tour, and everything else that went with being an airborne infantry soldier in Vietnam.

During my recuperation at the hospital, I was granted a pass to visit a friend of mine in Philadelphia. It seemed like everyone was against me, and it was only when I wore the uniform. The discharge board, taxi drivers, average people on the street—everyone I came in contact with—gave me strange or dirty looks and treated me like a second-class citizen. You know, the old baby killer stories about Vietnam veterans must have surely been in their minds. Because of it, I myself developed a bitter attitude, compounded with the fact that I already was upset from my Vietnam experiences. What made it worse was knowing what I had gone through to survive, and now I was being treated so poorly by my own countrymen.

After I was discharged from the service, I walked down a hallway at the hospital and I went into the men's room. I took off the uniform. With the exception of my jump boots and fatigue jacket, I threw all my stuff, medals included, into the trash receptacle. I then put civilian clothes on. This was how I was dressed when I hitchhiked home. I didn't get any more dirty looks all the way back to Newport.

Salvatore T. Raffa, *Airman Second Class, U.S. Air Force, 377th Security Police Squadron, Tan Son Nhut Air Base, Saigon, 1967–68*

I arrived back in the States a few days earlier than expected, and I remember telephoning my wife from T. F. Green Airport to let her know I was back.

She said, "You can't be home yet."

"What do you mean?"

"You're not supposed to be back for a few more days," she said.

"Well, I'm sorry, but I'm here."

Time makes me forget who picked me up at the airport besides my wife, but one thing I do remember: it was the greatest feeling in the world.

Betsy Wylie, *Lieutenant, U.S. Navy, Management Information Center, Headquarters, Naval Forces Vietnam (NAVFORV), Saigon, 1967–68*

Less than two months after I got home, I did have a very unpleasant encounter here in Newport. I was at the Bellevue Shopping Center, and I was in uniform and coming out of a supermarket with two grocery bags, one in each arm, and I had somebody walk up to me and say, "You're a baby killer!" and spit on the ground in front of me.

I knew that there was nothing I could do because I was in uniform. So I just said, "You're wrong!" and walked off.

A year later, in 1969, during the Jazz and Folk Festivals, both the Women Officers' School and the Officer Candidate School authorized the wearing of civilian clothes for their students for both of those weekends. This was to protect them, as much as possible, from harassment.

Doug Johnson, *Specialist Four, U.S. Army, 25th Infantry Division, 2nd Battalion, 12th Infantry, 1968*

I was flown from Japan to Andrews Air Force Base just outside of Washington, D.C. I was very relieved to be back in the United States again, and it felt like a heavy burden had been lifted from me to be back home safe and somewhat sound. My fiancée lived in Washington, so there could not have been friendlier soil for me to touch down on. It wasn't long after I arrived that my pretty prospective bride arrived at the hospital with her parents, and I was able to hold her close to me and hope that we would never be parted under such circumstances again. I remember that the conversation was somewhat strained, probably because we had existed in two worlds that couldn't possibly have been more removed. In fact, I don't think we talked that much, but rather held each other and were very thankful that we were able to be with each other again. Because I flew from Japan to the hospital at Andrews, I did not encounter anyone but other soldiers and the medical personnel on the plane and at the hospital.

I returned home in pajamas instead of olive drab and was therefore temporarily isolated from the abuse or taunts of those who were opposed to the war and anyone who fought in it. From Andrews Air Force Base, I was sent to Walter Reed Army Hospital in Washington about long enough to be quickly checked out and get a cup of coffee. The next leg of the long journey home took me to Newport Naval Hospital. It seems that an uncle of mine who was an officer in the army reserves had been able to pull some strings and get me into the closest military hospital to my home.

When I arrived in Rhode Island, it was raining pretty hard. I remember as if it were yesterday how eerie it was when they took me off the plane. I was on a stretcher, and because it was raining, they put the blanket over my head to protect me from the rain as they carried me from the plane to an awaiting ambulance. My thoughts flashed back to Vietnam and how close I had come to being killed, and I felt blessed that this blanket over my head was a temporary protection from the elements instead of a sign that my earthly existence had come to an end.

It seemed like I had no sooner arrived at the Newport Naval Hospital and gotten settled when my parents and brothers and sisters were there to greet me. What a wonderful day it was when I was able to see them again face-to-face and try to catch up on what had been going on in their worlds while I was gone. My parents were somewhat shocked to see my emaciated and weakened condition, as I didn't much resemble the robust son they had last seen at the Newport Air Park in January of 1969. I weighed about 135 pounds, down from probably 170, and looked every bit like a person who had had an argument with a mortar shell and lost.

By this time, late November or early December 1969, I was able to walk and get around under my own power. The doctors who were in charge of my case treated me very well. I recall how, when they reviewed my medical records and examined me, they expressed amazement that I had survived my wounds. They informed me that I was very lucky indeed, and that they knew that a lot of soldiers in my condition had not survived. After I had been at the hospital only a short time, the doctors began to allow me to go home on weekends to continue my recuperation in the comfort and warmth of my own home.

Looking back, I was very fortunate to have had a month between leaving Vietnam and arriving back in Newport. It allowed me the opportunity to do a lot of thinking and to begin to sort out the complicated pieces of where I had been and where I wanted, or more importantly needed, to go. I can't imagine how difficult it must have been for most of our troops when they returned home and were probably sitting at their kitchen table within days of their arrival. How could you possibly communicate, or even want to communicate, the experiences of war and survival to those who never had and probably never would have to face it?

My weekend visits home were very therapeutic, and lots of the neighbors came to visit and bring me cakes and lots of other goodies. I really got a kick out of my two youngest brothers, Kevin and Paul, who were in elementary school at the time and full of the energy, wonder, and curiosity associated with kids at that age. They appointed themselves head of publicity for awards and decorations, and no one who came to visit would be allowed to leave before they were shown my medals.

My fiancée came to visit on many weekends, and my parents pulled their own version of guard duty by making sure the door to my room was always open when the two of us were together. One of the highlights of my visits at home was when my dad took slides of my wounds and scars, even the ones on my derrière. The store that developed these photos must have thought that some pictures got mixed up, and that Mr. Johnson had somehow gotten some detailed photos of the moon with sharply defined craters that were taken by the Mount Palomar Telescope. You can imagine how much fun we have had with those slides in our family slide shows!

A strange but true incident involving one of our neighbors was also relayed to me after I got back to Newport. This man told my parents that he
had a dream that something traumatic had happened to me. At the time he
had the dream, he did not know that I was in the army and that I was serving in Vietnam. In fact, I am quite certain that it had been months or perhaps years since I had last seen him or talked to him. When my parents
inquired when the dream had taken place, they were amazed to discover
that it was on the very evening I was wounded.

The ward at the Newport Naval Hospital where I completed my physical recuperative process was known unofficially as the dirty surgery
ward. The majority of the patients on the ward were navy enlisted guys
who were there to undergo surgery for removal of pilonidal cysts, cysts
which grew in the area of the tailbone. I guess you could say that the thing
I had in common with all of them was a persistent pain in the ass.

There were two other patients on the ward who were recuperating
from wounds in Vietnam. A navy-enlisted man had been ambushed along
the road by the VC while in a Jeep with others. He was hit in the chest
and the leg by AK-47 rounds, and his Jeep went off the road and turned
over. He told a harrowing story of how he had to play dead while the VC
took his boots off him and his dead comrades and left him for dead. How
he managed to play dead with a sucking chest wound is something I've
been able to figure out. He was a good guy and really suffered a lot,
not only from the effects of his wounds, but also horrible nightmares
about his experience. On many nights I would be awakened by his blood-
curdling screams as he relived this terrible experience.

The other one was a marine who had been hit by fragments from a
grenade and apparently had a portion of his anatomy partially severed in
a manner that would give any guy nightmares. To put it gently, his distinctly male organ had been *cut short* in the prime of life. Fortunately, the
wonders of modern medicine being what they are, he had the damaged
appendage repaired. I still recall the first time that he was able to go out
on a date after his surgery. The burning question that I had upon his return to the ward was whether he had had the opportunity to test the effectiveness of his surgery. His beaming smile and thumbs-up signal told
me that all was well.

Michael Toner Farrell, *Specialist Five, U.S. Army, 544th Replacement
Company, Cam Ranh Bay, 1969–70*

I was processed out of the service in Fort Lewis, Washington. When we
left the base, we wore our dress green uniforms. Our welcome-home

greeting was given to us by a bunch of protesters at the airport. It was terrible. I mean we got spit on, called names, you know, the whole bit. I don't know exactly how many there were, but there were lots of them. It must have been something they did every time a plane came in from Vietnam. It was bad; I couldn't believe it.

One of the ironic things is, I became a protester, but not like them. I never spit on or dishonored a soldier—it was our government and its policies that I found objectionable.

Mike Pinksaw, *Specialist Four, U.S. Army, 60th Land Clearing Company, 62nd Engineering Battalion, 20th Engineering Brigade, Long Binh, Bien Hoa, Lai Khe, 1968–69*

My parents and grandfather were shocked to see what I looked like when they saw me for the first time at Fort Devens. I was not a pretty sight. I really can't remember much more about what happened that day.

Ken Garthee, *Private First Class, U.S. Marine Corps, 3rd Battalion, 3rd Marines, 3rd Marine Division, Da Nang, Rock Pile, 1966–67*

When I finally arrived at the hospital, I called my parents to let them know when visiting hours were. I was lying on my bed in the middle of the hospital ward, just prior to visiting hours, when I heard someone running down the aisle. It was Mom. When she reached my bed, she gave me a big hug. Shortly thereafter, we went in the visiting area to meet with the rest of my family. Everyone was there—my dad, my brothers, aunts, and uncles.

David Rossi, *Specialist Four, U.S. Army, 1st Infantry Division and 25th Infantry Division, Di An, Tay Ninh, and Cu Chi, 1969–70*

When I came back, about the only negative reaction I can remember was at my father's house. There was a party given for me upon my return. My father and this kid, who was younger than I, got into an argument about the war.

This kid said that I was over there for nothing, and that the war was a waste of time and a waste of money.

I didn't get involved, and it eventually ran its course.

Bill McCollum, *Sergeant, U.S. Army, 173rd Airborne Brigade, Charlie Company, 4th Battalion, 503rd Infantry, LZ-English, 1969–71*

I was at a train station in New York, and several of us took some negative comments while we were sitting on a bench. You know, things like,

"You guys are baby killers," and that kind of stuff. It wasn't really directed at any one of us in particular; it was meant for all of us in a group.

The number-one question when I came home went something like this: "Hey, did you kill anybody?" You know, guys just wanted to know about it.

After my first tour, I arrived home to find out that my mother was in intensive care. I remember getting ready to go back to finish my last six months, and my father and I went to the All-American Cafe down on Thames Street to have a beer.

He said to me, "So what are your plans now?" Up until then I hadn't told my family that I was going back to Vietnam. I told him I was going back.

"What do you mean, you're going back? They can't send you back there, can they?"

I said, "Dad, they're not sending me back. I asked to go back."

"What do you want to do something f—in' stupid like that for?" he replied.

I had six months left to serve in the military, and I didn't want to come back to the States and go back to a place like Fort Riley, Kansas, and experience spit-shined shoes, clean uniforms, inspections, and all that.

My father's next question to me was, "How are you going to tell your mother this, or how am I going to tell her this?"

I ended up telling her. She took it about how you would expect.

Before I left for Vietnam again, my mother got out of the hospital.

One morning I can remember her cooking breakfast for me, and my stupid brother said, "Ma, look at Billy's pictures."

I had sent them home earlier, and many were pretty graphic.

She never said she saw them; all she said was, "You should talk to a priest."

"What do I want to do that for?"

She said, "Those pictures."

"What pictures?"

"The pictures your brother showed me."

I was thinking to myself, "What do I say here?"

She continued, "I hope that was your photography and not your artwork."

I said, "Mom, it's over, I'm home, it's finished."

My father used to ask me questions about it, especially after he read a couple of articles in the local newspaper about my decorations. He was kind of proud of it and told all his friends about me.

My oldest sister use to say, "This is Billy. He was in Vietnam!"

So what, who gives a shit? For me, I'd still rather have Ralph back than any decoration.

Howard North, *Lieutenant j.g., U.S. Coast Guard, Coast Guard Squadron One, USCGC* Point Clear *(WPB 82315), An Thoi and Cat Lo, 1967–68*

I departed Maguire Air Force Base for the Philadelphia International Airport, and when I got there, I booked the first available flight to Providence. I tried to get in touch with my parents to let them know I was on my way home, but my folks were out of town. Finally, I made contact with one of my cousins, and he located my folks. They all met me at T. F. Green Airport. It was fun to be back and great to see my parents and relatives again. I also came home with a lot of money in my wallet because we didn't have any place to spend it in Vietnam.

TEN

THE HEALING PROCESS

And seeing the multitudes, he went up into
a mountain: and when he was set, his
disciples came unto him:
And he opened his mouth, and taught them,
saying,
Blessed are the poor in spirit: for theirs is
the kingdom of heaven.
Blessed are they that mourn: for they shall
be comforted.

Ask, and it shall be given you; seek, and ye
shall find; knock, and it shall be opened
unto you:
For every one that asketh receiveth; and he
that seeketh findeth; and to him that
knocketh it shall be opened.

—Matthew 5:1–4, 7:7

IN his book *Brothers in Arms: A Journey from War to Peace*, William Broyles writes, "When they [veterans] came back, their contemporaries who went to college were still in the first semester of their sophomore year, worrying about political science tests and getting a date for homecoming. The veterans returned utterly changed to an unchanged world—no wonder it was hard to adjust."*

---

* William Broyles, *Brothers in Arms: A Journey from War to Peace* (New York: Knopf, 1986), p. 136.

243

Experiencing the horrors of war firsthand undoubtedly had an incredible impact on a person's psyche. Although many recovered over time, some found the recovery process a lengthy and uncomfortable one.

Newport County veterans were no different in this respect from all the others who served. They would also suffer from numerous physical ailments and psychological illnesses.

THE PHYSICAL TRAUMA

Combat injuries healed and, in most cases, left only bodily scars. In other cases, although the outside skin had healed, the veteran continued to suffer from muscle aches and pains requiring periodic doctor's care. The discomfort remained, although it was not nearly as severe as when the wound was first inflicted.

Illnesses which surfaced long after the war plagued some of the veterans. Viruses could have been caused by a number of factors, and it can only be speculated that drinking impure water or living and fighting under poor sanitary conditions had a damaging effect. Diseases such as cancer could have been caused by overexposure to ultraviolet rays or from the exposure to the poisonous herbicide most commonly referred to as Agent Orange.* This chemical had been liberally sprayed as a defoliant in the South Vietnam jungles during much of the war. It was nearly impossible for soldiers to avoid walking through areas that had been sprayed. Worse, there were no warnings extended to the veterans that this herbicide was toxic. Unfortunately, it was years after the war had ended before manufacturers were found liable for the effects their chemicals wreaked upon humans in South Vietnam.

All too frequently, physicians back in the States had difficulty determining how Vietnam veterans contracted particular illnesses. Although many causes could be medically deduced, there was one overshadowing factor: some of these illnesses could have been contacted by the veteran while serving in Vietnam. It was an accepted fact that Vietnam's tropical climate was a breeding ground for numerous vector-borne diseases.

---

* The chemical composition of Agent Orange included equal parts of 2, 4-dichlorophenoxyacetic acid and 2, 4, 5 -trichlorophenoxyacetic acid. Dioxin was later determined to be one of its toxic substances.

Ken Garthee, *Private First Class, U.S. Marine Corps, 3rd Battalion, 3rd Marines, 3rd Marine Division, Da Nang, Rock Pile, 1966–67*

In the remaining year that I was in the marine corps, I spent more time in the hospital than out. I had surgery on my chest, removing the remaining bone fragments of ribs that were shattered when the bullet went through my chest. I received constant care and attention for my skin grafts, which were very painful at the time. The exit wound and my lower back required constant medical care and physical therapy.

Today, I still experience pain and discomfort in my lower back. I've learned to live with it.

Recuperating on the hospital ship USS Repose, *Ken Garthee poses for the camera less than four months after he was wounded. Ken's shirt covers a cage-like device he wore to help facilitate the healing of skin grafts on his back. (Courtesy of Ken Garthee)*

Mike Pinksaw, *Specialist Four, U.S. Army, 60th Land Clearing Company, 62nd Engineering Battalion, 20th Engineering Brigade, Long Binh, Bien Hoa, Lai Khe, 1968–69*

Today, I am totally blind in my right eye. My left eye is fine. I have a plastic surgical plate permanently embedded in my forehead. There's still pain in my arm from the shrapnel wounds and occasional pain in the right knee. Three of my fingers are numb and tingle constantly. Of course, I have a number of scars from the shrapnel, but these are mostly cosmetic.

When I first got out, I was receiving 100 percent disability compensation. Now I've been cut back to 80 percent after I went to work as a civilian fire department dispatcher for the navy. Instead of giving me a medical discharge, they medically retired me, and that gives me all the benefits at all the military installations.

Today, I still have lots of steel in me from the shrapnel. Occasionally, some works its way out. When I go for a chest X-ray, I've got to tell the X-ray technician that I have steel in my chest.

One day, I forgot to tell them, and this nurse came out and said, "Mr. Pinksaw, were you in a war?"

"Yeah," I responded.

She said, "That explains the spots on your X-ray."

Rob Roche, *Sergeant, U.S. Army, 101st Airborne Division, Da Nang, 1967–69*

I have no physical problems from either one of my injuries. I get 10 percent government compensation for disfigurement scars. I just found out that I've got hepatitis C; the guy I joined with also has it. Now, hepatitis C, they didn't even know it existed until '86. I had a physical at work a little over a year ago, and they found it.

So I went to my doctor and asked, "How did I get this?"

He said, "It's most likely from Vietnam."

My doctor said a lot of vets have hepatitis C from there, and they don't even know they have it. You have to be careful with it. There is really no cure, and it can kill your liver, but they can give you interferon shots. My friend is taking those. That has been known to put it into remission, but it's not a cure. My doctor has advised me against it.*

Doug Johnson, *Specialist Four, U.S. Army, 25th Infantry Division, 2nd Battalion, 12th Infantry, 1968*

Considering the severity, location, and magnitude of my wounds, I consider myself to be a very lucky guy. After being discharged from the Newport Naval Hospital and having a short period of leave, I was assigned to complete my remaining six months of active duty in Virginia at Fort Belvoir with the 91st Engineer Battalion. If you had some medical condition or injury that would prevent you from performing certain activities, the army medical personnel would issue you a piece of paper, called a profile, which would list your physical limitations and the activities to avoid. I had an amazing profile—no standing, stooping, bending, crawling, etc., etc., etc.

---

* Dr. Paul Donohue, in his syndicated column which appeared in the January 14, 1997, issue of the *Providence Journal-Bulletin,* had this to say about interferon: "Interferon is a small protein that body cells make to stop proliferation of viruses. Its effectiveness against the hepatitis virus has been shown to be between 30 percent and 50 percent." He went on to list the side effects, such as headaches and diarrhea, and also relapses if the patient stopped taking the injections. He concluded that "Interferon is a ray of sunshine in the hepatitis treatment landscape."

—the list seemed to go on endlessly. It meant that I did not have to march or do any other physical activities that would work up a sweat. In essence, I was semi-retired. On those occasions when some frustrated lifer would get on my case for some insignificant reason, I would remind them of my profile and threaten that I would get "no breathing" added to the list if they didn't leave me alone.

I continued to get terrible shooting pains down the entire length of my left leg, like someone was applying an electric shock. I also got terrible stiffening of the calf area of my left leg, worse than the most painful charlie horse that I had ever experienced. My digestion wasn't what it used to be before I was wounded, and I had trouble with foods with which I hadn't previously had any problems. Objectively speaking, I had nothing to complain about—I was lucky to be alive, and the pain was something I was happy to be able to deal with when I considered what might have been.

I occasionally have a random shooting pain down my leg and an occasional charlie horse. I have also lost some sensitivity in the areas where I had surgery, especially the left buttock and upper leg. My digestion remains troublesome, and I have been a major contributor to those pharmaceutical companies that manufacture antacids. I also have to avoid certain foods because although I know they taste good going down, the eventual pain will not be worth the temporary enjoyment.

All in all, I am a very lucky man, and I thank God for the twenty-seven plus bonus years he has given me since that fateful day. I also frequently ask His blessings on those who were not so fortunate—those who died; the physically, emotionally and psychologically impaired; and the relatives who have had to bear these terrible losses for so many years.

Stephen Butler, Lance Corporal, U.S. Marine Corps, 7th Marine Combat Engineers, Da Nang, 1966–67

Because of the job I did over there, handling water and such, I got some kind of a bacterial infection which got into my blood. I had to go for treatment and took a good deal of antibiotics. It lasted a long time. Even to this day, if I get run down, it still surfaces, but I haven't had any real problems with it in the last ten years.

I never got jungle rot* or any of that shit.

---

* Jungle rot is a skin fungus brought about by walking in a damp environment for an extended period of time without a change of clothes.

David Rossi, *Specialist Four, U.S. Army, 1st Infantry Division and 25th Infantry Division, Di An, Tay Ninh, and Cu Chi, 1969–70*

Eight years ago I came down with cancer. It was melanoma from overexposure to the sun. It started on my cheek and traveled down to my neck. Initially, the tumor was spotted during a normal doctor's visit. It was removed; laboratory tests were conducted, but it was misdiagnosed as benign. Another tumor showed up less than a year later, and this time the lab report showed the malignancy. I had surgery at Mass General Hospital to have the tumors removed. Whether the cancer was the direct result of my being in the field so much in Vietnam, I really don't know. My mother felt it was. Today, I still go for checkups on a regular basis.

Betsy Wylie, *Lieutenant, U.S. Navy, Management Information Center, Headquarters, Naval Forces Vietnam (NAVFORV), Saigon, 1967–68*

I was told later that some of the medications we were given routinely were not the best quality, and they were not sure what the reactions were going to be. We took malaria pills and got shots for this and that and whatever else. So, I don't know! But I can't say for certain that anything was a result of my being in Vietnam.

Dick Turner, *Boatswain's Mate Third Class, U.S. Navy, River Assault Squadron 15, River Division 152, Task Force 117, Dong Tam and My Tho, 1968–69*

I've got this rash down in the groin area and on my feet from having being constantly exposed to the wet conditions on the rivers. Eventually, all the clothes I had on the boat I had to throw away because they all had mildew and mold on them. There was no way I could have brought them home.

Bill McCollum, *Sergeant, U.S. Army, 173rd Airborne Brigade, Charlie Company, 4th Battalion, 503rd Infantry, LZ-English, 1969–71*

Believe it or not, I suffer from headaches every day. They call them cluster headaches. I've been to everybody, and I've taken all kinds of medication for them. I've used an ice pack on my head and a heat pack on my neck, and not much seems to help. This morning I was a basket case. I had them again. Some days it feels like pressure, other days my head just bangs.

I never had these headaches until right after I came home from Vietnam. I was up at that outpost, and I used to fire that .90 caliber recoilless rifle from a tripod. You know, that's a pretty big tube to be firing right next to your head.

I live with the headaches every day. Some days it's just the pressure and not as bad as other days.

THE PSYCHOLOGICAL SHOCK

The condition was diagnosed as early as World War I, if not before. During World War I it was known as shell shock, and during World War II and the Korean War it was called combat fatigue. After Vietnam, it was given a more specific name—post-traumatic stress disorder (PTSD). PTSD is not an easy medical condition to define. It is a puzzling and complex illness to recognize and treat.

Although only a small percentage of veterans were diagnosed with PTSD (normally those individuals who witnessed heavy combat), many others had to deal with unpleasant memories of their Vietnam tour of duty. Some veterans have suffered periods of depression or anxiety; others experienced infrequent nightmares or an occasional flashback. Many found that memories of their experiences in Vietnam were triggered by a sound or a feeling experienced in their civilian lives and that these reminders of the time they spent at war continued to crop up unexpectedly. Other veterans suffer from survivors' guilt.

The psychological impact of their Vietnam experience has made it difficult for some veterans to put it into their past. Some have learned to live with it and eventually rise above it. There are those who have achieved acceptance of their role in the war; others are still dealing with it.

Rob Roche, *Sergeant, U.S. Army, 101st Airborne Division, Da Nang, 1967–69*

When I was recuperating in Valley Forge, my mother and stepfather came down to visit me. I was already in pajamas and was able to walk around; however, I still had to wear the big neck brace. I was screwed up in the head from the combat, being wounded, and smoking grass.

Theirs were the first familiar faces I'd seen in over a year. It was just strange. I was screwed up and didn't know how to react. Even afterwards my mother said she knew something was wrong. I wasn't myself.

I had three really good friends come down to see me when I was there, and I couldn't react to them either. I was really out of it. What really bothered me was they treated me as if I were retarded or something 'cause I wasn't reacting like the same old Robbie that they knew. As a matter of fact, after I got discharged and hitchhiked back home, it took me a while to really get back into the groove of being a person again.

I do have flashbacks and dreams about Vietnam, but I try to bury it. People say "Go to therapy," "go to the VA," that kind of shit. Well, everybody I've gone to just rehashes it and rehashes it. Maybe that's the right way. For me, it's not.

You know, you change, especially with age. The war screwed me up. I'm an alcoholic, I'll tell you that right now. I've gone through two wives. Now I'm single, but I've got four kids that I try to do my best for. I can't blame my drinking on Vietnam alone; alcoholism runs in my family. I can't blame it all on that, but I think Vietnam had a lot to do with it. I really do! I just can't, you know, get rid of it. I try to bury it, try to bury it and go on with everything, but it keeps coming back.

Mike Pinksaw, *Specialist Four, U.S. Army, 60th Land Clearing Company, 62nd Engineering Battalion, 20th Engineering Brigade, Long Binh, Bien Hoa, Lai Khe, 1968–69*

I've had a couple of nightmares over time but nothing really frequent. I feel I'm pretty well adjusted, although I did have some problems back around 1981. I just felt like I was tired of the way we as veterans were being treated and the lack of recognition. And then I started getting depressed. I was going downhill after that. Fortunately, I got the help I needed.

It's changed a lot since then, but there are still people out there who feel we didn't deserve what we eventually worked so hard to get; that is, the recognition we all so justly deserved.

Bill McCollum, *Sergeant, U.S. Army, 173rd Airborne Brigade, Charlie Company, 4th Battalion, 503rd Infantry, LZ-English, 1969–71*

I'll think about Vietnam the rest of the night tonight, tomorrow being the anniversary of the day Ralph got killed. I'll think about it on Valentine's Day, the day he was buried. I can't even imagine what it must have been like for his mother back in Texas. Since his death, his mother has written to me three times. I've talked to her on the phone, but I've never seen her. As far as I know, she's still alive.

You see a movie like *Platoon,* but it doesn't have to be that direct because any little thing could trigger memories. It's always there!

When I first came home, I used to wake up with nightmares. When I went to a club, I wouldn't sit with my back to anyone. It was like I didn't want anyone behind me, and I always wanted to see everything in front of me. What it really came down to was, I just wanted to feel like I was in control of my own life and destiny.

Salvatore T. Raffa, *Airman Second Class, U.S. Air Force, 377th Security Police Squadron, Tan Son Nhut Air Base, Saigon, 1967–68*

I can honestly say I never was able to put the war behind me. I don't mean that it affected me in such a way that I think about it all the time. But something always seems to happen which triggers a memory. When you think it's all behind you, something happens, either to you or someone else, which brings it all back again. It's never over with.

Dick Turner, *Boatswain's Mate Third Class, U.S. Navy, River Assault Squadron 15, River Division 152, Task Force 117, Dong Tam and My Tho, 1968–69*

My real problem is the PTSD. It's affected my performance on the job. I no longer can drive government vehicles because I had a recent rash of accidents on the base.

I was actually retired from the navy for PTSD. I was given a ten percent disability, and the VA increased it to thirty percent.

Last year, after all these accidents, I had a nervous breakdown, and I said to my supervisor, "I think I'll go home, drive the truck up into the garage, leave the engine running, read a magazine, and just go to sleep." Immediately, he took me right to the Providence VA Hospital.

The doctor looked at me and said, "We don't hospitalize people here, but we will definitely do an evaluation." That's when they put me on medication.

The psychiatrist that I see up there said that I looked and seemed very depressed, and because of it, he changed my medication to an antidepressant. I feel a lot better now, I mean, I'm a different person. It gives you that I-don't-give-a-f— attitude.

I still have flashbacks. It's very hard for me to watch movies about Vietnam. I'm better now. At least now I can usually watch the whole thing.

Peggy R. Zarek, *Lieutenant Commander, U.S. Navy, U.S.S.* Sanctuary *(AH-17), Coastal Waters off South Vietnam, Military Region 1, 1969–70*

You know what's funny? If I'm outside hanging clothes and I hear a helicopter, immediately I think of it. In my mind, I can hear the announcement, "Stand by for Helo-ops!"

I haven't thought about it much, but that's the truth; if I hear a helicopter, it's the first thing that comes to my mind. It amazes me, because, that's how many years ago?

Betsy Wylie, *Lieutenant, U.S. Navy, Management Information Center, Headquarters, Naval Forces Vietnam (NAVFORV), Saigon, 1967–68*

I think about Vietnam only when someone asks me about it, except when I hear a helicopter. I'm alert to the sound, but it does not bother me like someone who was in combat or went through some type of traumatic experience. For a lot of the health-care professionals, hearing a helicopter is still a very tense experience. For me, it's not tense, but still I can spot one of those things a mile away.

I was at a navy dance after I had been home about three or four months. I was dancing with my date when somebody outside lit off a string of firecrackers. I remember absolutely going rigid.

My date asked me, "What's wrong?"

And I said, "What was that sound?"

He said, "What sound?" He hadn't even heard it.

Stephen Butler, *Lance Corporal, US Marine Corps, 7th Marine Combat Engineers, Da Nang, 1966–67*

I just made up my mind, that I, myself, would solve my Vietnam problem by not admitting that there ever was a Vietnam problem. So I just went about trying to build a life.

Doug Johnson, *Specialist Four, U.S. Army, 25th Infantry Division, 2nd Battalion, 12th Infantry, 1968*

It took a while for me to recognize that I did suffer from some psychological problems in trying to deal with my experience in Vietnam. The first recollection I have of the effect took place shortly after I arrived back in the States. One evening, not long after arriving at Fort Belvoir, I went to see a movie on post. I don't recall the name of the movie or what it was about, but I remember there was a sad part, and that I started crying uncontrollably. It hadn't dawned on me before this episode that I had been literally moving through my existence with little emotion and, in fact, had succeeded in burying my emotions. In hindsight, I recognized that this was one of the ways I protected myself from the inner turmoil that constantly seethed beneath the surface in Vietnam. I immediately called my fiancée, and, still very emotional, described to her how I had begun feeling some emotion again. It was a small step on the beginning of the journey to truly return home.

I would have to say that among the things that hurt me the most and caused the most psychological pain was the treatment we received when we returned home. It seemed to me that, no matter where I went, if the Vietnam War was discussed, all the so-called experts came out of the woodwork. I wish that I had a dollar for every person who told me what an illegal, immoral war we had been waging and how we had no right to be there killing innocent people. No one ever spit in my face or called me a baby killer, but there are many other effective ways of demoralizing those of us who gave our all in an unpopular cause, especially if the words come from those who called themselves friends. It seemed that I was spending half my life arguing about the war and the other half wondering why I bothered.

Nothing was more bothersome than those who would say that Vietnam was not a real war—it was undeclared and was only a *conflict*. I remember clearly one particularly angry outburst at work when I practically got up on a coworker's desk, a veteran of World War II, after he reminded me that Vietnam was not really a war. I reminded him that we were being shot at, killed, and wounded in staggering numbers and he could call it whatever he wanted, but to me it was and always would be a war. I never felt like I got through to these people, and after many heated arguments, I just decided not to argue about it any more. I know that World War II and all other wars were just as nasty as Vietnam, but at least most other wars (except probably Korea) enjoyed the support of the American people, and the soldiers returned home as conquering heroes. The public support of Vietnam ended long before the war did, and this was the first time that America had lost a war. That loss was pinned on the soldiers, who fought with all they had, instead of on those who were responsible for ensuring that we could never win because of their lack of strategy, foresight, and clear objectives.

I grieve for all those who returned home broken in body and spirit. Many returned physically but, in fact, they too died in Vietnam. I remember a guy in my unit who had spent his year in Vietnam out in the field with an infantry unit and was about ready to be shipped home. My guess would be that he was about nineteen at that time and had probably been whisked off from the carefree days of high school, compliments of the draft, and been given an all-expenses-paid tour of Vietnam. Even after what had been a grueling experience, he still looked young and fragile. I remember observing him in the company area one day, walking around almost in a circle and staring at the ground. I approached him and asked what he was doing.

He looked at me with a look of confusion and fear that I still remember to this day.

"Can you see them?" he asked me.

"See what?"

"The footprints . . . Charlie's footprints . . . can you see them?" he shouted nervously.

I never did see the footprints, and I honestly don't know whether I told him I did or I didn't. Shortly after this incident, he returned to the States to try to get back to a normal life. Somehow, I fear that he's still seeing footsteps some twenty-seven years later unless he managed to get some type of help. I relate this story because I think that many such men returned to the world carrying their own demons and ghosts due to the nature of the war and its aftermath. They are not part of the official statistics but nevertheless are part of the walking wounded who carry the effects of the war even today. My survivors' guilt encompasses and grieves for them because they suffer today, while I have been loved and blessed to have returned to a full and productive life.

I know that I will never know why my life was spared in Vietnam, but I do fervently believe that all of us are put on this earth for a reason. I have tried to remain open to opportunities to serve others as my way of thanking God for sparing me on October 7, 1969.

I have worked for years with my youth group at church because in them I see the hope for the future of this world. It is also my way of contributing to our youth in the memory of so many of our young, promising, talented, and loving soldiers who breathed their last in Vietnam.

ELEVEN

OUR FALLEN HEROES

I would rather to have had you for 21 years, and all the pain that goes with losing you, than never to have had you at all.—Mom (excerpt from a letter placed at the Vietnam Veterans Memorial)

U NQUESTIONABLY, one of the most difficult tasks undertaken while editing this book was to interview surviving family members. As twenty-five years or more have passed since hostilities ended, only a few parents are alive today. Several surviving sisters and brothers have moved out of the immediate area. Also, it was difficult to find family members who were willing to discuss this unfortunate and heart-wrenching time in their lives. It was of the utmost importance to include their thoughts and feelings in this endeavor. Newport County families experienced the sorrow of the Vietnam War firsthand, and as in all wars, the reality of death hit home with a crushing blow.

AN ELDERLY MOTHER REMEMBERS

In the early morning hours of January 31, 1968, Mrs. John P. Braga woke up from what had been a restless night of sleep. Suddenly, she felt a sharp stabbing pain in her back and experienced a strange feeling that something was not right. When she got out of bed that morning, she told her husband that they should delay their vacation trip to California, as she feared something was wrong with their son, who had been in Vietnam for more than eight months. They agreed that the trip should be postponed.

A few days later, Mr. and Mrs. Braga went to Sunday services. Driving back from the church to their home, they noticed two men dressed in military uniforms standing at the front door. The army recruiters had been there for a while, waiting for them to come home. The frightening premonition that Mrs. Braga had experienced was about to be confirmed. Their son, John Paul Braga, Jr., had been killed in action in Saigon on January 31, 1968, during the Communist Tet Offensive. The official government telegram received later by the family simply reported that he had been killed by gunshot wounds.

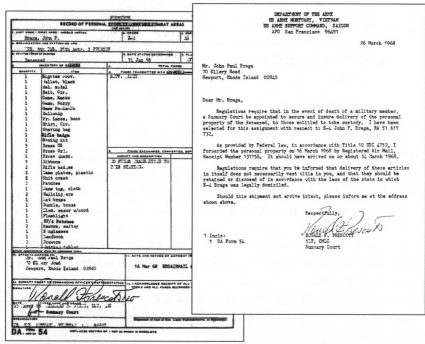

Right, the letter advising Mr. John Braga that the personal effects of his son, John Jr., were being mailed to him from Vietnam. The enclosure (left) inventoried all items. (Courtesy of Mrs. John P. Braga)

It was the afternoon of January 15, 1997, when I first made contact with Mrs. Braga. When I called her, she was on her way out the door to take care of an elderly friend who was convalescing. Briefly, I explained my intentions and, I hope, made her feel somewhat at ease. She told me that her husband had passed away nine years ago, in November 1988. He had been a navy Seabee. She was proud to say that the Bragas were a true military family.

We talked briefly and agreed to meet at a later date. Because both of us had busy schedules, we were unable to get together until the morning of March 14, 1997.

Mrs. Braga did not look her age (nearly eighty), in spite of her white hair. She appeared to be in excellent health.

During our conversation, she told me that John Jr. was born in Newport on May 25, 1947. In his youth, he loved to play baseball and was a member of one of the local Little League teams. He also had a paper route delivering the local newspaper, the *Newport Daily News,* to his neighbors. In his teens, John Jr. was a member of the ROTC program during the mid-60s at Rogers High School in Newport. He was also involved in several school activities and was extremely well liked.

John Braga, Jr., when he was about five years old. (Courtesy of Mrs. John P. Braga)

According to Mrs. Braga, "He was a good boy who had many friends at the high school and in the neighborhood." She continued, "He was always clowning around, and the kids loved him because of it." Since meeting Mrs. Braga, I have spoken with a few of John Jr.'s friends who attended Rogers High School with him. They all confirmed that he was very well liked and extremely popular among his classmates. One person said that John always had a smile on his face.

After graduation in 1965, he worked for a local tire company. In 1966 he was drafted into the army.

John Jr. received his basic training at Fort Dix, New Jersey, and attended the Army Ordnance School at Fort Carson, Colorado. Later he attended the U.S. Army Quartermaster School in Fort Lee, Virginia, where he successfully completed a training course on January 27, 1967, and was awarded a certificate as an ordnance supply and parts specialist.

Sergeant Braga's premature death came less than four months before he was scheduled to rotate back to the States. He had come so close, yet God had decided he was not to come back home alive. Sergeant Braga was only twenty years and eight months old at the time of his passing.

Mrs. Braga remembers her son's body coming home to Newport, and the wake and funeral, just as if it were yesterday. She described the attendance at the wake as being a wonderful tribute to her son, as many of his friends from high school were there. She remembered how she, her husband, and daughter, Marie Louise, grieved during that time. But she also wanted it to be known that she was appreciative, as appreciative as any mother would be under these terrible circumstances, that the casket was open and she could gaze upon her son's face and touch him for one last time. She recalled that his hair was combed in the same way she always remembered it. She said, "He looked like he was only sleeping." We can only imagine how great her grief must have been.

In memory of
JOHN PAUL BRAGA, JR.
Born May 25, 1947
Died in Military Service
at Saigon, Vietnam
January 31, 1968

The obverse of a prayer card handed out at the wake for John Paul Braga, Jr. (Courtesy of Mrs. John P. Braga)

"It was a very sad and difficult time in our lives," Mrs. Braga concluded.

She wanted everyone to know that a park was dedicated and named in memory of John—Braga Park on Kay Street in Newport. Should the reader visit this park, perhaps he or she will take a moment to reflect upon the memory of

Mr. and Mrs. John P. Braga at the dedication ceremonies for the John P. Braga, Jr., Park. (Courtesy of Mrs. John P. Braga)

John P. Braga, Jr., a sergeant in the U.S. Army, a mother's loving son, who gave his life as the ultimate sacrifice for his country.

THE SPORTS CAR THAT WAS NOT TO BE

"Donald was the most happy child I think I ever knew. He never got angry. He teased the daylights out of everyone and enjoyed doing it," said Nancy (Sisson) Winning about her deceased younger brother.

They were very close—so close that more than once, Nancy more than willingly covered for him when he came home late at night after having had a few too many beers.

Donald was one of six children, four boys and two girls. The Sisson family lived in Portsmouth.

Donald attended all the Portsmouth schools and was in the first graduating class at Portsmouth High School. In high school he played football, but only for a very short time—he had forged his mother's signature in order to play.

Nancy remembers her brother as intelligent, but stressed that he never really applied himself at school, at least not to any great degree. "He squeaked by. He just didn't put a huge amount of effort into it, as school wasn't his favorite thing to do."

Cars were Donald's passion. Learning automotive mechanics at a local gas station allowed him to apply his skills in restoring a 1939 Chevy. Both he and his friend Frankie worked on the car, got it running reasonably well, and eventually painted it black. It was Donald's pride and joy. No one was allowed to smoke in it, as that was his baby. Nancy said, "When it came to cars, he could fix anything. When I had a problem with my car, he'd ask me a few questions and was able to diagnose the problem even before touching it. He was a wonderful mechanic."

Donald Sisson's high-school graduation picture. (Courtesy of Mrs. Nancy Winning)

When Donald completed high school, he realized that his days as a civilian were numbered, and he decided to enlist for three years in the hope

of securing a better military occupation. After basic training, he attended a military specialty school and successfully completed training as a radio repairman.

After receiving orders for Vietnam, Donald went home on leave in mid-July 1968 and spent the next thirty days of leave with his family and friends. He left Portsmouth for Vietnam in August.

Donald had been in Vietnam several months when he wrote home to tell his family that he was looking forward to going on R & R. He had made tentative plans to visit Hawaii, and Nancy and Donald's girlfriend, Brandie, most likely would have met him there.

Donald Sisson in basic training. (Courtesy of Mrs. Nancy Winning)

Donald and Brandie were very much in love. As Nancy describes it, after Donald's death, Brandie left the community on the advice of her doctor. She eventually became a nurse and, ironically, went to stay with a friend in Hawaii, settled there, and married.

Donald had saved nearly enough money to buy himself his dream sports car—a new Corvette—and was making plans to pick it up in California with his sister. They were going to drive it back to the East Coast.

At Christmas time Donald managed to call home on a communication system employing both telephone lines and ham radio senders and receivers. When he called, he appeared to be in good spirits. Nancy said, "He was always in a good mood!" She reminisced, "He never seemed to be afraid of his predicament at any particular time."

Nancy received a final letter from her brother in late January, and we have included an excerpt here (see page 262). The following month would be Donald's last. Nancy relates:

> It was the most difficult situation you could ever imagine because we were in the middle of one of the worst New England blizzards up to that time. I was working at

a law firm in Providence, and it was either early afternoon or late morning, and the snow was so bad that my
boss said, "You've got to get out of here." When I got
home, the driveway was covered with two feet of snow.
I pulled the car in as far as I could get it, and I left the
motor running, thinking, "I'll get a shovel and clear a
path in order to pull the car in far enough so that my
brother Paul could get in behind me." And I ran up the
steps into the house to see where the shovel was; and as
I opened the door, my mom and dad came to the door in
tears, I knew something awful had happened. My father
received the news about Donald's death while he was at
work by a chaplain from the Newport War College. I
turned around to run back out to turn the car off, and they
thought that I was panicking, and they came back out
after me. I managed to turn the car off and went inside
and found out what happened. And then I had to start
calling people—all my brothers at work—to get them
home. I told them that there had been an emergency
without telling them what had happened. Then I started
calling friends, at least those who could make it. My aunt
and uncle from Jamestown managed to make it to the
house; and my cousin, who just returned from a tour in
Vietnam two weeks previous, also came by. They all
stayed at the house until about three in the morning.

My mother was hysterical and it was difficult to calm
her down and get her to bed. Because of the snowstorm,
the phone lines were down; and my aunt and uncle didn't
make it back to their home until four the next afternoon.
They had to go all around through Providence, as the
bridge was closed. It was a horror show!

While at the house, one of Donald's best friends was
plowing snow across the street and kept driving by while
Paul and I were shoveling the driveway. He kept tooting
[the horn] and waving. And the two of us were just dying
inside; we knew when we told him how upset he was
going to be.

The timing of the whole thing was really horrible.
Also that afternoon, I received a phone call from a friend
who said that another friend of ours just had a baby; and

I'm in tears trying to explain to her that I was happy for
her, yet I'm not happy.

According to a letter sent home from Donald's company commander,
Donald was killed by an incoming mortar round while running from one
foxhole to another so he could repair a radio. The shrapnel hit him in the back, apparently killing him instantly.

It took several weeks for Donald's body to return home—an unusually long time, even considering the distance. Apparently the delay, as Nancy remembers it, was that they didn't have a casket long enough to hold his remains for transport back to the States.

The wake and funeral for Sergeant Donald Sisson were very well attended. The police were called to control the influx of traffic at the funeral home. Parking, in fact, was at a premium. The family in the reception line never had an opportunity to sit down; and as Nancy tells it, "There was a steady stream of people from the opening until the doors closed later that evening."

Frankie, Donald's mechanic friend, had a son who used to look up to Donald. This nine-year-old boy took his own money from his piggy bank and donated it to a church to have masses said in Donald's honor.

"I think the toughest thing that happened to us," Nancy related, "was when his personal effects were sent home; and they hadn't cleaned his boots— there was blood on them. And that was really . . . Mom stayed in the other room, and Dad, Paul, and I found the boots. The three of us just held each other and cried. It was an awful thing. It really brought it home; the war, you know."

Looking back, Nancy said, "If I had to do it all over again, instead of

> 16 JAN. 68
>
> Dear Nancy,
>
> It's been a long time since I wrote you last and I'm sorry for not writing sooner. I'm feeling fine. I hope everyone back home is feeling the same.
>
> I got your package about two weeks ago with the books and I thanks you very much for it. It made me real happy when I got it. I don't know what I would do without you. You do anything I asked you to do and that means a lot to me. I also would like to thank you for getting me a christmas gift for Brandi and also tell me how much more money I owe you. I have one more favor I would like to asked you to do for me. Her birthday is coming up in Feb. so if you can come up with some idea's write and let me
>
> -2-
>
> know. Don't laugh but I forgot her birthday I can't remember dates any more but I know its in Feb. so maybe some how you can find out and tell me. How about sending her some flowers, I don't know what kind you ought to know, more or less your a girl, and something else to go along with it. Write me and let me know soon.
>
> Nancy write me and tell me how your car is running and if you ever got your radio working. I will let you know how much my new car will cost when I figure it out.
>
> Nancy maybe you can tell me what Brandi has been doing you know what I mean about going out with other guys. I know I don't have any strings on her but I'm jealous you know how it is. Also

driving Donald to the bus station before his flight, I would have taken him
to Canada. That war wasn't worth his life. If things would have been different, then I would have said it was worth it. It really wasn't.

Nancy concluded the interview saying, "I don't think he knew he was
going to die, but I always think his whole life was spent enjoying every
single minute of it. No matter what he did, he had fun doing it."

"MOM, DO I HAVE TO GO?"

When John Glover was very young, not much older than an infant, he went
to live with his godparents in Georgia. Because his mother had a large family with six boys and four girls, she thought it best that he go. The agree-
ment between Mrs. Glover and the godparents was that John would be
returned when he turned five years old. However, John actually lived with
his godparents until he graduated from high school. His diploma carried the
full name he was going by at the time: John Glover Henry.

John decided to return to his family in Newport. In time, he dropped
the name Henry and was known by his baptismal name, John Glover.

When John arrived home—that is, the one he never knew—he liked
what he saw. He met all of his brothers and sisters and enjoyed their company immensely. It was obvious he was pleased that he returned to his an-
cestral roots. Ella, one of his sisters, remembers seeing her brother John
for the first time, while he was sitting at the dining room table.

She said, "When I saw him the first time, he looked exactly like my
brother George."

As Mrs. Glover tells it, "John looked out for his sisters, like any good
brother would."

Ella added, "John looked and acted like a brother even from the start."

Ella also remembered him keeping to himself when he first got home,
not because he was a loner, but because he was new in the neighborhood,
"still feeling his way around," as Ella put it. Others had the advantage of
forging friendships over many years; John was given only a few months.

"He loved to clown around and play practical jokes," Ella continued.
"He'd tell jokes to make us laugh." She'd had stored away several letters
that John had written to her, and they reflected his sense of humor. She
also added, quite proudly, "For a guy, he had great handwriting."

John never neglected his mother. Mrs. Glover related, "He'd put his arm around me, and he kept saying to me, 'Are you my mother?'"

"Yes! Why?"

John Glover, on the left, clasping hands with a friend. (Courtesy of Mrs. Frances C. Glover)

"Because you're too young and good looking!"

"He also asked me why he went to Georgia to live, and I tried to explain the situation to him the best I could. I told him he was just a little baby boy at the time, and he was better off living with his godparents."

Soon John joined the air force. His oldest brother, Jack, had been in the air force, and John was influenced by Jack's choice. After basic training, he was sent to Sheppard Air Force Base for a seven-week course. He completed it and qualified as an Air Cargo Specialist. Not long after, John received orders for Vietnam.

Just prior to departing from his home in Newport, he asked his mother, "Mom, do I have to go?"

Mrs. Glover responded to her son by saying, "Yes, John, you have to go. You have an obligation to the service you belong to."

After saying his good-byes, John departed for Vietnam on Friday, March 5, 1971. It wasn't long before his mother and his sister Ella received their first letters from John. The letters were upbeat and displayed John's terrific sense of humor.

Shortly thereafter, Mrs. Glover received another letter from her son. Ella received one the same day. Mrs. Glover next remembers hearing a knock at her front door. She opened it to see two men dressed in military uniforms.

They said, "Mrs. Glover?"

"Yes."

"Mrs. Glover, we have some sad news about your son. He was killed in action in Vietnam."

"I said, 'No, he's not! I just got a letter from him today.'"

Mrs. Glover tried to get some information—to get some answers—asking, "Where did he die?"

"But all they would say was, 'It's a sad thing,' and they wouldn't say any more. I couldn't say any more either."

Ella was told of her brother's passing by her mother when she came home from school that day. As to be expected, it was devastating news for Ella and the rest of the Glover household.

The official record listed John's death as a ground casualty, caused by explosive devices. The date was Thursday, April 8, 1971, only thirty-five days from the day he first stepped foot in-country.

John's father and one of his brothers were summoned to Providence to receive the body. They would not let Mrs. Glover accompany them.

They escorted the hearse back to Newport, where the wake and funeral were held. Mrs. Glover remembers the wake being well attended. His casket was open but covered with a glass dome. As Mrs. Glover remembers, "His body was lying way, way down in the casket." She said that the experience was very draining for her and the entire family.

Before concluding the interview, the family showed me John's Purple Heart and the accompanying certificate.*

Just before parting, Ella spoke these final words: "He was a loving brother. I wish we had had him longer."†

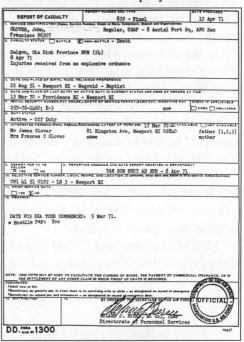

Air force casualty report for John Glover, who was killed in action. (Courtesy of Mrs. Frances C. Glover)

---

* I was troubled that John's name was not engraved on the Purple Heart. All the money that was wasted during the war, and the military didn't have a regulation or find the time to engrave John's name on it.

† John was one of two African-American soldiers from Newport County who lost his life in Vietnam; the other was Richard E. Greene, Jr., a marine, also from Newport.

FAMILIES MEET TO SHARE THEIR GRIEF

Several Newport County families, along with friends of the local veterans killed in Vietnam, met on the evening of January 25, 1973, to share their grief about the loss of their sons and discuss their feelings about the war. The meeting was held two days before a cease-fire was to take effect in Vietnam, which for all practical matters eventually ended America's combat role there. Their sentiments were published by the *Newport Daily News* in an article titled "Residents Air Gripes on Draft, War, Death."

At the gathering, Mrs. Harrison Manchester, mother of Jay Manchester of Portsmouth, said, "Jay didn't want to go. He was drafted. Our boys went because they had to . . . what our boys went over there for had been accomplished." She then began to cry.

Jay had graduated from Bryant College and recently had been married. He planned to attend law school in Boston after his graduation but was drafted into the army instead. Not long after, he was sent to Vietnam.

In March 1969, Jay, a private first class who had been in-country for less than two months, was killed in Saigon. At the time, he was assigned to a combat infantry unit. He was twenty-two years and five months old when he was killed in action.

Mrs. Manchester said, "I feel like all mothers who lost their sons. It's an emotional thing that mothers and fathers never get over. We lost three boys in Portsmouth. It will be a relief to us mothers that other boys won't have to go. I don't want other mothers to go through this."*

THEIR SPIRIT LIVES ON

It felt so good to meet and converse with Mrs. Mary Braga, Mrs. Nancy Winning, and Mrs. Frances Glover and her daughter Ella.† I felt I had

---

* David M. Korb, "Residents Air Gripes on Draft, War, Death," *Newport Daily News,* January 26, 1973. Actually, four men from Portsmouth died.

† I regret that I could not locate or make contact with all the families of our Newport County heroes. To those people, I offer my sincere apologies and sympathy on their loss.

known them for years, although we had only met recently. Their treasured recollections and photographs have given a special dimension to this book, and I am grateful that I had the opportunity to memorialize these young men in this modest way. Certainly they deserve so much more.

I can conceive of few more tragic ways to lose a son or brother than through a war. But these "gold star" families have managed to go on with their lives, never forgetting their loved ones, who are frozen in time as infants, boys, and young men in photographs and memories.

It has also been difficult for those of us who survived the Vietnam experience. We miss our friends, our comrades in arms, our brothers, who were not afforded the opportunity of life's continued pleasures and surprises as we were. We veterans share your grief and honor their memory for the sacrifice they made in the name of freedom.

TWELVE

YEARS LATER

For the first time in American history, the soldiers who fought for us are now our teachers. Unlike any other warriors of any other age,'they are telling us about their war and their anguish and how they sense their own Government betrayed them. The passage of time has not dimmed their recollection of what happened, and they do not glamorize Vietnam. They are trying to tell us the truth as they see it and feel it, and they do it more effectively than could any historian or journalist or social critic. . . . Sometimes they abrade us with their anger and their insistence. But when they tell us what really happened to them, they return to us the memory we lost, the memory that has failed us so often during the past two centuries. These veterans have thus taken upon themselves the responsibility to instruct us. Their lessons are too important for us not to listen.—Richard Severo and Lewis Milford, *The Wages of War: When America's Soldiers Came Home*

RETROSPECTIVES

OVER a quarter of a century has passed since the interview participants left Vietnam; certainly enough time to reflect upon and reevaluate their own involvement in the war. What were their more lasting wartime recollections, and how would they reflect upon them some twenty-five to thirty years later?

These veterans recalled an extraordinary number of memories. In fact, some of the stories they told surprised even the veterans themselves, as they thought they had forgotten many of the events and accompanying details. There was one factor, however, which universally bound each one of them together in their story telling. There wasn't an individual interviewed who hadn't been affected to some degree by the war. Most lost their youth; others witnessed the death of their best friends. Some sustained serious and life-threatening wounds, while a smaller percentage suffered the mental anguish associated with lingering memories of combat. Whatever their experiences, all were truly touched by their wartime service.

Vietnam was a terrible war from the standpoint of national guilt. It tore into the very soul of each and every American—those who served and those who remained on the home front—and it afflicted our fellow citizens with either a deep sense of shame or outright denial. These uncomfortable feelings continued for a number of years, long after the war officially ended.

It should come as no surprise, therefore, that several veterans mentioned that upon their return no one wanted to talk to them about their tours of duty. This was not an atypical experience by any means. Jan Scruggs, founder of the Vietnam Veterans Memorial (the Wall), had this to say:

> Even ten years after you came back, the easiest way to clear a room was to mention Vietnam. Friends and family only wanted you to quietly and happily join their sanitized, safe lives. "I was shocked," one vet said, "not by the fact that no one cared, but that no one even talked about it."*

After the war, a unique condition permeated much of America. Perhaps best described as mass amnesia, this psychological illness was most likely caused by national shame and guilt—either for losing the war and having to bear its legacy or for participating in it at all.† Conceivably, the nation simply wanted to forget all the horrors which its citizens had been subjected to, especially after being totally saturated for over a decade with media coverage of the war. Whatever the reason, the illness seemed to fester long after the war officially ended.

Quite frankly, very few Americans were eager to discuss any aspects of

---

* Jan C. Scruggs and Joel L. Swerdlow, *To Heal a Nation: The Vietnam Veterans Memorial* (New York: Harper & Row, 1985), p. 11.

† John S. Bowman, *Vietnam War, Day by Day* (New York: Holt, Rinehart & Winston, 1977), p. 6.

the war; and except for the veterans' immediate families, even fewer were willing to question them about it. It was as if the entire country had regressed into a post-war cerebral deep-freeze. For those who served, it was not only disheartening but appalling. Many who had witnessed traumatic events and sacrificed in silence rarely could find a sympathetic ear inclined to listen or a friendly shoulder to lean on. This situation would eventually take a dreadful toll on far too many veterans. Marriages failed at an alarming rate, incidents of PTSD increased substantially, suicides became considerably more prevalent, and a shameless number of troubled and lost souls became homeless. The emotional and psychological cleansing many veterans were seeking was simply not to be found.

This attitude changed, however, at about the time the Vietnam Veterans Memorial was being planned. Slowly the mental and emotional deep-freeze began to thaw. The nation was beginning to realize that veterans were not the real culprits of the war; they were in many cases unwilling pawns in the political scheme of things. Let there be no misconception: there were veterans who believed in the cause, and in many cases they may have been correct in their assumptions. These individuals went to Vietnam with the idea of helping an impoverished people fight the onslaught of communism. Unfortunately, the war was fought to be lost. But did the communist North Vietnamese and Viet Cong actually win? Even today, reunified Vietnam is not much better off than when the Americans first arrived in the early 1960s. Politically, the former South Vietnamese populace has little voice in the communist government. Even now, some still think of it as the war that nobody really won.*

Newport County men and women, as well as most veterans throughout the country, performed their patriotic duty in an admirable fashion. When their tours of duty ended, they quietly assimilated back into society, wanting nothing more than to continue with their lives and maybe, just maybe, have their wartime service better understood.

Thomas Finn, *Specialist Four, U.S. Army, Company A, 519th Military Intelligence Battalion, 525th Military Intelligence Group, MACV-J2, Saigon, 1966–67*

When I first came home, I tried to explain to others where I had been, what I had done there, but nobody really cared or wanted to listen. I felt a little hurt by this. I'd get the responses like, "Oh, you were over there." So for the longest time, for years, I would not talk about it.

---

* Ibid.

It helped me when I joined the army reserves in 1974, and I met a few fellow Vietnam veterans. There you could talk about it with people who understood. We were able to open up to each other. It made me feel good. However, I rarely talked about my experiences to others. In all, I did twenty years in the reserves.

In the 1980s the Vietnam stigma left me for the most part; and if anyone was interested, I'd talk about it.

Today, I serve as the chairman of my unit's reunion association, which I'm proud to say I founded. I'm still very much involved with this group of 500 members. We've had a number of reunions and also include the wives in the festivities. We've had reunions in Chicago, Fort Bragg, and at the Wall.

David Rossi, *Specialist Four, U.S. Army, 1st Infantry Division and 25th Infantry Division, Di An, Tay Ninh, and Cu Chi, 1969–70*

You know, we had guys who got killed out there. I remember it happening and how it happened, but I just can't remember their names. I don't know if you just kind of block that out. One of our guys stepped on a booby trap, and he was just blown away. Another was an ARVN soldier assigned to our unit who accidentally blew himself up while wiring batteries from a radio trying to set up a automatic claymore mine.

Rob Roche, *Sergeant, U.S. Army, 101st Airborne Division, Da Nang, 1967–69*

I really thought at the time, and being naive of course, that we were doing the patriotic thing like our fathers. After being there and seeing what it was about, and smelling it, and tasting it, and watching all the stuff, you know, my regret is just going over there, period! I don't think we should have been there. I really don't!

I used to say to myself, after someone would be killed and I'd look at him or would carry him to an area where we could get a chopper in and throw him on the chopper, I would just say to myself, "What the f— are we doing here?" You know, I'd look at the Vietnamese people and say to myself, "I've got nothing against these people, what am I killing them for?" You know, that kind of thing.

I seriously question what we were there for. If the same thing happened again today, I'd take my son to Canada, I really would. I have no doubts whatsoever that I'd do just that.

Ken Garthee, *Private First Class, U.S. Marine Corps, 3rd Battalion, 3rd Marines, 3rd Marine Division, Da Nang, Rock Pile, 1966–67*

It's interesting what you remember so many years later. While in-country, we never displayed our rank in the field for fear of being a VC target. In fact, I didn't even know that I had been promoted. Only after my tour was over did I find out that I was promoted to sergeant. I always wondered if they promoted me because I was among the few to survive the Rock Pile. The stripes didn't catch up to me until I was at the Great Lakes Naval Hospital.

When I got out of the marine corps, the Veterans Administration provided me with an opportunity I couldn't resist—a free education! It was called the Veterans Rehabilitation Program and my education was paid for in full, including books, tuition, and all fees. I was even paid to go to school. I decided to go to the University of Wisconsin, since I had spent the better part of my childhood in that state.

I found the transition from military routine to academic life very difficult. Initially I had wanted to be a farmer, but my disability prevented me from being one. Instead, I decided to become a teacher. One thing I knew for certain. I wanted to help, guide, and encourage children.

While attending school one day, I was going through the cafeteria line to get some breakfast when I saw a young woman ahead of me. She would change my life forever. It only took one look for me to know that I was going to marry her. I didn't officially meet her until our first class of the day—French 101.

At the end of the academic year, 1969, she moved to Newport and attended Rhode Island College. Quickly, I transferred to Rhode Island College. I always said I chased her until she caught me!

I graduated in 1973 with a bachelor of science degree in education and went on to obtain my master of education degree. My wife graduated with a bachelor of arts degree in sociology a few years later.

The best gifts of all, however, were presented to us later—the births of our two sons.

Every day we try to show our love for our family and do whatever it takes to keep our sons healthy, to encourage them to do their best, and to work together. Most of all, we want them to enjoy life and have fun.

Looking back to the time when I was in the hospital, shortly after being wounded, I remember saying to myself, "My God, why me? Why was I saved and given another chance?"

Now I understand.

Salvatore T. Raffa, Airman Second Class, U.S. Air Force, 377th Security Police Squadron, Tan Son Nhut Air Base, Saigon, 1967–68

What I remember most about Vietnam was the hundreds of coffins I used to see, on a daily basis, being loaded unto planes for the return trip back to the States. I lived right near the flight line at Tan Son Nhut Air Base, every day the coffins would come from the morgue and then were lined up before being loaded onto the plane. You just couldn't believe the number of caskets.

Also, I'll never forget the hospital buses taking the wounded soldiers (most on stretchers) to the flight line to have them put on airplanes for their final trip home. They all had blue hospital pajamas on; these were the guys with no arms, no legs, and no eyes, and I saw that every day. Oh, it was terrible. It was just unbelievable.

I'm very proud to see veterans and be one also. I've got friends who went to Canada to avoid the draft, but they are still my friends. That was their way of dealing with it. But, even to this day, there are some people close to me who have little regard for them. My reply is, "If I knew how the war was going to be, I probably would have gone to Canada, too."

It was something I was forced into. I didn't volunteer, and I wasn't a hero. I went over there as a scared-to-death little boy and came home a scared-to-death young man.

Vietnam was very different from any other war this country ever took part in. When you went over there, you knew immediately you only had to serve one year. So each man was defending his own life and interests so he wouldn't die and could make it back home. It was so different from World War II.* Some of those guys didn't come home for several years. When you've got a thousand guys protecting themselves, all with the ultimate goal of making that one year so they could be sent home, it's no wonder the war ended up the way it did. Now, I'm not saying we were any less patriotic, but that was the way Vietnam was.

Michael Toner Farrell, *Specialist Five, U.S. Army, 544th Replacement Company, Cam Ranh Bay, 1969–70*

Every time a movie about Vietnam is released, I go to see it to reflect on just how lucky and blessed I was. I've seen guys with post-traumatic stress disorder, other guys who were banged up physically, homeless guys, others who were totally screwed up mentally because of what our government did to them, and I realize that God knew I had had open-heart surgery and that I didn't belong in a jungle or in the war.

---

* In World War II, a point scheme allowed troops to rotate back to the States. Those in combat accumulated points faster than support troops through the award of medals (the higher ones gained more points) and by the amount of time served in a war zone. As the war continued, the government always appeared to be increasing the amount of points required to go home due to the difficulty of finding new replacements. Just when a soldier thought he had accumulated enough points to go home, the total was adjusted upward. So it was virtually impossible to reach the point-total goal in one year.

When I was operated on back in 1964, there were only about fifteen of us that had that surgery during that period of time, as the technology for open-heart surgery was relatively new and extremely risky. I was one of only two survivors—you have to feel blessed to have survived that kind of an operation and Vietnam as well.

Dick Turner, *Boatswains Mate Third Class, U.S. Navy, River Assault Squadron 15, River Division 152, Task Force 117, Dong Tam and My Tho, 1968–69*

We were actually sent over there to help those people. I guess today the United States has resumed relations with them. I know for a fact Briggs and Stratton has a big plant over there, and now a lot of big corporations are building plants over there. I think it's a good thing. It's time to bury the hatchet—life goes on.

I'd like to go back there, myself, and see what the place looks like today. I think it would be a great thing to do. Unfortunately, it can cost anywhere from thirty-five hundred to five thousand dollars to do it. How can you justify that kind of money?

I used to give talks to high-school students about Vietnam, but I haven't

lately. I'd show slides as well. In fact, the Naval War College showed considerable interest in them when I lectured in front of a group of officers.

I lost a good friend over there; his name was Bill, and he was from Arkansas. He was standing right next to me when he was shot. That's what caused some of my PTSD. It happened at dusk. We were in the Mang Thit Canal and were anchored there to stay overnight. Bill and I were up on the flight deck eating supper, and all of a sudden I heard this bang. The next thing I knew, Bill was lying on the deck, right next to me, dead! The sniper had shot from a bridge up over the canal. The bullet just missed hitting me. If I hadn't moved, I would have been hit. I've written his parents, and I have kept in touch.

Doug Johnson, *Specialist Four, U.S. Army, 25th Infantry Division, 2nd Battalion, 12th Infantry, 1968*

There has hardly been a week that has gone by that I have not thought about Vietnam. I had a lot of time for solitary reflection during my initial period of recuperation, and the recurring theme was always, "Why did I survive when so many were not so fortunate?" It is a question that I have been asking myself for over twenty-seven years and can't say that I have found the answer. It's a question that probably ranks right up there with, "What is the meaning of life?"

I think about how precious the gift of life is and how terrible it is to waste a second of it. I learned how quickly life can be snuffed out and how the difference between life and death can be just a millimeter. I remember that this was graphically illustrated by the experiences of some of the officers who served in my unit. One lieutenant was hit by shrapnel  from a mine. He apparently was struck by very little shrapnel, and what looked like minor wounds turned out to be a small piece in the heart which killed him. Contrast that with the experience of a captain who was grazed on both sides of his forehead by AK-47 rounds and lived to talk about it. He had matching nasty red scars on each side of his forehead as an everlasting reminder to him of the sanctity of life. I still wonder, as I'm sure he has wondered, what happened to the round in the middle that would have struck him right between the eyes.

There were also the many men who came back for second and third tours of duty hoping to get rank in a way that is not possible in the peacetime army. One such captain paid dearly for his decision. He left Vietnam during his second tour after losing an arm, both legs and an eye. These are the memories that you will never forget and yet will never truly understand or comprehend.

In my opinion, one of the most significant contributions to the healing process for Vietnam veterans has been the construction of the Vietnam Veteran's Memorial in Washington, D.C. I will be forever grateful for the vision and foresight of veterans like Jan Scruggs and the many others who had a dream for this memorial and set it in motion. Almost every Veteran's Day and Memorial Day, I join veterans and their families and friends, people from all walks of life, to honor the lives and sacrifices of the many brave soldiers on the wall.

It hurts to see so many veterans at the Wall from year to year who are still suffering from physical, mental, and emotional torments and especially those who are still attempting to extinguish these demons with alcohol and drug addictions. It is a constant reminder that many still suffer the effects of long-ago battles and, for them, the war is still not over.

Long ago, I vowed that I would not forget those who made the ultimate sacrifice, and I will never forget them as long as I live. All of us who participated in the Vietnam War have our own personal walls within us. By keeping the memory of those on our walls alive, we honor them and remain ever vigilant in our attempts to ensure that this carnage and personal sacrifice will not happen again. I believe that a part of all of us died in Vietnam and remains there as part of our collective experience.

Betsy Wylie, *Lieutenant, U.S. Navy, Management Information Center, Headquarters, Naval Forces Vietnam (NAVFORV), Saigon, 1967–68*

The time I spent in Vietnam was a superb learning experience. I worked with many aspects of the navy (and the other services) that I would not otherwise have known and understood. I saw funny situations as well as

the sad ones; and the horrendous ones. It gave me a greater understanding of my profession and a skepticism about obfuscation.

Those in positions of senior leadership had a great responsibility to be honest and forthright and true to their followers. There were many such leaders in Vietnam. There were also those who had none of these qualities. I resented those who lied to me, then and later. Professional military and politicians who regularly lie for self-aggrandizement do nobody any good. They need to find other employment. The business of arms is based on trust, and one cannot trust a liar.

One can do much more, and under more trying circumstances, than one thinks possible. I have the utmost respect for those who volunteered to take on onerous and frightening duties.

Bill McCollum, *Sergeant, U.S. Army, 173rd Airborne Brigade, Charlie Company, 4th Battalion, 503rd Infantry, LZ-English, 1969–71*

When I came back from Vietnam, I read an article in the military newspaper that said they needed drill sergeants. So I said, "Maybe I should do that. Maybe I can help someone like my drill sergeant helped me way back in basic training." So I did that for sixteen years, and I just retired with twenty-seven years of military experience (three years of active duty and twenty-four years of reserve duty). I enjoyed it.

Peggy R. Zarek, *Lieutenant Commander, U.S. Navy, U.S.S.* Sanctuary *(AH-17), Coastal Waters off South Vietnam, Military Region 1, 1969–70*

No one even asked you about it or wanted to hear about it, even my own peers, which surprised me. I was assigned to the navy hospital here in Newport, and I was in charge of the intensive care unit. I found it amusing that the staff would complain that they couldn't have a coffee break, and I just got in from a place where we couldn't even spell coffee break. You know what I mean? That kind of got to me. And it got to me that no one said, "Peggy, what was it like?" Except for one young nurse, whom I'm still friends with today; she was the only one who asked or showed an interest.

Eventually, this attitude changed. Several years ago, I was asked to speak at a Memorial Day service in Little Compton. The commander of the American Legion post came to my house specifically asking me to talk about Vietnam. I accepted.

I guess I wouldn't say it amazed me, but in a way it did; when the ceremony was finished, people came up to me and hugged me and kissed me, and cried, and said, "Thank you!"

A neurosurgeon visiting from New York came up to me and said, "I can't believe it, *I just can't believe it.*" He was genuinely touched at my speech and the numbers I had quoted.

When the Moving Wall came to Fall River, I went to see it. Now, you don't think of Vietnam every day; but when I saw that, it just hit me. I mean all those names, yet I couldn't remember any of them. I'd really like to know what happened to some of them. I mean, I really would love to know.

I went to the dedication ceremonies of the Vietnam Women's Memorial in Washington, D.C., and that was quite an experience. It was the most emotional four days of my life. Oh, the gamut of emotions—laughter, sadness, tears! But the thing that got to the majority of us as we walked down Pennsylvania Avenue (it was the most gorgeous day, you couldn't have asked for a better day), and as we walked where the veterans were standing on the sidewalks, they were all saying, "Thank you! Thank you!" And that got to us. They were coming up to us hugging us and thanking us.

Peggy Zarek, fourth from left, with glasses, looks over the banner carried in the parade celebrating the Vietnam Women's Memorial dedication.

Three or four years ago, a group of local Vietnam veterans asked me to march in the Bristol Fourth of July Parade. Of course, the first year the veterans marched in the parade, they were treated rather badly. Now, of course, it's a whole different story.

That year they were paying tribute to the nurses and had a replica of the Vietnam Women's Memorial. I had just had leg surgery, and I said, "Oh God, should I?" Anyway, I did it. That was quite an experience. I couldn't believe the people clapping and everything. It was just wonderful.

But in my opinion, the Vietnam War was senseless. These nineteen-year-old kids didn't even get a chance to live yet. I would have liked to have had the politicians spend some time in the ICU and see what we had to see every day.

Stephen Butler, *Lance Corporal, U.S. Marine Corps, 7th Marine Combat Engineers, Da Nang, 1966–67*

When I was in Vietnam I was only a kid, and that's why I think it was an awesome responsibility. It was an awesome responsibility for all involved, whether directly or indirectly for the soldiers themselves, the politicians, and the nation. I mean, an eighteen- or nineteen-year-old kid was trained to do his job, and that's all it was. I myself didn't know why we were there. I didn't know if it was right or wrong. When I got back, I was nineteen; your life experiences were limited, even with the war behind you.

Speaking today as a father and an adult, I feel that the way we as a nation went about handling that conflict was absolutely and totally unacceptable. I would hope that if something like that ever happened again: one, we would make certain that we were totally committed; and two, that we made a positive determination not to fight it on a part-time basis, especially with cavalier attitudes. If we make the decision to fight, we should do it one hundred percent.

I hope this nation never lets a war like that happen again; I know I could never let it happen again in my lifetime. I hope my son and future generations will do the same.

The following poem was composed by Doug Johnson. Initially, he wrote it for his own personal reflection and catharsis. It is a Vietnam veteran's tribute to his friends and fellow comrades who never returned home and affirms why their sacrifice will never be forgotten. It is also a veteran's retrospective of the war. But in a greater sense, it is a lasting tribute to all those who served, living or deceased. The poem is published here for the first time.

REFLECTIONS ON VIETNAM MEMORIAL DAY—1988

It could be any Memorial Day
since 1969.
  The emptiness engulfs
me.
  It rises from deep
inside me—
  from a part of me that
was and remains a long
way from home.
  It will always be
a part of me—kept at bay
by the passage of time and
people and events.
  I want to explore and
roam its musty corridors—
but pain and hurt are
unwelcome companions—
I just pass on.

Images bombard my
  mind's eye:
  of a pastoral land of beauty,
  of a people condemned to death,
   of faith and hope and love,
  of bravery and sacrifice,
   of uncommon valor,
  of death,
   destruction,
    fear,
   hopelessness,
    futility . . .
A war in which youth was
wasted on the young
  not wasted by life but
    death.
    The canvas of life is
  painted with images of
proms, graduations, young
love, promises and hope . . .

the school dances of
joy and abandonment
    replaced by the macabre
dance of death and destruction.
    The canvas rent, the
curtain falling,
    promises, hope, life—
ebbing out with the blood
    of sacrifice.
    Dreams destroyed,
innocence lost.
    The mournful echo of Taps
escorts another young warrior
to an early grave.

I walk The Wall—
 God's gift of reconciliation
to us all.
    In my reflection I see the
names of those left behind.
    I search for answers.
    I pray for peace.
Each inscription not just a
name but a precious memory—
    a life.
    Someone's son, daughter,
brother, sister, husband, wife,
fiancée—
a fellow dreamer in the
dreams of life.
    They are all our sons.
    Their dreams are extinguished
but the flickering light of
their memories burns
brightly in our hearts.

I watch the pain and anguish
and tears at The Wall.
    I want to reach out and
touch them—

But I, too, hurt and I
can't let go—
   wanting to be a part
of the healing and move on,
   yet desperately wanting
to never forget.

With my fellow wanderers
drifting on a journey of memories
and confusion,
   we join in the cavalcade of
history.
   We march proudly with
brothers and sisters from battles
and wars past.
   The years have not erased
 their hollowness and pain—
they still see the youthful faces
of those who decades ago
passed through the portals of
death.

We alone are left to honor
their memory—
   and honor them we will!
   They marched through the
valley of death and now
rest peacefully in verdant pastures.
   We, alone, are not at peace.
I will see their faces and hear
their voices in the songs of our
youth blaring wistfully on the radio.
Memories will stir whenever a
flag is raised and the bugler
sounds his sad refrain.
   You are gone but will *never*
be forgotten.
   You gave your last full
measure of life
   and we vow to live our

last full measure of life in
your memories.
I love you.
May God hold you in the
palm of His Hand.
Peace is now yours,
you have not died in vain.
Your memory and your
sacrifice are eternally
etched on the walls inside
of all of us.
Rest in Peace!

INTERESTING ENCOUNTERS

It never failed. Just when an individual thought he had put the whole Vietnam experience behind him, something totally unexpected would happen.
He would meet someone he knew from Vietnam, he would read an article
in the newspaper, or his senses would trigger some type of memory about
it. Fortunately, some of the recollections were positive, and friendships
were made in Vietnam have continued to last over several decades.

Thomas Finn, *Specialist Four, U.S. Army, Company A, 519th Military
Intelligence Battalion, 525th Military Intelligence Group, MACV-J2,
Saigon, 1966–67*

I'm still friends today with a number of guys I served with. Since leaving Vietnam, I stayed on a Christmas card list with many of the guys. In
the late '80s I contacted a few and asked if they thought a reunion was
possible. Prior to that, I had seen two individuals from my unit. One of
them, who was one of my first friends in Vietnam, I still see fairly frequently. I've been to his house in Chicago a number of times, and he's
been to mine. We're really close, and our wives are, too.

Dick Turner, *Boatswains Mate Third Class, U.S. Navy, River Assault
Squadron 15, River Division 152, Task Force 117, Dong Tam and My
Tho, 1968–69*

Two years ago, when the *Normandy* was here, I ran into one of my old shipmates from Vietnam. I was on the pier one day working as a rigger when I ran into him. He looked at me and I looked at him, and I put my arms right around him. I knew him right off the bat. He was a gunner's mate on the boat, and today he was still in the service as a master chief.

Michael Toner Farrell, *Specialist Five, U.S. Army, 544th Replacement Company, Cam Ranh Bay, 1969–70*

One morning in Cam Ranh Bay I was in the mess hall cooking breakfast. I had the first shift that day because, I guess, one of the cooks was sick. I happened to look up, when these two grunts walked in. I mean, you could tell they were grunts by their disheveled clothes, their mannerisms, the way they carried themselves, which was all in keeping with the typical stereotype of an infantry soldier.

The next thing I know, they're coming through the mess line to order their breakfast. We used to prepare eggs to order.

All of a sudden this guy says, "Holy shit, it's Michael Farrell!"

I looked at him and thought, "Who the hell are you?"

He continued, "I know you because I went to school with you and even prayed for you with the other kids when you had your open-heart surgery. What the hell are you doing in Vietnam?"

It was embarrassing because I still couldn't remember his name. He had to introduce himself.

Anyway, he continued, "What are you doing here?"

"I'm the mess sergeant."

He looked at me and said, "Do you think you could get us some milk?"

I said, "You want milk? I'll get you some milk."

Remember now, milk wasn't an easy commodity to get in Vietnam, especially for an infantry soldier.

I went to the back cooler, got them both half-gallons of ice-cold milk, and put them in bags. I got back to the front line and handed it to them, saying, "You've got to go hide because if you drink it here, you'll get me in trouble."

After that I never saw him again. The year was 1969.

While on vacation in 1988, I was invited to a private party at Gooseberry Beach in Newport. At the time, I was living in Florida. On the spur of the moment, I was asked if I wanted to go to the opening festivities for the summer season at the beach. I said, "Sure, I might even see some people I know from Newport."

So we arrived at the beach, and of course I met a lot of people I knew. All of a sudden, this guy comes up to me.

"Michael Farrell," he says. "You don't know who I am, do you?"

I said, "No I don't." I had no idea who he was.

"I've been looking for you for almost twenty years."

Now I'm thinking to myself, "What the f— did I do to this guy?"

Then he says, "I'll never forget you. I was in Vietnam and going through a mess hall line, and I asked you for some milk, and you gave me and my friend a half-gallon each. I want to thank you so much because that was liquid gold to us. We hadn't had cold milk for months."

I had absolutely forgotten that incident in Vietnam, as it didn't mean much to me at the time; obviously, it meant a great deal to him.

That's one of my best Vietnam stories. Here's a guy I gave a half-gallon of milk to, which meant nothing to me, I mean nothing. I had all the milk I ever wanted, and I ate like a king and he kept that in the back of his mind for all those years until he could thank me personally.

It just makes me feel good to tell that story. You know what I mean? To this day, it gives me goose bumps when I tell it.

EPILOG

A FTER the publication of the hard-bound edition of this book, I received the usual number of compliments. Some correspondence, however, was totally unexpected. Within six months of the book's release, a letter arrived at my home from a Korean War veteran residing in Florida. In it the gentleman thanked me for opening his eyes to the realization that the Vietnam grunts were not unlike the Korean War soldiers he remembered. He apologized to me for not having understood the plight of the Vietnam veteran during and after the conflict.

From St. Petersburg, Russia, I received a congratulatory letter from a veteran of the Afghanistan War. He wrote to say that the book was extremely uplifting for him and his friends who served in that war. He went on to describe how he as a soldier was received home in exactly the same manner as many of the Vietnam soldiers were: with extreme indifference. To often we forget that all war veterans, no matter where they served or for that matter, what country they represented, are in fact one and the same—bound by an unselfish devotion to duty and country, yet subject to those who could not, or did not want to, understand them.

In the summer of 1999, at a military awards ceremony conducted in Rhode Island, William McCollum, one of the participants in this book, was awarded two Purple Hearts and a Bronze Star for his valor in Vietnam. I suspect that telling his story for this book played an instrumental role in his decision to seek his hard-earned decorations. Not only were they long in coming but, more importantly, well deserved.

This past year I said my good-byes to two fellow veterans, both of whom I considered good friends. William Sullivan and his wife moved to Idaho to care for an elderly family member. Rob Roche retired from the fire department and moved to the sunny skies of Florida.

Perhaps my most unforgettable encounter occurred at a Barnes and Noble book signing. A lovely and gentle lady introduced herself to me. Her name was Shirley Saulnier. At first, I was unaware of who she was. Hesitantly, and somewhat reluctantly, she described her mission that day. I forget her exact words, but I do remember the generalities of the conversation. She said something like: I am very nervous about being here today, but I felt I had to come. My husband was one of the men listed in the appendix of your book. He was killed in action in Vietnam. She told me about the last time she saw her husband alive. That was when she visited him in Hawaii on his R&R. She went on to tell me that I had incorrectly spelled his surname and asked if I could make the correction in the subsequent printing. Almost in the same breath, she proudly talked about her children and how well they had adjusted in life without a father. During our conversation, I never detected a tone of bitterness in her voice. In the end, I was left nearly speechless and truly humbled for being in her presence. I can't remember exactly what I said that day; hopefully they were the right words for the occasion.

For me, it has certainly been a remarkable year. I consider myself fortunate to have met so many wonderful people (veterans and non-veterans) as a direct result of this book.

PERSONAL BRIEFS

Butler, Stephen D.

Lance Corporal, U.S. Marine Corps,
Combat Engineer, 7th Marine Combat Engineers, Da Nang
September 1966–November 1967

Steve is employed as a management analyst and union steward for the Department of Defense, United States Navy. In his spare time, Steve operates a home construction business. He is a member of the B.P.O. Elks and the Rhode Island Builders Association. He is married and has a son.

Farrell, Michael Toner

Specialist Five, U.S. Army
Cook, 544th Replacement Company, Cam Ranh Bay
June 1969–December 1970

Toner, as he is now known, is still working in the food profession, but is no longer a cook. He serves as a waiter in a local restaurant. When not working, he is attending college to pursue a career in social work. Toner enjoys sky diving, horseback riding, chess, backgammon, and, of course, cooking. Toner is engaged to be married.

Finn, Thomas M.

Specialist Four, U.S. Army
Military Intelligence, Company A, 519th Military Intelligence Battalion, 525th Military Intelligence Group, MACV-J2, Saigon
May 1966–June 1967

In 1974 Tom joined the U.S. Army Reserves and served until his retirement in May 1995. When he retired, he was a staff sergeant with over 23 years of active duty and reserve service. Tom is now a retail store manager in Massachusetts. He still remains in contact with several of his fellow Vietnam veterans by serving as the chairman of his unit's reunion association. Tom is married and has two sons. One is in the army, currently stationed in Germany after serving seven months in Bosnia; and the other is working at a ski resort in Colorado.

Garthee, Kenneth

Private First Class, U.S. Marine Corps
Infantry, 3rd Battalion, 3rd Marines, 3rd Marine Division, Da Nang
January 1966–February 1967

Ken is employed by a defense contractor and works in the field of human resources. He holds a BS and an M.Ed., both with majors in education. Ken has donated considerable hours to the Boy Scouts of America and Little League Baseball. He is married and has two sons.

Johnson, Douglas L.

Specialist Four, U.S. Army
Radio/Telephone Operator, 25th Infantry Division, 2nd Battalion, 12th Infantry, Cu Chi, Fire Support Base Stuart, Fire Support Base Pershing
February 1968–October 1968

Doug is employed as an attorney for a transit authority. His hobbies include theater, play writing, reading, and performing youth service work. He is affiliated with the Virginia Bar Association and the D.C. Bar Association. Doug is married and has three children (two daughters and a son) and two grandchildren.

McCollum, William

Sergeant, U.S. Army
Infantry, 173rd Airborne Brigade, Charlie Company, 4th Battalion, 503rd Infantry, LZ-English
September 1969–April 1971

Bill is a captain in a fire department located at a naval government facility. In his spare time, Bill enjoys making videos and playing golf. He is married and has a son.

North, Howard

Lieutenant j.g., U.S. Coast Guard
Executive Officer, Coast Guard Squadron One, USCGC *Point Clear* (WPB 82315), An Thoi and Cat Lo
April 1967–May 1968

Howard is a high-school assistant principal. Previously, he taught mathematics on the secondary education level for more than 20 years. Howard enjoys fishing and gardening. He is a member of the National Education Association, the National Association of Secondary School Principals, and the Reserve Officers Association. Howard is married and has a daughter and son.

Pinksaw, Michael D., Jr.

Specialist Four, U.S. Army

Engineer, Heavy Equipment Operator, 60th Land Clearing Company, 62nd Engineering Battalion, 20th Engineering Brigade, Long Binh, Bien Hoa, and Lai Khe

July 1968–May 1969

Mike is a fire department dispatcher for the Department of Defense, United States Navy. In his spare time he is a volunteer at a local community fire department. Mike also enjoys lawn and gardening work. He is married and has three children.

Raffa, Salvatore T.

Airman Second Class, U.S. Air Force

Security Police, 377th Security Police Squadron, Tan Son Nhut Air Base, Saigon

December 1967–December 1968

Salvatore is employed by a local school department and works on the maintenance staff. At home, Salvatore enjoys yard work. For thirteen years, he was an auxiliary policeman in Newport. Currently Salvatore is a member of the Democratic City Committee. He is married and has three daughters.

Roche, Robert

Sergeant, U.S. Army

Infantry, 101st Airborne Division, Da Nang

August 1967–January 1969

Rob is employed as a fireman for the Department of Defense, United States Navy. In his spare time, Rob enjoys golfing. He is divorced and has three daughters and a son.

Rossi, David

Specialist Four, U.S. Army
Medic, 1st Infantry Division and the 25th Infantry Division, Di An,
Tay Ninh, and Cu Chi
July 1969–July 1970

Dave is vice president of an ice company. He enjoys wind sailing in the summer and ice boating in the winter, and one of his ice boats is an antique from the 1920s. Dave likes to use his mechanical skills whenever he has the opportunity, both at home and at work. He is a member of the National Ice Association. He is married and has two daughters.

Sullivan, William

Lieutenant Commander, U.S. Navy
Naval Flight Officer, Fighter Squadron 213, U.S.S. *Kitty Hawk* (CVA-63), U.S.S. *Intrepid* (CVA-11), *U.S.S. Paul Revere,* U.S.S. *Blue Ridge,* Tactical Air Control 12, Amphibious Forces, U.S. Seventh Fleet
October 1965–June 1966; September 1966–May 1967; September 1967–June 1968; and November 1971–June 1972

Bill attained the rank of captain before retiring after serving his country on active duty for more than 31 years. He is currently employed as a project manager for a defense contractor. When he finds the time, Bill enjoys doing carpentry work. He is married and has eight children (six sons and two daughters) and two grandchildren.

Turner, Richard P.

Boatswain's Mate Third Class, U.S. Navy
Boatscoxswain, Well Deck Gunner, and Radio Operator, River Assault Squadron 15, River Division 152, Task Force 117, Dong Tam and My Tho
May 1968–July 1969

Dick is an automotive worker for the Department of Defense, United States Navy. He belongs to several veterans' organizations: the Fleet Reserve Association, the Retired Enlisted Association, the Veterans of Foreign Wars, the Disabled American Veterans, the American Legion, Post 18 in Portsmouth, and the Vietnam Veterans of America. Dick likes canoing and camping. He also enjoys woodworking, operating his computer, and listening to classical and country/western music. He is single.

Wylie, Elizabeth G.

Lieutenant, U.S. Navy

General Unrestricted Line Officer, Management Information Center
Headquarters, Naval Forces Vietnam (NAVFORV), Saigon

June 1967–July 68

Betsy retired as a captain after serving over 30 years in the service of her country. She is currently an executive director of a military educational foundation. Betsy is a member of the Women Officers' Professional Association of Washington, D.C.; is a trustee at St. Michael's School; and serves as a member of the Board of Directors for the Potter Animal League and the Battleship Massachusetts. Also, she is a member of the Newport Rotary Club and is chairman of the Glen Farm Authority. In her leisure hours, Betsy enjoys gardening and travel. She is single.

Zarek (Barry), Margaret R.

Lieutenant Commander, U.S. Navy

Registered Nurse, U.S.S. *Sanctuary* (AH-17), Coastal Waters of
South Vietnam, Military Region 1

December 1969–December 1970

Peggy retired from active duty as a registered nurse with the rank of lieutenant commander. She is a member of the New England Navy Nurse Association and the Retired Officers' Association. In her spare time she enjoys gardening and doing volunteer work in the community. Her husband is also a retired navy veteran.

HOME OF RECORD/ NAME OF SERVICEMAN	MIL. GRD.	MIL. SERVICE
MIDDLETOWN		
Kelley, John Patrick	PFC	Army
Lavallee, Robert C. Jr.	PFC	Army
NEWPORT		
Braga, John Paul Jr.	SP4	Army
Cochrane, Blanchard Ward	SSGT	Army
Dupere, Joseph Rene	SSGT	Army
Glover, John	A1C	Air Force
Greene, Richard Edward Jr.	SGT	Marines
Mosher, Robert Lloyd	CAPT	Army
Potter, Alfred N.	SGT	Air Force
Saulnier, Jeremiah John	SGT	Army
Vandevender, Joseph Thomas	CPL	Army
PORTSMOUTH		
Augustine, Frank Francis	SGT	Army
Manchester, Jay Harrison	PFC	Army
Sisson, Donald Henry	SGT	Army
Upton, Stephen Louis	LCPL	Marines
TIVERTON		
Jerome, Paul Andrew Jr.	1LT	Army
Lewis, James Earl	CPL	Marines
Sylvia, Michael Alan	SP5	Army

Note:
(A) Joseph Thomas Vandevender is listed in several sources with his home of record as Newport. According to a reliable source, he was born and raised in Jamestown, R.I.
(B) All reported deaths were in South Vietnam, with the exception of Alfred N. Potter, who died in Thailand.

RESIDENTS OF NEWPORT COUNTY
WHO DIED DURING THE VIETNAM WAR

DATE OF DEATH	AGE AT DEATH	TYPE OF CASUALTY
27APR68	20yr. 8mo.	KIA
19 NOV67	20 yr. 1mo.	Hostile, Died, Missing
31JAN68	20yr. 8mo.	Hostile, Died, Wounds
12MAY66	31yr. 1mo.	KIA
12NOV65	32yr.	KIA
08APR71	19yr. 8mo.	KIA
22JUN67	24yr. 1mo.	KIA
26MAY67	29yr. 3mo.	Non-hostile, Died, Other
10APR70	28yr. 6mo.	Non-hostile, Died, Other
15JUL68	38yr. 7mo.	Hostile, Died, Wounds
02JUN68	21yr. 2mo.	KIA
28SEP69	24yr. 4mo.	KIA
17MAR69	22yr. 5mo.	KIA
23FEB69	20yr. 10mo.	KIA
28MAY69	20yr. 5mo.	Non-hostile, Died, Other
22AUG68	24yr. 6mo.	KIA
07SEP67	19yr. 8mo.	KIA
12JUN69	22yr. 1mo.	Non-hostile, Died, Illness, Injury

Source:
Combat Area Casualties, Current File, as of November 1995, Records of the Office of the Secretary of Defense, Record Group 330, National Archives Building, Trust Fund, Washington, DC 20408

APPENDIX C

GLOSSARY

AFSC. Air force specialty code.

AIT. Advanced infantry training.

AK-47. A Russian or Chinese assault rifle.

APC. Armored personnel carrier; a track vehicle which usually had a .50 caliber machine gun mounted to it.

ARVN. Army of the Republic of Vietnam (South Vietnam).

ASAP. As soon as possible.

AWOL. Absent without leave; to leave a post or position without official authorization.

BA. Bachelor of arts degree.

base camp. A semi-permanent administrative and logistical center of operation for a military unit.

basic training. Initial training of recruits into the military way of life (both physical and mental). In the marines it was called boot camp.

beaucoup. French word meaning "many"; used by both Vietnamese and Americans.

Bde. Brigade.

Bn. Battalion.

body bag. A plastic or canvas bag used to transport soldiers' bodies from the field.

boonies. Short for boondocks—the jungle.

BOQ. Bachelor officers' quarters.

BS. Bachelor of science degree.

bush. Slang for remote area or jungle.

BX. Base exchange (air force).

C-130. A four-engine, turbo-prop airplane used to carry heavy cargo; also carried troops within Vietnam.

cache. Equipment or supplies hidden by the enemy.

carbine. A short-barrelled rifle which could be fired as a semi- or automatic rifle.

Charlie. Slang name for Viet Cong taken from phonetic initialing: Victor/Charlie.

cherry. A new in-country replacement.

chopper. A helicopter.

claymore. An antipersonnel land mine which, when detonated, sent shrapnel in a 60-degree, fan-shaped pattern.

click. A hundred meters in distance.

clip. A spring-loaded metal cartridge which held 20 rounds of ammunition and could be quickly inserted into a weapon. Also called a magazine. A banana clip, so named because it was curved, held approximately 30 rounds.

CO. Commanding officer.

concertina. A razor-sharp, roll-like steel barbed-wire used as fortification around compounds and base camps to delay enemy ground attacks.

conscientious objector. An individual opposed to serving in the military due to religious, moral, or ethical beliefs.

corps. South Vietnam was divided into four military regions; I Corp was the most northern area and IV Corps the most southern.

corpsman. A navy medic, assigned to either a navy or marine unit.

coxswain. A name given to the individual who steers a ship.

CP. Command post.

DEROS. Date of expected return from overseas.

DI. Drill instructor (army).

dink(s). Derogatory name GIs called Vietnamese.

dong. Vietnamese monetary unit.

doughnut dollies. Slang nickname given to Red Cross female volunteers who served coffee and doughnuts and provided moral support to the troops.

deuce-and-a-half. A military 2 1/2-ton truck.

dud. Any explosive devise that did not detonate.

DMZ. Demilitarized zone. The 17th parallel line on a map that separated North and South Vietnam.

Evac. Evacuation, as in "evacuation hospital."

F-4 Phantom. A jet plane used as a fighter-bomber.

fatigues. A military uniform used for work and combat.

firefight. A skirmish between opposing forces that usually involved rifle and other types of gunfire.

first shirt. First sergeant.

fleshette. A clustered projectile placed in a warhead.

FNG. F—n' new guy, a term used to describe fresh replacements in Vietnam.

FO. Forward observer

Freedom Bird. Name given to any plane which carried troops back home from Vietnam.

FSB. Fire support base.

gook. Derogatory name GIs called a Vietnamese civilian.

grunt. Name given to infantry soldiers (army or marine) in Vietnam; taken from the sound a soldier would make when lifting his rucksack.

guerrillas. Name given to soldiers of a resistance movement such as the Viet Cong.

gunship. Referred to Cobra Gunship, an attack helicopter.

H & I. Harassment and interdictory fire.

helo(s). Short for helicopter(s).

hooch. A shanty hut or tent.

hot LZ. A landing zone experiencing enemy fire.

huey. Slang name given to the UH-series troop-transport helicopters.

Hurdy-gurdy. An M79 percussion-type, single-shot, hand-held grenade launcher that had to be cranked in order for it to be fired.

ICU. Intensive care unit.

ID. Identification.

in-country. Being in the country of Vietnam.

incoming. Receiving enemy rocket or mortar fire.

ITR. Infantry training reserve.

IV. Intravenous.

j.g. Junior grade.

KIA. Killed in action.

klick. A kilometer. This term came from adjusting the sights of an M16 and the sound the device made while turning it.

KP. Kitchen police; the cleanup detail in the kitchen.

LAW. M72 light antitank weapon.

LBJ. Usually used to refer to the Long Bien Jail; also the initials of President Lyndon B. Johnson.

lifer. A derogatory name given to a career soldier.

LRP. Long-range reconnaissance patrol.

LST. Landing ship, tank

Lt. Lieutenant.

LZ. Landing zone.

MAC. Military Assistance Command.

MACV. Military Assistance Command, Vietnam.

mad minute. A time set when everyone fired his weapon to upset and confuse the enemy. Usually a considerable amount of ammunition was expended during these moments.

mama-san. Slang term to describe a female Vietnamese peasant.

medevac. Evacuation by helicopter, usually because of combat wounds.

M.Ed. Master of education degree.

MI. Military Intelligence.

MIA. Missing in action.

MOS. Military occupational specialty.

MP. Military police.

NBC School. Nuclear, Chemical, and Biological Warfare School.

neutralize. To use military action to cause an enemy force to be ineffective.

Number one. Slang term used by the Vietnamese to call a GI the best.

Number ten. Slang term used by the Vietnamese to call a GI the worst.

nuoc-mam. A pungent fish sauce produced by the Vietnamese and eaten with rice dishes.

NVA. North Vietnamese Army (regulars).

OCS. Officer Candidate School.

ONI. Office of Naval Investigation.

OP. Phonetic spelling for Oscar/Papa; also means outpost.

P38. Collapsible can opener designed to be worn on a chain.

papa-san. Slang used to describe a male Vietnamese peasant.

PBR. Patrol boat, river.

PDQ. Pretty damn quick.

PFC. Private first class.

platoon. A military unit of two to four squads of 25 to 45 men.

point man. The lead position in a platoon; usually the most dangerous because of the individual's full frontal exposure to the enemy.

POW. Prisoner of war.

PT. Physical training.

PTSD. Post-traumatic stress disorder.

Puff the Magic Dragon. A C-47 up-gunned air force support aircraft.

Purple Heart. Military decoration awarded by the U.S. government for wounds received in action.

PX. Post exchange (army).

R & R. Rest and recreation.

ROTC. Reserve Officer Training Corps.

RPG. A rocket-propelled grenade launcher.

RTO. Radio/telephone operator.

rucksack. A military backpack carried by an infantry soldier.

Saigon tea. A weak Vietnamese alcoholic beverage consisting mostly of Coca-Cola or diluted with water.

SAM. Surface-to-air missile.

sapper(s). VC or NVA who performed suicide missions with explosives carried in backpacks.

search & destroy. An offensive operation planned to destroy the enemy.

SEER. Survival, escape, evasion, and resistance.

shake-down. A surprise inspection usually performed to find contraband among the troops.

short, short-timer. A serviceman with very little time left to serve in his enlistment or in-country.

shrapnel. Pieces of steel expelled from an explosive device.

starlight scope. An image intensifier used at night to locate the enemy.

Tet. Vietnamese word short for *Tet nguyen dan,* or Lunar New Year; a Vietnamese holiday celebrating Buddha's birthday.

The World. What the troops affectionately called America; their homes back in the States.

TI. Training instructor (marines).

TOC. Tactical operations center.

tracers. Incendiary bullets, fired at night, that left an illuminated trail to help a soldier better aim at his target. American tracers were red, while Russian tracers were green or white.

Tunnel rat. A soldier, of small build, who descended into tunnels to locate and exterminate the enemy.

USAF. United States Air Force.

USARV. United States Army, Vietnam.

USCG. United States Coast Guard.

USCGC. United States Coast Guard cutter.

USMC. United States Marine Corps.

USN. United States Navy.

USO. United Services Organization.

VA. United States Veterans Administration.

VC. Viet Cong—derived from the term Viet Cong Son (Vietnamese Communist).

waste or wasted. To kill or be killed.

WAVES (Women Accepted for Volunteer Emergency Service). Acronym devised during World War II to identify commissioned women officers in the naval reserve. The name was retained after the war to identify any naval woman officer, whether active duty or reserve.

WEST PAC. Western Pacific.

WIA. Wounded in action.

Willie Peter. White phosphorus; an incendiary used in grenades or shells.

WPB. (Coast Guard) patrol boat.

XO. Executive officer.

COMMON VIETNAMESE WORDS AND PHRASES
USED BY AMERICAN SOLDIERS

Dung lai	Halt
Buong sung xuong	Lay down your gun
Dee-dee	Leave quickly
Dinky dau (slang)	Crazy
Dua tay len	Put up your hands
Duia tay len dau	Keep your hands on your head
Toi klam ong	I will search you
Dung noi chuyen	Do not talk
Lai dang kia	Walk there
Xay ben phai	Turn right
Xay ben trai	Turn left
Doi	Wait
Den	Come

SELECTED BIBLIOGRAPHY

INTERVIEWS & MEMOIRS

Braga, Mary. Interview by editor. March 14, 1997.

Butler, Stephen. Interview by editor. April 8, 1997.

Farrell, Michael Toner. Interview by editor. January 22, 1997.

Finn, Thomas M. Interview by editor. December 9, 1996.

Garthee, Ken. Interviews by editor.

————. Unpublished memoirs. January 1997.

Glover, Ella. Interview by editor. April 27, 1997.

Glover, Frances C. Interview by editor. April 27, 1997.

Johnson, Douglas L. Unpublished memoirs. May 1997.

McCollum, William. Interview by editor. February 4, 1997.

North, Howard. Interview by editor. December 31, 1996.

Pinksaw, Michael D., Jr. Interview by editor. January 18, 1997.

Raffa, Salvatore T. Interview by editor. February 11, 1997.

Roche, Robert. Interview by editor. December 11, 1996.

Rossi, David. Interview by editor. December 10, 1996.

Sullivan, William. Interview by editor. January 23, 1997.

Turner, Richard P. Interview by editor. March 24, 1997.

Winning, Nancy. Interview by editor. July 6, 1997.

Wylie, Elizabeth G. Interview by editor. May 21, 1997.

Zarek (Barry), Margaret R. Interview by editor. May 12, 1997.

BOOKS

Appy, Christian G. *Working-Class War: American Combat Soldiers and Vietnam*. Chapel Hill: University of North Carolina Press, 1993.

Bowman, John S. *Vietnam War, Day by Day*. New York: Mallard Press, 1989.

Broyles, William. *Brothers in Arms: A Journey from War to Peace*. New York: Knopf, 1986.

Caputo, Philip. *A Rumor of War*. New York: Holt, Rinehart & Winston, 1977.

Davidson, Phillip B. *Vietnam at War: The History, 1946–1975*. Novato, Calif.: Presidio Press, 1988.

Duncan, David Douglas. *War without Heroes*. New York: Harper & Row, 1970.

Ebert, James R. *A Life in a Year: The American Infantryman in Vietnam, 1965–1972*. Novato, Calif.: Presidio Press, 1993.

Edelman, Bernard, ed. *Dear America: Letters Home from Vietnam*. New York: Holton, 1985.

Evans, Diane Carlson, et al. *Celebration of Patriotism and Courage*. Washington, D.C.: Vietnam Women's Memorial Project, 1993.

Gettleman, Marvin E., ed. *Viet Nam History, Documents, and Opinions on a Major World Crisis*. Greenwich, Conn.: Fawcett Publications, Inc., 1966.

Herr, Michael. *Dispatches*. New York: Knopf, 1977.

Karnow, Stanley. *Vietnam: A History*. New York: Viking Press, 1983.

Legrand, Jacques, Pub. *Chronicle of America*. Mount Kisco, N.Y.: Chronicle Publications Inc., 1993.

Levy, Charles J. *Spoils of War*. Boston: Houghton Mifflin Company, 1974.

Littauer, Raphael, and Norman Uphoff, eds. *The Air War in Indochina*. Boston: Beacon Press, 1972.

O'Brien, Tim. *If I Die in a Combat Zone*. New York: Delacorte, 1973.

Regan, Geoffrey. *Blue on Blue: A History of Friendly Fire*. New York: Avon Books, 1995.

Scruggs, Jan C., and Joel L. Swerdlow. *To Heal a Nation: The Vietnam Veterans Memorial*. New York: Harper & Row, Publishers, 1985.

Severo, Richard, and Lewis Milford. *The Wages of War: When America's Soldiers Came Home: From Valley Forge to Vietnam*. New York: Simon and Schuster, 1989.

Stanton, Shelby L. *Vietnam Order of Battle*. New York: Galahad Books, 1986.

Thompson, A., et al. *Another Kind of War Story: Army Nurses Look Back to Vietnam*. Lebanon, Pennsylvania: Ann Thompson, 1993.

Thu, Nguyen Xuan. *Vietnamese Phrasebook*. Oakland, Calif.: Lonely Planet Publications, 1996.

Wilcox, Fred A. *Waiting for an Army to Die*. New York: Random House, 1983.

ENCYCLOPEDIAS

Bahr, Lauren S., and Bernard Johnson, eds. *Collier's Encyclopedia.* Volume 23. New York: P. F. Collier, 1995.

Cornish, George A., et al., eds. *Encyclopedia Americana International Edition.* Volume 28. New York: Encyclopedia Americana Corp., 1970.

NEWSPAPERS

Newport Daily News. Newport, Rhode Island.

New York Times. New York, New York.

Providence Journal-Bulletin. Providence, Rhode Island.

Washington Post National Weekly Edition. Washington, D.C.

THE AMERICAN MILITARY EXPERIENCE
OTHER TITLES OF INTEREST
FROM PURDUE UNIVERSITY PRESS

Vietnam

Four American Perspectives

Lectures by George S. McGovern, William C. Westmoreland,
Edward N. Luttwak, and Thomas J. McCormick
edited with an introduction by Patrick J. Hearden
Paper; ISBN 1-55753-003-3

Seeds of Hope

An Engineer's World War II Letters

by William O. Sabel
Cloth; ISBN 1-55753-131-5

RAF Wings over Florida

*Memories of World War II Air Cadet Training
in Arcadia and Clewiston*

by Will Largent
Cloth; ISBN 1-55753-203-6